The Mexico-U.S.
Free Trade Agreement

The Mexico-U.S.
Free Trade Agreement

edited by Peter M. Garber

The MIT Press
Cambridge, Massachusetts
London, England

HF
1756
.M49
1993

Second printing, 1995

This book was set in Palatino by Asco Trade Typesetting Ltd., Hong Kong and
was printed and bound in the United States of America.

Library of Congress Cataloging-in-Publication Data

The Mexico-U.S. free trade agreement / edited by Peter M. Garber.
    p.   cm.
  Papers prepared for a conference held at Brown University on October 18–19, 1991.
  Includes bibliographical references and index.
  ISBN 0-262-07152-5
  1. Free trade—United States—Congresses. 2. Free trade—Mexico—Congresses.
  3. United States—Foreign economic relations—Mexico—Congresses. 4. Mexico—
  Foreign economic relations—United States—Congresses. 5. Wages—United
  States—Congresses. 6. United States—Industries—Congresses. I. Garber, Peter M.
  II. Title: Mexico-United States free trade agreement.
  HF1756.M49   1993
  382'.917—dc20
                                                                      93-8946
                                                                         CIP

Contents

1 Introduction

Peter M. Garber

The laborious part of a negotiation of a free trade agreement concerns how much protection will remain in place and the rate at which it will be reduced. Much necessary effort is devoted to rules of origin prescribing minimums on local content, transitional protection, the degree of permissible subsidization, the permissible degree of foreign ownership of an industry or of market share, and the method of resolving disputes on the adherence to the agreement. In this regard, the negotiation for a North American Free Trade Agreement (NAFTA) is no different: industries or interests that are most affected—typically most negatively affected—naturally influence the direction of negotiation and the final result. Nevertheless, in the end numerous dimensions of trade are opened among the countries in the trade agreement.

The chapters in this volume are intended to examine the impact of a free trade agreement with Mexico on the U.S. economy in those dimensions that are likely to experience significant opening to trade. The contributions range in content from the general sources of comparative advantage between Mexico and the United States to regional and local effects on production and employment to the effect on production in particular industries. A first group of chapters considers how some sources of comparative advantage that cut across industries—differential environmental regulations and wage differentials—may affect the outcome. These, of course, are among the most frequently raised issues in the debate about the NAFTA. The second group of chapters considers the locational effects on U.S production of an agreement—either from the empirical viewpoint of which U.S. metropolitan areas will gain employment or on the theoretical basis of the scale effects–transportation cost trade-off. The third group of chapters considers the effect of the NAFTA on several individual U.S. industries. It was taken as a point of departure for the conference at which these papers were first presented that since the U.S. economy is large relative to Mexico's, and since there is already unhindered trade with Mexico for many goods, the initial impact of a free trade agreement on U.S. aggregate income would be small. Therefore, the researchers sought to study in detail some of those industries that will be affected in a large way— agriculture, autos, financial services—if free trade is opened indefinitely.

Sources of Comparative Advantage

Two sources of comparative advantage for Mexican industries have emerged in the debates around the NAFTA. First, the traditional large supply of low-wage Mexican labor benefits Mexican industrial activities intensive in labor. Second, if free trade arises between two countries with different environmental standards, a new source of comparative advantage may arise, as polluting industries migrate to the country with the looser standard. To protect U.S. industries subject to strict environmental controls from the disadvantage of lax Mexican standards and to avoid a general degradation of the Mexican environment, environmental standards and enforcement have become part of the free trade debate.

Environmental Standards

Gene Grossman and Alan Krueger address the question of whether the NAFTA will foment the movement of polluting industry to Mexico, thereby reducing Mexican environmental quality and perhaps increasing pressures to reduce U.S. standards. They divide the environmental effects of free trade into three components. First is a scale effect through which increased aggregate economic activity in Mexico may lead to increased pollution. Second is a composition effect through which the composition of output of Mexican industry may change toward more polluting industries. Third is a technique effect through which a shift may occur toward production techiques with different emissions of pollutants.

The nature of the scale and technique effects can be determined by examining the general empirical relationship between economic growth and pollution across countries. With data for several cities from each of forty-two countries, Grossman and Krueger estimate the relationship between gross domestic product and pollution levels measured in terms of concentrations of sulfur dioxide or suspended particulate matter. With sulfur dioxide, for example, pollution levels peak at about $5,000 per capita of GDP (using Summers and Hesten GDP data standardized for international prices) and then fall. Since Mexican GDP is $4,970 per capita, the scale effect should lead to a decline of pollutants in Mexico as the Mexican economy expands.

Compositional effects can be measured by determining whether pollution-intensive industries derive other sources of comparative advantage from locating in Mexico. By finding the relationship between U.S. imports from Mexico in general or imports under the *maquiladora* program in particular and human capital intensity, physical capital intensity, pollution abatement costs, tariff rates, and injury rates, Grossman and Krueger conclude that goods produced by U.S. industries intensive in human and physical capital are less likely to be imported from Mexico. Also, both pollution abatement costs and injury rates do not significantly affect imports from Mexico, so pollution abatement costs are a much smaller determinant of comparative advantage than labor intensity.

Given that comparative advantage depends on factor intensities, it is possible to estimate which sectors will expand or contract in both Mexico and the United States under the NAFTA and to determine the net impact on pollution from the pollution intensities of the affected industries. Since energy-intensive industries are also capital intensive, they should tend to move to the United States, actually reducing pollution in Mexico.

Thus the environmental impact of the NAFTA should be to reduce pollution in Mexico. Indeed, the NAFTA itself may represent a political mechanism through which an environmental regulation regime usually desired by middle-income countries is attained. Further growth will lead to greater attention to environmental standards in the usual pattern for a middle-income country. Perhaps more important, labor-intensive industries in which Mexico has a comparative advantage are not also pollution intensive.

 Low-Wage Labor

International wage differentials are a major force driving international commerce. Such trade in turn generates a convergence of wages in countries open to trade. Edward Leamer studies the effect that the NAFTA, viewed as a permanent commitment to free trade, will have on the wages of U.S. low-wage workers. Even without the NAFTA, relatively open international trade has put serious downward pressure on the earnings of U.S. low-wage workers. Trade barriers are traditionally a means of effecting a desired income distribution by protecting such workers. Barring some other method of redistribution or compensation such as retraining programs, it is easy to envision a continuation of existing barriers to trade vis-à-vis the rest of the world or even an expansion. Nevertheless, committing the United States to permanent free trade with a low-wage country like Mexico need not undermine the goals of such protection if Mexican exports do not dominate U.S. imports. In that case, the effect of the NAFTA will be to divert trade away from Asian or other producers to Mexico. Through trade diversion, Mexico will gain by coming in under U.S. protectionist barriers, but the gain will include the tariff revenue equivalents that now accrue to Asian producers under voluntary restrictions. If post-NAFTA Mexican exports take 100% of U.S. imports in specific products, so that U.S. trade actually expands, then U.S. protection will be circumvented, and there will be an effect on U.S. low-wage workers.

To determine whether the NAFTA will foment trade diversion or trade expansion, Leamer considers how important Mexico is in supplying U.S. imports for specific products. He finds that currently Mexican output is large relative to U.S. import demand for many goods, but not large enough to have a great impact on U.S. prices if imports from Mexico expand somewhat. Nevertheless, as Mexico specializes in labor-intensive products and in those products protected in the U.S. market, there is a potential for a large impact on U.S. prices, which will affect the ability of the United States to use commercial policy as a redistributional tool. As a result, Leamer concludes that the NAFTA will lead to a substantial income redistribution in the United States.

Locational Effects on Production

The NAFTA will certainly not affect all areas of a country evenly. The impact of a trade liberalization will be concentrated, depending on the industrial makeup of a particular city or region. It should be stronger with proximity to the border because of the impact of transportation costs on trade. To determine empirically the locational distribution of the gains and losses from the NAFTA, it is necessary to disaggregate industrial output at the city or regional level by industry. Moreover, to infer the long-run regional impacts, it is helpful to turn to theories of industrial location within a country.

U.S. Regional and Metropolitan-Area Effects of NAFTA

Vernon Henderson examines location patterns of output in the United States and trade patterns to assess the geographical impact of the NAFTA. He selects several industries—including textiles, computers, and electronic components—that are generally expected to be affected favorably by a permanent opening of free trade with Mexico to find the cities where the gains in employment will be concentrated. Cities with a high percentage of the work force employed in these industries will experience a significant gain, with the gain declining because of transportation costs as the distance of the city from Mexico increases.

Henderson concentrates on the employment effects of increased Mexican demand predictable on the basis of reduced prices facing Mexico after the NAFTA. From data on export patterns by state to Mexico, estimates of Mexican demand for U.S. products can be derived, where demand depends on distance. From such demand estimates, U.S. export expansion and the percentage changes in U.S. regional prices by product can be obtained. From estimates of U.S. supply elasticities, it is then possible to predict the employment effects by industry and by location in the directly affected products. Adding to the direct employment effects in a given location are interaction effects across industries. For example, if employment increases in computers in a location, it will also increase in electronic components used as inputs, though there need be little increased Mexican demand for components directly.

The expansion in the positively affected industries will be felt most strongly in the southern and western regions of the United States, as the transportion cost of location view implies. Also, within a region, cities nearer Mexico are likely to experience a stronger impact than more distant cities. Specifically, from the increased exports of high-tech industries, textiles, plastics, and machinery, such cities as Austin, Houston, Anaheim, Los Angeles, San Jose, Phoenix, Boulder, and Dallas will each gain thousands of jobs.

Location with Scale Economies in Production

Most analyses of the effects of the NAFTA on production patterns have employed standard trade theoretical methods to infer likely outcomes. Paul Krugman and Gordon Hanson shift the focus to the central importance of scale economies in current theories of location. The NAFTA will be implemented in a system of current or potential trade barriers where the relatively small Mexican economy operates side by side with a large U.S. economy. The changed regime will turn the Mexican economy inside out: a core-periphery economy—that is, the current Mexican economy divided into the Mexico City area and the north of the country—will continue its evolution to an outward-looking economy where the mass of industrial production intended for the expanded market is located near the border zone.

To underpin this scenario, Krugman and Hanson construct a model that operates on an interaction among economies of scale in production, transportation costs, and the mobility of factors of production. Scale economies create a tendency to locate production facilities in a central location and leads to a circular process of industrial location: firms locate in a central area to minimize transport costs, bringing labor and intermediate goods producers with them. In turn, facilities to produce consumer goods also locate in the central area. The model consists of a primary producing sector with diminishing returns to scale of a mobile factor and a monopolistically competitive industrial sector with a increasing returns to scale technology.

Suppose that two countries—one large and one small—trade freely and that because of local cost advantages, large-scale output in some industries occurs in the small country and supplies demand in both countries. If the two countries move from free trade to a system of equal tariffs, firms in these industries will locate away from the small country to avoid the tariffs of the large country where most of the output will be sold. Still higher tariffs in the small country, however, will move the firms back into the small country to produce for local consumption on a small and costly scale. Thus, moderate tariffs in the large country will lead to a reduction in production in the small country unless met by large tariffs by the small country. Mexico has traditionally been an importer of manufactured goods into a protected domestic market, and the United States has imposed moderate tariffs on manufactures or might do so in the future in the absence of a free trade agreement. Standard trade theory implies that free trade will cause a general decline in Mexican manufacturing output and an increase in imports. From a locational viewpoint, however, manufacturing may well relocate to Mexico as a relative advantage of Mexican production sites attracts large-scale operations to serve the now unprotected, large economy. Thus manufacturing may expand in Mexico. In quantifying these effects, Krugman and Hanson find that Mexican manufacturing output will expand under free trade, though the trade deficit in manufactured goods may increase somewhat.

Krugman and Hanson also consider the locational pattern of manufacturing in Mexico. The pattern is shifting from a core-periphery arrangement, in which the Mexico City area had about 60% of manufacturing employment in the 1965 heyday of import substitution, to an export-oriented economy in which about 20% of manufacturing employment was in Mexico City in 1988. This shift in orientation was brought about by the fall in internal demand during the Mexican adjustment of the 1980s and the implementation of a policy to expand exports. A free trade agreement would carry this shift to a new level, moving the center of Mexican manufacturing to the northern states of Mexico.

Some Affected Industries

Although a large number of industries will inevitably be affected by the NAFTA, the authors in this volume concentrated on three that have been the source of a large political input, either for or against the NAFTA: California agriculture, automobile manufacture, and financial services. The aim is to determine how opening to Mexican competition or, alternatively, allowing access to the Mexican market, will affect these industries. Generally it is believed that low Mexican wages will cause labor-intensive industries to relocate to Mexico, and this should negatively affect protected industries like horticultural products. Similarly, there should be an incentive for labor-intensive processes to move south of the border even in unprotected industries like automobiles. At the same time, the United States has an advantage in supplying professional services, notably financial services, so a free trade agreement should lead to the entry of U.S. financial firms into the currently protected Mexican market, with little increase in Mexican firms entering the open U.S. market.

California Agricultural Products

Agricultural products constitute a large fraction of world and U.S. trade, and between the United States and Mexico there is now $5 billion in agricultural trade. U.S. exports of some foods, notably grains, should expand under a free trade agreement that eliminates protection for Mexican grain producers. Alternatively, other U.S. products such as fruits and vegetables, which have some import protection, would be expected to suffer from increased competition from imports. In their chapter, Robert Feenstra and Andrew Rose focus on the effect of a trade agreement on California agricultural products—tomatoes, citrus, and other vegetables—which, protected by tariffs, quotas, marketing orders, and health and sanitary regulations, would face competition from Mexican products in a free trade agreement. Although these crops would be negatively affected by a free trade agreement, other California crops would be largely unaffected.

Feenstra and Rose estimate that there would be social gains on the order of magnitude of $100 million per year accruing to U.S. consumers in a free trade agreement from the effects on California horticultural products. Nevertheless, the gains that may accrue to the United States may, through a switch from California production of horticultural products to such products as grains, be more than offset by an associated misallocation of scarce, sudsidized water resources to relatively low-value activity. For example, if land use shifts from horticulture to more water-intensive pasture, alfalfa, or rice, available water for municipal or industrial use may decline, thereby offsetting the direct welfare gains to consumers. If the agreement can be tied to a more efficient allocation of water resources, perhaps through allowing California agriculture to market water rights and thereby compensating itself somewhat for direct losses to the three horticultural products, Feenstra and Rose estimate an additional social gain of about $150 million annually.

The Automobile Industry

The automobile industry is expected to be among those most strongly affected by the NAFTA. Steven Berry, Vittorio Grilli, and Florencio Lopez de Silanes examine the question of whether the NAFTA will lead to a large movement of the U.S. automobile industry to Mexico in search of lower wages. Because U.S. tariffs are already quite low and the Mexican market has been virtually closed to U.S. imports, Berry et al. argue that the largest effect should arise from the opening of the Mexican market to U.S. exports. In Mexico, the automobile industry is actually two industries: an import-substitution industry that will be threatened by U.S. producers and an export-oriented industry. Assembly for export is undertaken in border plants with imported parts. Less efficient plants located around Mexico City generally produce for domestic consumption and also foster an auto parts industry around Mexico City. Since much of the worldwide output of U.S. automobile manufacturers is already located outside the United States, it is unlikely that the NAFTA will lead to any substantial relocation of production to Mexico.

Mexico has experienced a large recent increase in production for export, but this need not imply that U.S. output will relocate to Mexico. Indeed, much of this export increase arose from a 1983 decree that forced producers located in Mexico to have a positive balance of trade, leading to a large increase in exports to offset an increase in imports. Similarly, the 1989 relaxation of the automobile decree, which permitted imports up to 15% of domestic production, led to a large increase in automotive imports.

Berry et al. examine the effect on Mexican demand for automobiles if prices fall to near U.S. levels and Mexican incomes rise. They find that elasticities of demand are high and predict large Mexican demand increases if automobile prices fall to near U.S. levels. They conclude that restructuring of the industry can be expected on both sides of the border, but the greater impact will be on the Mexican side, with production located on the U.S. side generally expanding.

Financial Services

Because of a general belief that the United States has an advantage in the provision of financial services, the U.S. side has adopted the opening of financial markets as a goal in the NAFTA. For example, U.S. banks believe that their internal risk management systems are superior to those of their foreign counterparts, so that an importation of their operational methods into a protected market like Mexico will provide an opportunity to acquire whatever market share is permitted in the NAFTA. Based on the real rate of return to Mexican bank equity in recent years, it is believed that profit opportunities for U.S. banks are substantial.

In their chapter, Peter Garber and Steven Weisbrod examine the sources of bank profitability in Mexico. They argue that in retail and wholesale peso markets, the banking business is essentially local and therefore Mexican financial institutions are at no disadvantage in providing financial services in these areas. Since there are no capital or exchange controls in Mexico and since foreign banks can already establish booking offices in Mexico, the dollar-denominated wholesale banking market is already open to U.S. banks, which can book loans and deposits from Mexican entities offshore. Thus U.S. banks have already taken their potential share in the market in which they have the greatest advantage, the provision of wholesale dollar liquidity.

Because banks are providers of liquidity and Mexican peso-denominated markets are relatively illiquid, banks are more valuable in Mexico than in the liquid U.S. markets. Several features of Mexican financial markets signal their illiquidity. In Mexico, securities dealers engage heavily in repurchase agreements with banks because banks are better able to deliver cash for a security than are other dealers. In the United States, only a small fraction of bank security holdings are used for repurchases with dealers, an indication that dealers in securities markets do not lean heavily on banks for short-term finance. In Mexico, banks hold a higher percentage of assets in non-interest-bearing central bank accounts than U.S. banks, though they are not required to hold reserves. This indicates that payments are not as regular and interbank markets are not as liquid as in the United States. The trend in Mexico is toward a reduced amount of government debt and an increased amount of private financial claims. Since private claims are less liquid than claims on the government, Mexican banks' liquidity provision services will become more valuable as they are called on to provide more liquidity to customers. Nevertheless, the provision of liquidity to local customers is always a local business in which U.S. banks have no special advantage in Mexico. Citibank, for example, currently can operate in Mexico; but it concentrates almost entirely on the wholesale market. The innovative products provided by U.S. banks will be useful for the higher end of the Mexican financial services market but not for peso loans, but U.S. banks will not have a large impact on the peso-denominated Mexican market under the NAFTA.

Acknowledgments

The chapters in this volume were prepared for a conference on the Mexico-U.S. Free Trade Agreement held at Brown University on October 18–19, 1991. Planning for the conference began before Canada joined the negotiation, so the authors concentrated on the impact of an agreement between Mexico and the United States. Limitations on the size of the conference precluded a comprehensive coverage of all the issues under negotiation; instead, the authors were asked to deal either with individual sectors of importance or with questions that had not been covered by the rapidly growing literature on the free trade agreement based on general equilibrium calculations. The conference was funded by SECOFI, the Mexican Ministry of Commerce.

I would like to express my gratitude to William Niskanen for presenting the after-dinner lecture for the conference and to the discussants of the papers for their contribution to the conference. These included Robert Barro, Rudiger Dornbusch, Andrew Feltenstein, Raquel Fernandez, Robert Hodrick, Peter Hooper, James Levinsohn, Santiago Levy, Jeffrey Mackie-Mason, Michael Murray, and Toby Page. I also greatly appreciate the participation of Jagdish Bhagwati, David Munro, Javier Murcio, and Clinton Shiells in the roundtable discussion. Finally, I wish to thank Robert Reville for serving as the rapporteur and Carlotta Baptista for administering the operation of the conference.

Sources of Comparative Advantage

2 Environmental Impacts of a North American Free Trade Agreement

Gene M. Grossman and Alan B. Krueger

Environmental advocacy groups in the United States have voiced their concerns about a potential North American Free Trade Agreement (NAFTA). Some went so far as to oppose the congressional granting of fast-track negotiating authority to the president to enable American negotiators to enter into talks with their Mexican counterparts. The reservations of the lobbying groups mirror a growing perception on the part of environmentalists worldwide that an open world trading system may be inimical to the goal of preserving a clean, healthy, and sustainable global commons.

The arguments linking trade liberalization with environmental degradation have not been fully articulated.[1] With regard to a NAFTA, the environmentalists have expressed a number of reasons for fearing that freer trade and direct investment flows between the United States and Mexico may aggravate pollution problems in Mexico and in the border region.[2] At the least-discerning level, some have argued simply that any expansion of markets and economic activity inevitably leads to more pollution and faster depletion of scarce natural resources. A more pointed argument recognizes that pollution already is a severe problem in Mexico and that the country's weak regulatory infrastructure is strained to the breaking point. Under these conditions, it is feared that any further industrialization that results from the liberalization of trade and investment will exacerbate an already grave situation.

Other environmentalists draw their conclusions by extrapolating the experience of the maquiladora sector in Mexico. The maquiladoras are predominantly foreign-owned firms that produce largely for export to the United States under a Mexican policy that allows duty-free imports of foreign components for further processing and reexport. Originally, maquiladoras were required to locate within a 20-kilometer strip along the U.S.-Mexico border in order to qualify for special customs treatment. The sector grew rapidly and with little governmental oversight, and now is widely regarded as being a major contributor to the perilous environmental and social conditions in the border region. Environmental groups point to this sector as a prime example of how unregulated expansion in response to trade opportunities can create risks to worker safety and public health. They argue that investments in this sector have been encouraged by the lax enforcement of environment and labor protection laws in Mexico and fear that any further expansion in trade and investment flows between the United States and Mexico will be motivated by firms' desires to avoid the high costs of meeting U.S. regulations.

A further concern of some environmental groups is that a NAFTA may undercut regulatory standards in the United States. Spokespersons have made the political-economic argument that, with freer trade, industry groups in the United States will demand less stringent pollution controls in order to preserve their international competitiveness, so that environmental standards will tend toward a lowest common denominator. The environmentalists worry, moreover, that existing environmental protection laws in the United States may be seen as nontariff barriers to trade in the context of a regional trade agreement.

Although the environmental groups have raised a host of valid questions, they have so far been unable to provide convincing and well-supported answers to these questions. Many of their arguments fail to recognize all of the implications of trade liberalization for resource allocation and natural resource use in each of the trade-partner countries. Moreover, the empirical claims that have been made rely mostly on anecdotal evidence and on extrapolation of the experience in one region or industry to the entirety of economic activity in Mexico. Indeed, relatively little is known at any level of generality about the relationship between a country's trade regime and its rate of environmental degradation, or even about the relationship between a country's stage of economic development and its output of pollution. Theoretical investigation of these topics has been limited, and empirical studies are virtually nonexistent.

It is useful to distinguish three separate mechanisms by which a change in trade and foreign investment policy can affect the level of pollution and the rate of depletion of scarce environmental resources.[3] First, there is a *scale* effect, capturing the simple intuition espoused by the environmental advocates. That is, if trade and investment liberalization causes an expansion of economic activity, and if the nature of that activity remains unchanged, then the total amount of pollution generated must increase. The environmental groups point, for example, to the deleterious environmental consequences of the combustion of fossil fuels and to the air pollution that is generated by the trucking industry. To the extent that economic growth gives rise to an increased demand for energy, which then is generated by means similar to the prevailing methods, there will be an increased output of harmful pollutants that attends an increase in economic output. Similarly, to the extent that expanded trade gives rise to an increased demand for cross-border transportation services without there being any change in trucking practices, increased trade will contribute to a deterioration in air quality.

Second, there is a *composition* effect that results from any change in trade policy. When trade is liberalized, countries specialize to a greater extent in the sectors in which they enjoy competitive advantage. If competitive advantage derives largely from differences in environmental regulation, then the composition effect of trade liberalization will be damaging to the environment. Each country then will tend to specialize more completely in the activities that its government does not regulate strictly, and will shift out of production in industries where the local costs of pollution abatement are relatively great. On the other hand, if the sources of international comparative advantage are the more traditional ones, namely cross-country differences in factor abundance and technology, then the implications of the composition effect for the state of the environment are ambiguous. Trade liberalization will lead each country to shift resources into the sectors that make intensive use of its abundant factors. The net effect of this on the level of pollution in each location will depend upon whether pollution-intensive activities expand or contract in the country that on average has the more stringent pollution controls.

Finally, there is a *technique* effect. That is, output need not be produced by exactly the same methods subsequent to a liberalization of trade and foreign investment as it has been prior to the change in regime. In particular, the output of pollution per unit of economic product need not remain the same. There are at least two reasons to believe that pollution per unit of output might fall, especially in a less developed country. First, foreign producers may transfer modern technologies to the local economy when restrictions on foreign investment are relaxed. More modern technologies typically are cleaner than older technologies due to the growing global awareness of the urgency of environmental concerns. Second, and perhaps more important, if trade liberalization generates an increase in income levels, then the body politic may demand a cleaner environment as an expression of their increased national wealth. Thus, more stringent pollution standards and stricter enforcement of existing laws may be a natural political response to economic growth.

In this chapter we explore some of the empirical evidence that bears on the likely environmental impacts of a NAFTA. In section 1, we shed some light on the relative magnitudes of the scale and technique effects. We use a cross-country sample of comparable measures of pollution in various urban areas to explore the relationship between economic growth and air quality. After holding constant the identifiable geographic characteristics of different cities, a common global time trend in the levels of pollution, and the location and type of the pollution measurement device, we find that ambient levels of both sulfur dioxide and dark matter suspended in the air increase with per capita GDP at low levels of national income, but decrease with per capita GDP at higher levels of income. The turning point comes somewhere between $4,000 and $5,000, measured in 1985 U.S. dollars. For a third measure of air quality, namely the mass of suspended particles found in a given volume of air, the relationship between pollution and GDP is monotonically decreasing.

Sections 2 and 3 address different aspects of the composition effect. In section 2 we ask whether and to what extent the sectoral patterns of U.S. foreign investment in Mexico and of Mexican exports to the United States are affected by the laxity of environmental regulations in Mexico as compared to the stricter enforcement of controls in the United States. We relate the sectoral pattern of maquiladora activity, of U.S. imports from Mexico under the offshore assembly provisions of the U.S. tariff codes, and of total U.S. imports from Mexico to industry factor intensities, U.S. tariff rates, and the size of pollution abatement costs in the U.S. industry. We find that the traditional determinants of trade and investment patterns are significant here, but that the alleged competitive advantages created by lax pollution controls in Mexico play no substantial role in motivating trade and investment flows.

Finally, in section 3 we begin with the premise that resource allocations in the United States, Mexico, and Canada have been guided by competitive advantages generated by differences in factor endowments. We borrow from Brown, Deardorff, and Stern (1991) their estimates of the change in resource allocation that might result from a NAFTA, and discuss the implications of these predicted changes in the structure of production for levels of pollution in each country.

1 Economic Growth and Urban Air Pollution

As we noted above, economic growth has offsetting implications for the anthropogenic generation of air pollution. On one hand, some pollutants

are a natural by-product of economic activities such as electricity generation and the operation of motor vehicles. As economic activity expands,
emissions of these pollutants tend to grow. On the other hand, firms and
households can control their pollution to some degree by their choice of
technology. Cleaner technologies produce less pollution per unit of output.
As a society becomes richer, its members may intensify their demands for
a more healthy and sustainable environment, in which case the government
may be called upon to impose more stringent environmental controls.

Little is known about the empirical relationship between national income
and concentrations of various pollutants. Investigation of this issue has
been hampered by the paucity of data on pollution that are available on a
comparable basis for a representative sample of countries. However, since
1976 the World Health Organization (WHO) has collaborated with the
United Nations Environment Programme in operating the Global Environmental Monitoring System (GEMS). The goal of this project has been to
monitor closely the concentrations of several air pollutants in a cross-
section of urban areas using standardized methods of measurement. This
data set, which to our knowledge has not previously been analyzed by
economists, provides us with an opportunity to examine how air quality
is affected by economic growth.[4]

In the next subsection we describe the GEMS project, the types of
pollution that it monitors, and the data that it has generated. Section 1.2
gives the details of the statistical analysis that we have performed. Our
findings are presented in section 1.3 and the implications for Mexico are
discussed in section 1.4.

1.1 The GEMS Data

The GEMS monitors air quality in urban areas throughout the world. Daily
(or, in some cases, weekly) measurements are taken of concentrations of
sulfur dioxide (SO_2) and suspended particulate matter.[5] Data on particulates, which are gases and liquids suspended in the air, are collected by
different methods (described further below) that alternatively measure the
mass of materials in a given volume of air and the concentration of finer,
darker matter, sometimes referred to as "smoke."

Sulfur dioxide is a corrosive gas that has been linked to respiratory
disease and other health problems.[6] It is emitted naturally by volcanoes,
decaying organic matter, and sea spray. The major anthropogenic sources
of SO_2 are the burning of fossil fuels in electricity generation and domestic
heating, and the smelting of nonferrous ores (World Resources Institute,

1988). Other sources in some countries include automobile exhaust and the chemicals industry (Kormondy, 1989). Sulfur dioxide emissions can be controlled by the installation of flue gas desulfurization equipment (scrubbers) on polluting facilities, and by switching electricity-generating and home-heating capacity to lower sulfur grades of coal or away from coal altogether.

Particulates arise from dust, sea spray, forest fires, and volcanoes. Most of these naturally produced particles are relatively large. Finer particles are emitted by industry and from domestic fuel combustion (World Resources Institute, 1988). Larger particles reduce visibility but have a relatively minor health impact, whereas the finer particles can cause eye and lung damage and can aggravate existing respiratory conditions (U.S. EPA, 1982). Particulate emissions from anthropogenic processes can be reduced via the installation of control equipment and by switching to fuels that, when burned, emit fewer particles.

The GEMS sample of cities has been changing over time. Sulfur dioxide was monitored in 47 cities spread over 28 different countries in 1977, 52 cities in 32 countries in 1982, and 27 cities in 14 countries in 1988. Measurements of suspended particles were taken in 21 cities in 11 countries in 1977, 36 cities in 17 countries in 1982, and 26 cities in 13 countries in 1988, while data for darker matter (smoke) are available for 18 cities in 13 countries for 1977, 13 cities in 9 countries for 1982, and 7 cities in 4 countries for 1988. In all, there are 42 countries represented in our sample for SO_2, 19 countries in our sample for dark matter, and 29 countries in our sample for suspended particles. The participating cities (listed in the appendix) are located in a variety of developing and developed countries and have been chosen to be fairly representative of the geographic conditions that exist in different regions of the world (Bennett et al., 1985). In most of the cities included in the project, air quality measurements are taken at two or three different sites, which are classified either as center city or suburban, and as commercial, industrial, or residential. Multiple sites in the same city are monitored in recognition of the fact that pollutant concentrations can vary dramatically with local conditions that depend in part upon land use. Observations at most sites are made on a daily basis and the data set includes measures of the mean, median, 80th, 95th, and 98th percentile of daily observations in a given site for a given year.

Sulfur dioxide concentrations have been determined by a number of well-accepted methods (see WHO, 1984). The reliability of these methods has been checked in independent studies, and an intercomparison exercise was performed using one particular method as a reference point (Bennett et al., 1985). It was concluded that the measurements by alternative methods are roughly comparable, although particular meteorological conditions can affect the various methods differently. With these results in mind, we have chosen to pool our sample of observations of SO_2 concentration, but to allow for a dummy variable to reflect the method of measurement at each site.

Suspended particles are measured by two main methods. High volume gravimetric sampling determines the mass of particulates in a given volume of air, whereas the smoke-shade method assesses the reflectance of the stain left on a filter paper that ambient air has been drawn through. The former method measures the total weight of suspended particles, while the latter is predominantly an indication of dark material in the air. As the two methods yield incomparable measures that capture different aspects of particulate air pollution, we treat the data generated by gravimetric and smoke-shade methods separately in our analysis.[7]

Table 2.1 provides the mean, median, and standard deviation for the 50th and 95th percentiles of daily observations in our sample of cities for each of the three types of pollution. Figure 2.1 displays the corresponding histograms. The median of daily observations on SO_2 range from a minimum of zero to a maximum of 291 micrograms per cubic meter ($\mu g\ m^{-3}$) of air whereas the 95th percentile of daily measures range from 0 to 1,022

Table 2.1
Descriptive statistics on air pollution in urban areas

Pollutant	Mean	Standard deviation	Median	WHO standard
Sulphur dioxide 50th percentile	33.08	33.11	26.2	40–60
Sulphur dioxide 95th percentile	117.17	112.71	87.0	100–150
Dark matter 50th percentile	42.22	41.92	29.5	50–60
Dark matter 95th percentile	127.47	101.45	102.0	100–150
Suspended particles 50th percentile	146.62	126.79	91.0	60–90
Suspended particles 95th percentile	301.01	268.01	187.0	150–230

Notes: Pollutants are measured in μg per cubic meter. World Health Organization standards listed for the 50th percentile are for the annual average measure, and those listed for the 95th percentile are for the 98th percentile of daily measures. Sample size is 1,370 for sulphur dioxide, 1,021 for suspended particles, and 506 for dark matter.

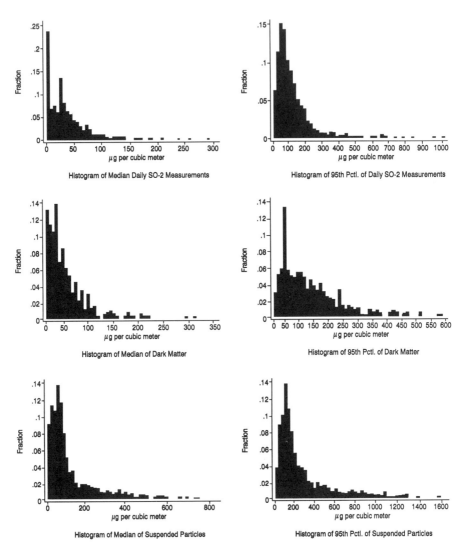

Figure 2.1
Histograms of air pollutants

μg m^{-3}.[8] These numbers can be compared with the World Health Organization recommendation that annual average SO$_2$ concentrations ought not to exceed 40–60 μg m^{-3} and that 98th percentile concentrations ought not to exceed 100–150 μg m^{-3}. The median of daily observations for suspended particles varied from zero to 715 μg m^{-3}, while that for the 95th percentile observation ranged from 15 to 1,580 μg m^{-3}. The WHO guidelines for suspended particles list 60–90 μg m^{-3} as the safe limit for the annual mean and 150–230 μg m^{-3} as the safe limit for the 98th percentile. Finally the median of daily observations of dark matter (or smoke) in the sample of sites varied from zero to 312 μg m^{-3}, while the 95th percentile observation varied from 2 to 582 μg m^{-3}. The WHO recommends that dark matter not exceed 50–60 μg m^{-3} in annual average and 100–150 μg m^{-3} in the 98th percentile of daily observations.

1.2 Estimation

Concentrations of pollutants in the air depend upon the amounts that are emitted by natural and anthropogenic sources and on the ability of the atmosphere to absorb and disburse the gases or particles. Thus our analysis of the relationship between growth and air quality must allow for an influence of city and site characteristics on the observed concentrations of the various pollutants in addition to the dependence on national product.

We have sought to explain the median and 95th percentile of daily observations for SO$_2$, suspended particles, and dark matter. As explanatory variables, we have included functions of per capita GDP in the country where the site is located, characteristics of the site and city, and a time trend. We used the Summers and Heston (1991) data for per capita GDP, which attempt to measure output in relation to a common set of international prices. Initially we allowed the coefficient on per capita GDP to vary across income ranges by including a dummy variable in our regressions for each $2,000 interval of per capita GDP. These relatively unrestricted regressions suggested that a cubic function of per capita GDP would fit the data fairly well. The cubic equations are the main focus of our subsequent analysis.[9]

In the equation for concentrations of SO$_2$, we included dummy variables for the location within the city (central city or suburban) and for the land use of the area near the testing site (industrial, commercial, or residential). We also included a dummy variable for the method of measurement (gas bubbler or otherwise). Another dummy indicated whether the city was located along a coastline or not (reflecting the disbursement properties of the local atmosphere). We included a variable for the population density of the city and a dummy variable for whether the city was located in a country ruled by a communist government.[10] Finally, a linear time trend was included to allow for the possibility that pollution has been abating (or worsening) worldwide, in response to increased global awareness or for other reasons.[11]

The regressions for suspended particles and dark matter included a similar set of right-hand-side variables, except that we did not include a dummy variable for the method of monitoring dark matter, because all measurements were taken in the same way. Because dust is an important natural source of particulate matter, we included as an additional explanatory variable a dummy that indicates whether the measurement site is located within 100 miles of a desert.[12]

Some commentators have argued that a country's level of pollution might be directly related to its openness to international trade, perhaps because environmental regulations tend to a least common denominator. To test this hypothesis, we estimated one set of regressions in which we included the trade intensity of the country in which the site is located (ratio of the sum of exports and imports to GDP) as a separate determinant of the concentration of the air pollutants.[13]

For each pollutant, we estimated a random effects model, allowing for a component of the error term that is common to a given year's observations at different sites located in the same city.[14] We find that the variance of the common-to-the-city component of the estimated residuals is relatively large in comparison to the idiosyncratic (site-by-time) component, so that ordinary least squares would give inconsistent estimates of the standard errors of the regressions. We also calculated one set of estimates that allowed for fixed site effects. In other words, we included a separate dummy variable for each of the different sites in our various samples. The fixed effects were intended to capture the unobservable topographical and meteorological conditions at a site that might contribute to its ability to absorb or disburse pollution. Of course, when we included the fixed site effects, we dropped the dummy variables reflecting the location of the site within the city and the location of the city on a coastline or near a desert, as these influences were no longer separately identified. The model with fixed site effects provides an especially stringent test of the relationship between national income and pollution, inasmuch as it ignores all information contained in the cross-country variation in pollution levels and relies instead only on the variation in air quality that resulted at the various sites from changes in GDP during the twelve years of GEMS observations (and then only that part of the variation that cannot be explained by a common linear time trend).

1.3 Findings

The results of our various estimates of the random effects models for the three pollutants are given in tables 2.2–2.4. These regressions do not include the model with fixed site effects, which we discuss separately below.

Figure 2.2 displays, for the median of daily observations on each pollutant, the estimated coefficients on the dummy variables indicating whether a country's per capita GDP falls in the range from $2,000 to $3,999, from $4,000 to $5,999, and so on. The coefficient estimates have been plotted above the midpoint in the range, for example, above $3,000 for GDP in the range from $2,000 to $3,999. These coefficients should be interpreted as indicating the amount of extra pollution a country with a per capita GDP in a given range is likely to have, holding constant the values of other explanatory variables (site location, city population density, etc.), relative to a country with a per capita GDP in the range from zero to $2,000. The figure also shows the estimated amount of extra pollution that is associated with a given level of per capita GDP (relative to a country with a per capita GDP of $1,000) that comes from regressing the pollution concentrations on per capita GDP, per capita GDP-squared, per capita GDP-cubed, and the remaining explanatory variables. The figure shows that, in each case, the cubic functional form approximates well the shape of the relationship between pollution and GDP that is indicated by the less restrictive regressions.

Figure 2.3 depicts the estimated relationship between per capita GDP and SO_2, derived from the cubic equations, for both the 50th and 95th percentile of daily observations. For both measures, the concentration of SO_2 rises with per capita GDP at low levels of national income, falls with per capita GDP in the broad range between $5,000 and $14,000 (1985 U.S. dollars), and then levels off or perhaps begins to rise again.[15] The turning point in the predicted relationship for the median of daily observations comes at $4,107, while that for the 95th percentile observation occurs at $4,635. We estimate that a country with per capita GDP of $5,000 will have a 20 $\mu g \ m^{-3}$ greater concentration of SO_2 for the 95th percentile of its daily observations, as compared to a country with a per capita GDP of $1,000, all else equal. Table 2.2 indicates that the hypothesis that SO_2 pollution is unrelated to the level of GDP can be rejected at the .01% significance level in the regression for the median observation and at the

Table 2.2
The determinants of sulphur dioxide air pollution, random effects estimates (standard errors in parentheses)

Variable	50th percentile			95th percentile		
	(1)	(2)	(3)	(4)	(5)	(6)
Per capita GDP $2,000–$3,999	4.70 (3.94)	—	—	3.28 (13.67)	—	—
Per capita GDP $4,000–$5,999	6.43 (4.19)	—	—	23.45 (14.57)	—	—
Per capita GDP $6,000–$7,999	−4.15 (5.31)	—	—	−15.00 (18.42)	—	—
Per capita GDP $8,000–$9,999	3.91 (4.55)	—	—	20.80 (15.79)	—	—
Per capita GDP $10,000–$11,999	−9.33* (4.40)	—	—	−3.58 (15.26)	—	—
Per capita GDP $12,000–$13,999	−19.07* (5.74)	—	—	−3.58 (19.82)	—	—
Per capita GDP $14,000–15,999	−11.82* (5.11)	—	—	−24.62 (17.61)	—	—
Per capita GDP $16,000–$17,999	−10.28 (6.63)	—	—	−11.35 (22.34)	—	—
Per capita GDP ($1,000s)		7.14* (2.50)	11.22* (2.64)		12.02 (8.66)	22.18* (9.22)
Per capita GDP-squared		−1.12* (0.34)	−1.44* (0.34)		−1.68 (1.53)	−2.42* (1.18)
Per capita GDP-cubed		0.041* (0.013)	0.047* (0.013)		0.055 (0.043)	0.068 (0.044)
Coast	−8.68* (2.39)	−6.68* (2.32)	−5.73* (2.32)	−52.62* (8.17)	−46.79* (7.94)	−45.27* (8.03)

	(1)	(2)	(3)	(4)	(5)	(6)
Central city	35.31*	34.33*	35.42*	8.94*	8.94*	9.45*
	(5.77)	(5.73)	(5.76)	(1.86)	(1.82)	(1.83)
Industrial	9.65	10.39	10.95	1.74	1.32	1.58
	(6.12)	(6.04)	(6.06)	(2.01)	(1.94)	(1.95)
Residential	−3.23	−5.45	−4.08	−4.97*	−5.71*	−5.30*
	(6.14)	(6.08)	(6.10)	(2.01)	(1.95)	(1.96)
Population density (10,000/sq. mi.)	49.81*	35.43*	41.74*	10.31*	4.09	5.54*
	(16.30)	(8.97)	(9.27)	(4.64)	(2.57)	(2.65)
Year	−5.12*	−5.32*	−5.38*	−1.77*	−1.79*	−1.69*
	(1.22)	(1.18)	(1.21)	(0.35)	(0.34)	(0.36)
Communist	90.77*	88.04*	88.05*	12.64*	11.47*	11.59*
	(13.61)	(13.32)	(13.47)	(3.86)	(3.83)	(3.88)
Trade intensity	—	—	—	−15.47*	—	—
				(4.38)		
p-value for all GDP variables	.007	.07	.06	.0001	.0001	.0001
Per capita GDP at which pollution reaches peak	$6,182	$4,635	—	$5,257	$4,107	—
	(2,963)	(3,309)		(1,179)	(1,327)	
σ_ε^2	5,555	5,575	5,593	579	554	556
σ_x^2	5,232	5,541	5,431	323	378	368
R^2	.138	.125	.132	.166	.150	.158

Notes: Equations also include an intercept, a dummy to indicate that the type of area is unknown, and a dummy to indicate that the measurement device is a gas bubbler. σ_x^2 is the estimated variance of the common-to-city component of the residuals, and σ_ε^2 is the estimated variance of the idiosyncratic component of the residual. Sample size is 1,370 for columns 1, 2, 4, and 5; sample size is 1,301 for columns 3 and 6.
*Statistically significant at .05 level for a two-tailed t-test.

Table 2.3
The determinants of dark matter pollution, random effects estimates (standard errors in parentheses)

Variable	50th percentile			95th percentile		
	(1)	(2)	(3)	(4)	(5)	(6)
Per capita GDP $2,000–$3,999	50.50* (11.77)	—	—	99.21* (31.77)	—	—
Per capita GDP $4,000–$5,999	58.25* (12.63)	—	—	118.05* (33.99)	—	—
Per capita GDP $6,000–$7,999	43.49* (13.10)	—	—	111.74* (35.23)	—	—
Per capita GDP $8,000–$9,999	21.26 (13.07)	—	—	39.85 (35.12)	—	—
Per capita GDP $10,000–$11,999	22.27 (13.04)	—	—	30.27 (35.17)	—	—
Per capita GDP $12,000–$13,999	27.29 (28.64)	—	—	16.10 (74.95)	—	—
Per capita GDP ($1,000s)		79.33* (13.04)	30.52 (16.79)		173.84* (34.32)	113.19* (47.45)
Per capita GDP-squared		−12.38* (2.05)	−5.08* (2.54)		−25.62* (5.38)	−16.45* (7.16)
Per capita GDP-cubed		0.56* (0.10)	0.233 (0.121)		1.09* (0.26)	0.68* (0.34)
Desert	40.19* (8.61)	42.11* (8.49)	−10.12 (14.21)	113.03* (23.24)	118.14* (22.67)	44.27* (41.85)
Coast	−21.29 (4.94)	−21.75* (4.55)	−17.68* (4.52)	−35.85* (13.00)	−41.44* (11.87)	−33.46* (12.50)

	(1)	(2)	(3)	(4)	(5)	(6)
Central city	9.55*	8.26*	10.95*	32.41*	20.32*	21.44*
	(4.05)	(3.96)	(3.86)	(9.38)	(9.18)	(9.50)
Industrial	0.25	-0.55	-0.13	-5.95	-6.37	-5.92
	(4.23)	(4.18)	(4.06)	(9.62)	(9.51)	(9.74)
Residential	-10.60*	-11.56*	-7.09*	-21.64*	-22.51*	-15.20
	(3.98)	(3.93)	(3.87)	(9.12)	(9.01)	(9.34)
Population density (10,000/sq. mi.)	1.32*	1.35*	2.92*	0.70	0.94	4.75
	(0.37)	(0.36)	(1.17)	(0.98)	(0.95)	(3.17)
Year	-0.26	-0.60	-0.59	0.41	-0.15	1.27
	(0.58)	(0.56)	(0.58)	(1.51)	(1.45)	(1.59)
Communist	-20.44*	-20.93*	-14.44	-0.98	-9.73	7.56
	(7.91)	(7.54)	(8.51)	(20.87)	(19.78)	(23.39)
Trade intensity	—	—	-6.57	—	—	-12.05
			(6.35)			(17.84)
p-value for all GDP variables	.0001	.0001	.0001	.0001	.0001	.0001
Per capita GDP at which pollution reaches peak	—	$4,721	$4,240	—	$4,970	$4,971
		(771)	(2,180)		(973)	(2,105)
σ_ε^2	598	953	864	4,865	4,828	4,772
σ_z^2	192	186	166	2,183	2,040	2,108
R^2	.345	.352	.210	.315	.315	.221

Notes: Equations also include an intercept and a dummy to indicate that the type of area is unknown. Sample size is 506 for columns 1, 2, 4, and 5; sample size is 457 for columns 3 and 6.

*Statistically significant at .05 level for a two-tailed t-test.

Table 2.4
The determinants for suspended particles pollution, random effects estimates (standard errors in parentheses)

Variable	50th percentile			95th percentile		
	(1)	(2)	(3)	(4)	(5)	(6)
Per capita GDP $2,000–$3,999	−102.4* (11.9)	—	—	−191.4* (25.4)	—	—
Per capita GDP $4,000–$5,999	−129.7* (13.5)	—	—	−247.4* (29.0)	—	—
Per capita GDP $6,000–$7,999	−101.9* (31.8)	—	—	−134.2 (69.2)	—	—
Per capita GDP $8,000–$9,999	−201.2* (22.4)	—	—	−348.8* (47.1)	—	—
Per capita GDP $10,000–$11,999	−221.1* (13.0)	—	—	−425.0* (27.7)	—	—
Per capita GDP $12,000–$13,999	−187.9* (14.6)	—	—	−368.1* (31.6)	—	—
Per capita GDP $14,000–15,999	−183.1* (12.5)	—	—	−366.2* (27.1)	—	—
Per capita GDP $16,000–$17,999	−184.5 (15.5)	—	—	−381.2* (32.9)	—	—
Per capita GDP ($1,000s)		−71.97* (8.02)	−72.54* (8.49)		−144.31* (17.81)	−146.48* (17.74)
Per capita GDP-squared		6.03* (1.08)	5.81* (1.10)		12.65* (2.28)	12.31* (2.28)
Per capita GDP-cubed		−0.157* (0.043)	−0.143* (0.040)		−0.353* (0.085)	−0.328* (0.084)
Desert	189.6* (19.0)	213.3* (18.6)	289.4* (34.3)	354.7* (40.7)	409.8* (39.6)	489.5* (68.9)

	(1)	(2)	(3)	(4)	(5)	(6)
Coast	0.42	4.47	2.90	-9.78	0.22	-4.39
	(7.73)	(7.58)	(7.41)	(16.41)	(16.01)	(15.43)
Central city	11.11*	12.99*	14.76*	32.52*	36.31*	39.11*
	(5.24)	(5.20)	(4.28)	(10.47)	(10.40)	(10.46)
Industrial	13.73*	15.23*	11.15	44.28*	47.55*	40.48*
	(5.79)	(5.77)	(5.91)	(11.55)	(11.49)	(11.66)
Residential	-12.17*	-9.67*	-9.45	-1.19	3.83	2.02
	(5.83)	(4.78)	(5.90)	(11.62)	(11.51)	(11.66)
Population density (10,000/sq. mi.)	5.20	-4.64	-17.55	-41.38	-43.97*	-74.43*
	(9.99)	(9.64)	(12.63)	(21.84)	(20.95)	(26.92)
Year	-2.06	-2.27*	-2.26*	-1.41	-1.65	-1.27
	(1.20)	(1.14)	(1.15)	(2.58)	(2.43)	(2.41)
Communist	90.52*	108.37*	107.81*	221.51*	256.46*	251.12*
	(13.21)	(12.65)	(12.54)	(28.68)	(27.28)	(26.52)
Trade intensity	—	—	-12.39	—	—	6.49
			(15.17)			(31.23)
p-value for all GDP variables	.0001	.0001	.0001	.0001	.0001	.0001
σ_ε^2	3,379	3,350	3,482	12,950	12,793	13,085
σ_z^2	3,353	3,754	3,073	18,043	17,218	14,894
R^2	.581	.577	.574	.569	.582	.590

Notes: Equations also include an intercept, a dummy to indicate the type of area unknown, and two dummies to indicate the kind of instrument used to measure suspended particulate matter. Sample size is 1,021 for columns 1, 2, 4, and 5; sample size is 971 for columns 3 and 6.

*Statistically significant at .05 level for a two-tailed t-test.

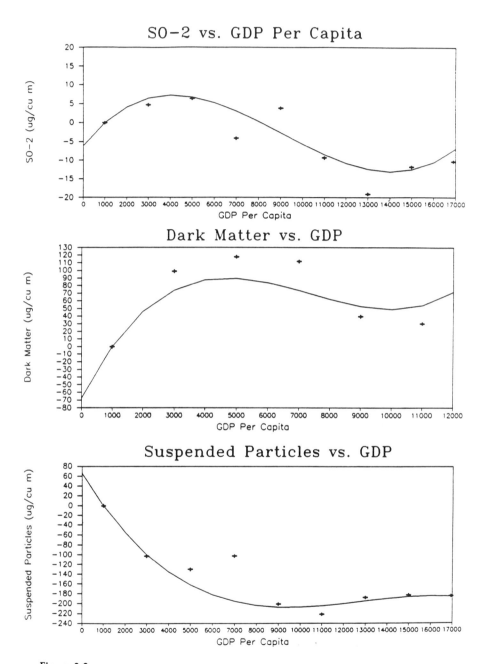

Figure 2.2
Fitted cubic and unrestricted dummies

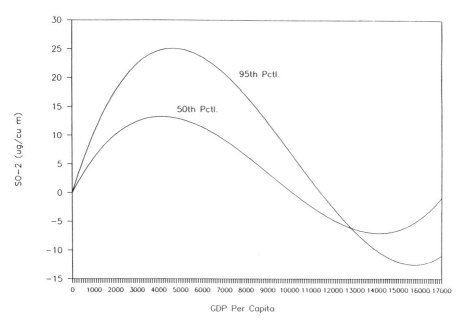

Figure 2.3
SO$_2$ vs. GDP per capita

7% level in the regression for the 95th percentile observation (see columns 2 and 5).

Table 2.2 reveals that several other variables contribute significantly to the cross-city variation in concentrations of SO$_2$. For example, cities located on a coastline are estimated to have lesser concentrations of SO$_2$: 6.68 μg m^{-3} lower for the median of daily observations and 46.79 μg m^{-3} lower for the 95th percentile observation. Concentrations of SO$_2$ are higher in the center city than in the suburbs, lower in residential areas than in commercial areas, and higher in industrial areas than in commercial areas (although this effect is not statistically significant at conventional significance levels). More densely populated cities suffer greater concentrations of SO$_2$, all else equal. We also find that SO$_2$ pollution has been significantly greater in cities located in communist-ruled countries. Finally, we note that SO$_2$ levels have been trending downward in our sample of cities even after controlling for the effects of income and other variables. The downward trend may reflect an increasing global awareness of the health problems associated with SO$_2$, and the expanding efforts that are being made worldwide to limit sulfur emissions.

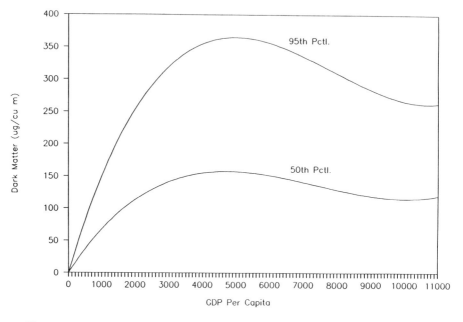

Figure 2.4
Dark matter vs. GDP per capita

Columns 3 and 6 of table 2.2 present estimates of a model for SO_2 determination that includes trade intensity as an additional explanatory variable. Contrary to the fears of some environmentalists, we find that SO_2 levels are significantly *lower* in cities located in countries that conduct a great deal of trade (relative to their GDP). We have no good economic explanation for this finding.

Figure 2.4 depicts the estimated (cubic) relationship between dark matter and per capita GDP for the median and 95th percentile of daily observations. Apparently the nature of the relationship is much the same as for SO_2. The concentration of smoke in the air rises with per capita GDP at low levels of income, peaks at around $5,000 (1985 U.S. dollars), and falls with GDP at higher income levels until it eventually levels off. We see in columns 2 and 5 of table 2.3 that the three GDP variables are jointly significant in the determination of dark matter pollution at the .01% significance level. Moreover, the size of the estimated effects are quite large. We estimate that a country with a per capita GDP of $5,000 will have a higher concentration of smoke by about 90 μg m^{-3} in its median of daily observations and 220 μg m^{-3} in its 95th percentile observation, compared to one with a per capita GDP of $1,000. Recall that the WHO recommends that

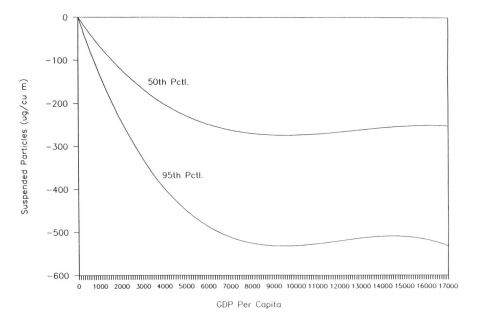

Figure 2.5
Suspended particles vs. GDP per capita

concentrations of smoke not exceed 50–60 μg m^{-3} for the mean observation and 100–150 μg m^{-3} for the 98th percentile observation.

Not surprisingly, the dummy variable indicating proximity to a desert has a positive and significant coefficient in the regressions explaining concentrations of dark matter. A location on a coast reduces a city's concentration of this type of pollution, and again the effect is statistically significant. We find that smoke pollution levels are greater in center cities than in suburbs, and smaller in residential areas than in commercial areas. Also, dark matter, like SO_2 rises with population density, although this effect is significant only in the regression for the median of daily observations. Finally, there appears to be neither a global trend in this type of pollution (once the upward movement in world incomes has been accounted for) nor a significant association with trade intensity.

Unlike the other two pollutants, the mass of suspended particles in the air appears to fall in response to increases in per capita GDP at low levels of economic development (see figure 2.5). This relationship continues until per capita GDP reaches about $9,000, whereupon economic growth has no further effect on the concentration of suspended particles. Again, the estimated effects are large in comparison to the WHO guidelines, and again

Table 2.5
Random effects estimates of the determinants of air pollution including fixed site effects (standard errors in parentheses)

Variable	SO$_2$		Dark matter		Suspended particles	
	50 pctl	95 pctl	50 pctl	95 pctl	50 pctl	95 pctl
Per capita GDP ($1,000s)	12.54*	−8.28	24.35	77.89	63.44*	142.18*
	(4.69)	(15.11)	(17.70)	(49.71)	(13.94)	(30.30)
Per capita GDP-squard	−1.74*	0.10	−4.15	−12.10	−2.84	−6.21
	(0.52)	(1.67)	(2.73)	(7.66)	(1.49)	(3.23)
Per capita GDP-cubed	0.05*	−0.00	0.19	0.51	0.04	0.07
	(.02)	(.06)	(0.13)	(0.36)	(0.05)	(0.11)
Year	−1.05*	−3.51*	−0.91*	−1.12	−3.60*	−5.58*
	(0.28)	(0.90)	(0.42)	(1.17)	(0.82)	(1.77)
Number of site dummies	239	239	87	87	161	161
p-value for GDP variables	0.0001	0.118	0.479	0.250	0.0001	0.0001
σ_ε^2	161	1,951	141	1,070	919	3679
σ_x^2	97	982	93	755	512	2473
R^2	0.76	0.77	0.87	0.82	0.91	0.91

Notes: Sample size is 1,370 for SO$_2$, 506 for dark matter and 1,021 for suspended particles. The SO$_2$ equations also include a dummy for the measuring device, and the suspended particles equations include two dummies for measuring device.
*Statistically significant at .05 level for a two-tailed t-test.

the three GDP variables are jointly significant in the determination of this measure of air quality.

As with dark matter, cities situated near to a desert are likely to experience higher concentrations of suspended particles than cities located elsewhere. This effect is both quantitatively large and highly significant. The coefficients on the communist dummy, the center-city dummy, and the industrial-area dummy all are positive and statistically significant in the regressions for both the median and 95th percentile of daily observations. The global trend in suspended particle pollution apparently has been downward, although the coefficient on the year variable is statistically significant only in the regressions for the median of daily observations. Finally, a country's trade intensity has a small and statistically insignificant effect on this form of pollution.

Table 2.5 reports the estimated coefficients from a random effects model for each type of pollutant that also allows for fixed site effects. The numbers of site dummy variables that were included in the various regressions are shown in the table. These estimates of the relationship between per

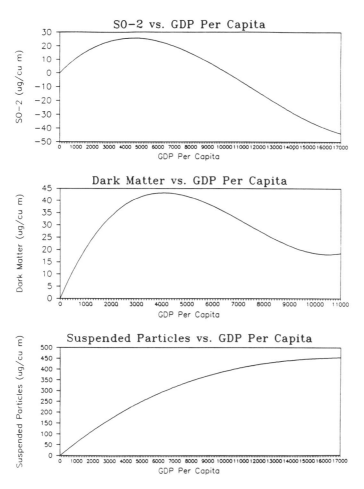

Figure 2.6
Fixed effects estimates—50th percentile

capita GDP and the various measures of air quality rely only on the covariation between GDP and concentrations of the pollutants over time within the individual sites, and not on the cross-country variation in pollution and GDP at a given moment in time. The estimated relationships for the median of daily observations of SO_2 and dark matter hold up remarkably well (see figure 2.6). In each case, the data continue to indicate an inverted U-shaped relationship between pollution and national income, with peak levels of pollution occurring for per capita incomes in the range from $4,000 to $5,000. Only the estimated coefficients from the fixed site effects model for suspended particles suggest a different relationship between per capita GDP and concentrations of the pollutant than is found in the regressions without site effects. In this case, the estimation indicates a monotonically increasing relationship between particulate pollution and national output in the sample range of output levels.

1.4 Implications for Mexico

Unfortunately, Mexico has not participated in the GEMS project and reliable measures of its air pollution are not available (U.S. GAO, 1991b). Thus predictions for Mexico must be inferred from relationships that hold in other countries at similar stages of development. Surely the available evidence suggests that air quality has deteriorated with economic growth in Mexico (U.S. GAO, 1991b). Our estimates indicate that this experience is common in poor countries, but that the positive association between two pollutants and economic output ceases when the typical country reaches a per capita income level of about $5,000 (1985 U.S. dollars). We note that Summers and Heston (1991) put Mexico's per capita GDP in 1988 (adjusted to reflect the purchasing power of its currency) at $4,996. Thus we might expect that further growth in Mexico, as may result from a free trade agreement with the United States and Canada, will lead the country to intensify its efforts to alleviate its environmental problems.

Recent measures taken by the government of Mexico suggest that the country already may have reached the turning point in terms of air pollution. In the last year, the Salinas government has reduced the lead content of petrol, ordered several power stations to burn natural gas instead of sulfur-generating fuel oil, and shut down oil refineries and private firms that were found to be major sources of air pollution (The *Economist*, May 18, 1991). Also, new cars are being fitted with catalytic convertors, a new fleet of cleaner buses has been introduced, and drivers have been banned from using their cars in Mexico City one day each week. To beef up enforcement, the budget of the environmental protection ministry has been increased sevenfold (*New York Times*, Sept. 22, 1991). Further growth may enable the government to implement fully its planned $2.5 billion, four-year program to clean up Mexico City.

2 Pollution Abatement Costs and the Pattern of U.S.-Mexico Investment and Trade

A main source of concern about a NAFTA is that it will enable firms to circumvent U.S. environmental protection laws. If the costs of meeting pollution controls are high in the United States and low or negligible in Mexico, then the asymmetry in standards or enforcement efforts can create a competitive advantage for Mexican producers and can motivate U.S. firms to relocate their production facilities south of the border. In these circumstances, liberalization of trade and investment flows can strengthen the incentives for "environmental dumping."

A number of authors, including Pethig (1976), Siebert (1977), Yohe (1979), and McGuire (1982), have studied the theoretical relationship between environmental regulations and the pattern of trade. They find that strict environmental standards or costly controls weaken a country's competitive position in pollution-intensive industries and diminish its exports (or increase its imports) of the product of such sectors. Countries that fail to regulate industrial pollution increase their specialization in activities that damage the environment. McGuire has extended these results to include direct foreign investment: controls cause firms active in the pollution-intensive industry to relocate their activities to the less regulated countries.

While these theoretical predictions are plausible and intuitive, they have found little support in previous empirical studies of trade and investment patterns. For example, Tobey (1990) has tested the hypothesis that environmental regulations have altered the pattern of trade in goods produced by "dirty" industries. He finds that a qualitative variable describing the stringency of environmental controls in twenty-three countries fails to contribute to the determination of their net exports of the five most pollution-intensive commodities. Similarly, Walter (1982) and Leonard (1988) conclude that there is little evidence that pollution abatement costs have influenced the location decisions of multinational firms. Apparently, the cross-country variation in the costs of meeting environmental controls is not so large as to be a major factor in the determination of nations' comparative advantages.

Our purpose in this section is to address this issue in connection with the pattern of U.S. imports from Mexico and the pattern of U.S. foreign investments in Mexico. There is some evidence from a GAO survey suggesting that a few American furniture manufacturers may have moved their operations to Mexico in response to the California's tightening of air pollution control standards for paint coatings and solvents (U.S. GAO, 1991c). But the question remains as to whether the overall sectoral pattern of U.S. economic relations with Mexico has been meaningfully affected by the higher cost of pollution abatement in the United States. If the pattern of specialization has been so influenced, then the composition effect of a further liberalization of trade and investment may be damaging to the environment.

Using data from the Bureau of Census's 1988 survey of pollution abatement costs in American industries (U.S. DOC, 1988), we have conducted three sets of tests. We have studied the 1987 pattern of U.S. imports from Mexico in three-digit SIC manufacturing industries, the pattern of 1987 U.S. imports from Mexico that have entered the country under the offshore assembly provisions (again at the three-digit SIC level), and the sectoral pattern of value added by maquiladora plants in (approximately) two-digit industry categories. In each case we have investigated whether pollution abatement costs in the United States help to explain the pattern of Mexican specialization and trade.

Our estimates of the determinants of the pattern of manufactured imports from Mexico are recorded in the first two columns of table 2.6. We use the ratio of 1987 U.S. imports from Mexico to total U.S. shipments in the same industry as the dependent variable. The explanatory variables include factor shares (reflecting the intensity of use of the various factors by the different industries; see Harkness [1978]), the U.S. effective tariff rate on imports of goods in the industry, and the ratio of pollution abatement costs (operating expenses) to total value added in the U.S. industry.[16,17] We also report another regression that includes the average injury rate in the industry as an additional independent variable. As firm outlays for worker compensation insurance are roughly proportional to injury rates (Krueger and Burton, 1990), the injury variable proxies for one (large) component of the cost to American manufacturing firms of U.S. labor protection laws.

We computed the factor shares as follows. We took the payroll expenses in an industry to represent a combined compensation for unskilled or "raw" labor and human capital. Payments to unskilled labor were defined as the product of the number of workers in the industry and the economywide average yearly income of workers in manufacturing with less than a high school education. We formed a share by dividing this amount by value added, and considered the remaining part of the total labor share to represent the payment to human capital.[18] Finally, we calculated the share of capital in value added as the difference between one and the total payroll share.[19]

Factor intensities figure prominently in the determination of the pattern of U.S. imports from Mexico. The ratio of imports to total U.S. shipments is smaller in industries that are highly intensive in their use of human or physical capital. This means, of course, that Mexico exports to the United

Table 2.6
The determinants of the pattern of U.S. imports from Mexico and of value added by maquiladora

Independent variables	Total U.S. imports from Mexico as fraction of U.S. shipments		Mexican value added in 807 imports as fraction of U.S. value added		Maquiladora value added as fraction of U.S. value added	
	(1)	(2)	(3)	(4)	(5)	(6)
Constant	.028* (.008)	−.027* (.009)	.019* (.006)	.021* (.007)	.010 (.007)	.015* (.007)
Human capital share	−.053* (.016)	−.053* (.016)	−.016 (.010)	−.015 (.010)	−.015 (.012)	−.016 (.011)
Physical capital share	−.024* (.010)	−.023* (.011)	−.026* (.009)	−.027* (.010)	−.011 (.010)	−.016 (.011)
Pollution abatement cost as fraction of U.S. industry value added	.014 (.060)	.012 (.061)	−.165* (.073)	−.151* (.074)	−.085 (.098)	−.077 (.090)
Tariff rate	−.002 (.028)	−.001 (.029)	—	—	—	—
Injury rate	—	.005 (.020)	—	−.001 (.016)	—	−.028 (.020)
R^2	.127	.127	.095	.095	.236	.392
Sample size	135	135	136	136	19	19
Mean of dependent variable	.0069	.0069	.0022	.0022	.0012	.0012

Notes: Standard errors are in parentheses. Columns (1) and (2) are OLS estimates. Columns (3), (4), (5), and (6) are maximum likely estimates of Tobit models. For the Tobit models, we calculated the reported values for R^2 as $1 − \sigma_\varepsilon^2/\sigma_0^2$, where σ_ε^2 denotes the estimated variance of the error from the Tobit model and σ_0^2 is the estimated variance of the residual from a Tobit estimation that includes only a constant on the right-hand side.
*Indicates statistically significant at .05 level.

States goods that have a relatively high share of unskilled labor in total factor cost. The coefficients on the physical and human capital variables both are statistically significant at the 5 percent level, but the latter coefficient is quantitatively much larger. We estimate that a 10 percentage point increase in the share of human capital reduces the ratio of imports to shipments by 0.52 percentage points, while a 10 percentage point increase in the share of physical capital lowers the import ratio by only 0.24 percentage points. Note that the mean ratio of imports to shipments across all manufacturing industries is 0.69%.

We estimate that the import ratio rises with the share of pollution abatement costs in U.S. industry value added, as would be predicted by a model of environmental dumping. However, the impact of these regulatory costs is both quantitatively small and statistically insignificant. Consider for example an industry that has the mean ratio of pollution abatement costs to industry value added and another that has a ratio that is two standard deviations higher. We estimate that the latter industry will have a greater ratio of imports to U.S. shipments by about 0.05%, which is less than .05 of a standard deviation in the import variable. This finding can be understood from the fact that pollution abatement costs average only 1.38% of value added across all manufacturing industries and rise to only 4.85% in an industry that is two standard deviations above the mean. The implied variation in competitiveness is small in comparison with that which arises from cross-industry variations in labor costs, for example.

We note that the injury rate has a positive coefficient when it is included in the import equation, but this variable too has a very small and statistically insignificant effect. Finally, the coefficient on the tariff variable has the theoretically predicted negative sign (imports are smaller in industries with high effective tariff rates), but also is not significant.[20]

We turn next to the determinants of the pattern of U.S. imports from Mexico under the offshore assembly provision (i.e., import category 807.00 in the old TSUSA tariff schedule). U.S. trade law provides for duty-free reentry of American-made components embodied in imported final goods. In cases where intermediate products are exported for further processing or assembly abroad, the applicable tariff rate applies only to the foreign value added. Nearly 44% of the value of Mexican exports to the United States qualified for this customs treatment in 1987 (Schoepfle, 1991). We study these imports separately, because much of the output by maquiladora plants enters the United States in this manner, and maquiladoras are the source of most of the item 807.00 U.S. imports from Mexico (Schoepfle,

1991). Thus the sectoral pattern of item 807.00 imports gives us an idea as to the pattern of maquiladora activity.

The middle two columns of table 2.6 report estimates of an equation for the ratio of the Mexican value added in imports entering under the 807.00 code in 1987 to the total value added by the U.S. industry. We would expect this variable to be high in industries where maquiladoras are especially active, that is those in which Mexico enjoys a competitive advantage. The independent variables in these equations are the same as before, namely the factor shares, the share of pollution abatement costs in U.S. industry value added, and in one set of estimates, the industry injury rate. The tariff variable was omitted from these regressions because our effective tariff rate applies to all imports from Mexico, and does not reflect the average tariff paid on imports that entered under the offshore assembly provision. We use a Tobit model to estimate these equations in view of the fact that item 807.00 imports are zero in 58 of the 136 industry categories. Because the import share cannot be negative, a censored regression model is appropriate.

The foreign content of U.S. item 807.00 imports from Mexico is highest in relation to total value added in the corresponding U.S. industry in sectors that make relatively intensive use of unskilled labor. This is not surprising, as many U.S. manufacturers attempt to outsource to maquiladora operations the most unskilled-labor-intensive phases of the production process. We find a negative association between the Mexican content of item 807.00 imports as a fraction of total U.S. industry value added and both the human capital share and the physical capital share in U.S. industry costs. The coefficient on the physical capital variable is estimated to be nearly twice as large in absolute value as that on the human capital variable (reversing the ordering found for total imports from Mexico), and the former coefficient is statistically significant at the 5% level, whereas the latter is statistically significant at only the 10% level.

Again, we fail to find a significant positive relationship between the size of pollution abatement costs (as a fraction of value added) in the U.S. manufacturing industry and the scale of sectoral activity in Mexico. In fact, the foreign content of item 807.00 imports from Mexico appears to be *lower* in relation to the size of the U.S. industry in sectors where U.S. pollution abatement costs are relatively high. The negative coefficient on the abatement cost variable is found to be statistically significant at the 5% level, although this may of course reflect a spurious correlation between these costs and some omitted variable. When the U.S. injury rate is included in the equation for item 807.00 imports, the estimated coefficient on this variable is also negative. This would imply that relatively little Mexican assembly activity takes place in those industries where the cost to U.S. employers of workers' compensation insurance and other accident-related costs are especially high. However, in this case, the estimated coefficient is not significantly different from zero, so we cannot reject the hypothesis that the association between injury rates and the pattern of Mexican assembly operations is nil.

The final set of estimates recorded in table 2.6 relate to the activity of Mexican maquiladoras. The Instituto Nacional de Estadistica Geografia E Informatica (INEGA) has surveyed all maquiladoras on the government's list of in-bond producers. Their publication, *Estadistica de la Industria Maquiladora de Exportacion, 1978–1988*, provides data on value added by maquiladoras in eleven different manufacturing industries. We developed a concordance of the available data to a two-digit SIC basis and sought to explain the ratio in 1987 of value added by maquiladoras to value added in the corresponding U.S. industry.[21] The explanatory variables are defined as before, except that now we calculate factor shares and pollution abatement costs as a fraction of value added at the two-digit SIC level.

The estimated coefficients from the models of maquiladora activity confirm our findings for total U.S. imports from Mexico and for imports under tariff item 807.00. Again we find that Mexican competitive advantage derives from an abundance of unskilled labor, and that value added by maquiladoras declines in relation to value added in the United States the greater are the shares of human and physical capital in industry cost. Although neither coefficient has been estimated precisely enough to allow for a clear rejection of the hypothesis that the associations are zero, the magnitudes of the coefficients are very much in line with what we have found before. Also, we find no evidence in support of the hypothesis that U.S. regulatory costs contribute to the explanation of the pattern of maquiladora activity. Neither the coefficient on the abatement cost variable nor that on the injury rate variable has the (positive) sign that one would expect if American firms are investing in maquiladora plants primarily to avoid the high costs of environmental and labor protection laws at home. Evidently, the costs involved in complying with these laws are small in relation to the other components of total cost that determine whether it is profitable to operate in the United States or Mexico.

3 Resource Reallocation: Implications for Pollution

Our findings in section 2 suggest that relative factor supplies govern the pattern of trade between Mexico and its neighbors to the North. We might expect, therefore, that trade liberalization will stimulate Mexican production in unskilled-labor-intensive industries, while the United States and Canada will shift resources into sectors that make relatively heavy use of capital and skilled labor. The removal by Mexico of barriers to direct foreign investment can have the opposite effect on international patterns of specialization, if foreign firms bring with them the factors that are scarce in Mexico. Then local production may expand in (moderately) capital and skilled-labor-intensive sectors. The question that arises is, what are the environmental implications of these potential resource reallocations?

To answer this question fully, we need several pieces of information. First, we need to know which sectors will expand in each country, and by how much. Second, we need to know the pollution intensities of the various industries. Finally, we must know how NAFTA will affect the production technologies used in each location, so as to gauge any changes in pollution generated per unit of output. Estimates of NAFTA impacts on the production structure in each country are available from computational modeling exercises. Brown, Deardorff, and Stern (1991), for example, have predicted resource movements for several different scenarios of policy change under a NAFTA. Unfortunately, the remaining informational requirements pose more serious difficulties. Concerning the pollution generated by different industries, the United States collects data only on releases of *toxic waste* (and that of questionable quality), while Mexico collects no such data whatsoever. And although our findings in section 1 suggest that production techniques might well change in response to a trade agreement that generates economic growth in Mexico, it is difficult to assess how these changes will be distributed across industries.

In this section we draw upon the detailed estimates of Brown, Deardorff, and Stern (BDS) to derive some possible environmental implications of the resource reallocations that would result from a NAFTA. After describing the BDS modeling exercise, we turn to two issues. First, we discuss the model's predictions about each country's demand for the services of utilities. Second, we use the information available in the U.S. EPA's *Toxic Resources Inventory* to analyze how a NAFTA might affect releases of hazardous waste by the manufacturing sectors in the three partner countries.

The BDS estimates are based on a computable general equilibrium model of the economic interactions between the United States, Canada, Mexico, a group of thirty-one other major trading nations, and an abbreviated fifth region comprising the rest of the world. The model aggregates production into twenty-three categories of tradable goods and six categories of nontradable goods and services. The industries are treated either as perfectly competitive or monopolistically competitive, with the latter set exhibiting economies of scale. Output in each sector is produced from intermediate inputs and an aggregate of capital and labor. The authors allow for varying degrees of substitution between capital and labor in the different sectors, but treat labor as a homogeneous input. The latter assumption is unfortunate in view of our finding in section 2 that human capital endowments play a central role in determining the bilateral trade pattern between the United States and Mexico.

Since it is not clear what policy measures will be included in a NAFTA, BDS explore a number of alternatives. In one scenario they assume the removal of all bilateral tariffs between the United States, Canada, and Mexico, and an easing of U.S. quantitative restrictions that generates a 25% increase in U.S. imports of agricultural products, food, textiles, and apparel from Mexico. In a second scenario they allow for these same forms of trade liberalization and also a relaxation of restrictions on direct foreign investment in Mexico. The liberalization of investment is assumed to result in an (exogenous) 10% increase in Mexico's capital stock. It should be noted that in both of these cases, the estimated impacts include not only the removal of existing barriers between Mexico and its trade partners, but also the ultimate implementation of the policy changes that comprise the already concluded Canada-U.S. free trade agreement.

It is well known that many pollutants, such as sulfur dioxide, nitric oxide, nitrogen dioxide, and carbon dioxide, are by-products of electricity generation, especially when fossil fuels are burned. Thus an important determinant of the net effect of trade liberalization on air pollution will be the induced change in the demand for electricity. Unfortunately, the disaggregation in the BDS model does not allow us to identify the likely impacts of a NAFTA on electricity use, inasmuch as the model treats electricity as a component of the broader category of utilities. It is interesting to note, nonetheless, that BDS predict a *decline* of 0.56% in output by the Mexican utilities sector in response to a hypothetical agreement involving an elimination of tariffs and an increase in U.S. import quotas. This prediction can be understood from the fact that the scenario generates output contractions in ten of twenty-one Mexican manufacturing sectors, and expansions are anticipated primarily in labor-intensive industries such as food, textiles, apparel, leather products, and footwear, which presumably are not the sectors that use energy most intensively. But just as Mexico will shift resources into activities that require relatively little energy input, the United States and Canada may be expected to do the opposite. The model predicts modest increases of 0.07 percent and 0.09 percent, respectively, in production by utilities in the United States and Canada.

Quite different conclusions emerge from the scenario that attempts to capture the effects of a potential liberalization of investment flows. The exogenous 10% increase in the Mexican capital stock that is taken to be the outgrowth of an easing of restrictions on foreign investment effects an expansion of every manufacturing industry there, with the implication that demand for utilities must rise. The experiment generates an increase in utilities output in Mexico of 9.31%. Presumably, air quality would deteriorate in this case, unless the associated income growth gave rise to political demands for more stringent standards and tougher enforcement.

We turn next to toxic waste. Our focus on this form of pollution is primarily a reflection of data availability. As far as we know, this is the only type of pollution for which data on releases are collected at the firm level. U.S. law requires all manufacturing firms with ten or more employees that use at least 10,000 pounds of one or more of over 300 chemicals to report their annual chemical releases to the EPA. Lines of business are recorded along with information on releases, enabling aggregation of the data to the industry level.

Several pitfalls in the use of the data contained in the Toxic Release Inventory (TRI) should be noted.[22] First, since the report reflects releases rather than exposures, it cannot reflect the great differences that exist in the rates at which different chemicals are dispersed or transformed. Second, releases are measured only in terms of weight, and no effort is made to account for the fact that some high-volume releases are relatively benign, while other lower-volume releases may create great health risks. Third, many toxic chemicals are omitted entirely from the inventory. Fourth, the inventory does not reflect emissions by firms outside the manufacturing sector or by federal facilities. Fifth, the EPA conducts relatively little verification of the information it receives and makes relatively little effort to ensure compliance with the reporting requirements. Finally, there is no way to know whether the relationships between toxic waste and industry outputs in Canada and Mexico mirror those in the United States, or whether there are great differences across countries in the industry-specific relationships between hazardous waste and quantities of output.

We have used the predictions of the BDS model and the data on the industry breakdown of toxic releases by U.S. manufacturing firms contained in the TRI to generate table 2.7. The table contains estimated impacts on total toxic releases by the manufacturing industries of Mexico, the United States, and Canada in response to two scenarios for a NAFTA. As

Table 2.7
Estimated impacts of NAFTA on toxic releases by manufacturing enterprises (pounds in thousands)

Industry	Trade liberalization only			Trade and investment liberalization		
	Mexico	U.S.	Canada	Mexico	U.S.	Canada
Food and tobacco products	5	17	40	129	10	39
Textile products	22	499	39	169	487	42
Apparel	6	18	28	15	57	28
Lumber and wood products	−13	86	−88	76	74	−88
Furniture	128	210	176	257	148	178
Paper products	55	1,198	−953	611	1,198	−971
Printing and publishing	−10	52	−49	56	40	−48
Chemical products	−1,430	12,198	−1,178	4,047	12,408	−1,180
Petroleum and coal products	62	93	19	29	70	19
Rubber and plastic products	−484	693	2,072	289	636	2,062
Leather products	37	−26	181	158	−38	182
Stone, clay, glass, and concrete	0	124	152	107	112	152
Primary metals	−15	−1,591	5,437	2,166	−1,452	5,494
Fabricated metals	+1	558	254	259	530	254
Nonelectrical equipment	−61	587	−103	62	569	−104
Electrical equipment	1,445	−1,101	217	1,490	−1,091	217
Transportation equipment	−178	−594	1,435	354	−594	1,424
Miscellaneous manufacturing	171	32	338	192	97	332
Total	−261	13,053	8,017	10,466	13,261	8,032

before, the scenarios distinguish a NAFTA that effects only trade liberalization and one that also includes investment liberalization measures in Mexico. In constructing the table we have assumed that an industry-specific fixed coefficient characterizes the relationship between the amount of toxic release and the quantity of output produced. We have calculated this coefficient using output and total release data for the United States in 1989.[23] To the extent that releases per unit of output are *uniformly* higher or lower in Mexico or Canada than they are in the United States, the estimates in table 2.7 for these countries can be adjusted upward or downward to reflect these percentage differences. But lacking data for Canada and Mexico, we cannot address the possibility that these countries have higher or lower pollution coefficients than the United States in some industries but not in others.

The table tells a similar story to the one told by the utilities sector. A liberalization of trade in the absence of increased capital flows causes Mexico to shift resources toward industries that, on average, generate less pollution than its current producers. In particular, the BDS model predicts contraction by the industries producing chemical products and rubber and plastics products, both of which generate great quantities of waste per unit of output. The beneficial environmental effects of these resource flows are largely offset by an expansion of the electrical equipment industry, but a small positive net impact remains. The reallocation of resources in the United States and Canada differ from those in Mexico, as these countries enjoy comparative advantage in a complementary set of activities. The model predicts an expansion of the chemical products industry in the United States, and of the primary metals industry in Canada, with the implication that aggregate chemical releases by manufacturing enterprises will rise in both of these countries.

Again, the scenario that assumes a 10% increase in Mexico's capital stock has quite different implications for Mexico. As noted before, such growth in the capital stock causes output to expand in every Mexican manufacturing industry. If the relationship between waste and output remains unchanged, then total chemical releases must rise.

Although our estimates in this section must be taken with a large grain of salt, they suggest conclusions that accord well with intuition. Because Mexico enjoys comparative advantage in a set of activities (agriculture and labor-intensive manufactures) that on the whole are "cleaner" than the average, the composition effect of trade liberalization may well reduce pollution there. On the other hand, a NAFTA will cause the United States and Canada to specialize more in physical and human capital-intensive activities, to the possible (slight) detriment of their local environments. On the global level, a net benefit may derive from the movement of the dirtier economic activities to the more highly regulated production environments.

4 Conclusions

Environmental advocacy groups have pointed to several risks that might be associated with further liberalization of trade between the United States and Mexico. While they raise a number of valid concerns, our findings suggest that some potential benefits, especially for Mexico, may have been overlooked. First, a more liberal trade regime and greater access to the large U.S. market is likely to generate income growth in Mexico. Brown, Deardorff, and Stern (1991), for example, estimate potential short-run welfare gains to Mexico of between 0.6% and 1.9% of GDP. We have found, through an examination of air quality measures in a cross-section of countries, that economic growth tends to alleviate pollution problems once a country's per capita income reaches about, U.S. $4,000 to $5,000. Mexico, with a (purchasing-power adjusted) per capita GDP of $5,000, now is at the critical juncture in its development process where further growth should generate increased political pressures for environmental protection and perhaps a change in private consumption behavior. Second, trade liberalization may well increase Mexican specialization in sectors that cause less than average amounts of environmental damage. Our investigation of the determinants of Mexico's trade pattern strongly suggests that the country draws comparative advantage from its large number of relatively unskilled workers and that it imports goods whose production requires intensive use of physical and human capital. The asymmetries in environmental regulations and enforcement between the United States and Mexico play at most a minor role in guiding intersectoral resource allocations. But as it would appear that labor-intensive and agricultural activities require less energy input and generate less hazardous waste per unit of output than more capital- and human capital-intensive sectors, a reduction in pollution may well be a side benefit of increased Mexican specialization and trade.

Our findings must remain tentative until better data become available. We have been unable to use any information about the pollution situation as it currently stands in Mexico, since environmental monitoring there has been unsystematic at best. Furthermore, the kinds of pollutants that we can examine are limited by data availability (e.g., there are no reliable data on emissions of carbon dioxide in different countries). Still, one lesson from our study seems quite general and important. The environmental impacts of trade liberalization in any country will depend not only upon the effect of policy change on the overall scale of economic activity, but also upon the induced changes in the intersectoral composition of economic activity and in the technologies that are used to produce goods and services.

Appendix: Cities included in sample

Sulphur dioxide		Dark matter		Suspended particles	
City	Country	City	Country	City	Country
Accra	Ghana	Athens	Greece	Accra	Ghana
Amsterdam	New Zealand	Auckland	New Zealand	Athens	Greece
Athens	Greece	Bogota	Colombia	Azusa	United States
Auckland	New Zealand	Brussels	Belgium	Baghdad	Iraq
Azusa	United States	Cairo	Egypt	Bangkok	Thailand
Baghdad	Iraq	Cali	Colombia	Beijing	China
Bangkok	Thailand	Caracas	Venezuela	Birmingham	United States
Beijing	China	Christchurch	New Zealand	Bogota	Colombia
Birmingham	United States	Copenhagen	Denmark	Bombay	India
Bogota	Colombia	Dublin	Ireland	Brussels	Belgium
Bombay	India	Fray Louis Beltran	Argentina	Calcutta	India
Brussels	Belgium	Glasgow	United Kingdom	Cali	Colombia
Cairo	Egypt	Gourdon	France	Caracas	Venezuela
Calcutta	India	Hong Kong	Hong Kong	Chattanooga	United States
Cali	Colombia	Lima	Peru	Chicago	United States
Caracas	Venezuela	Lisbon	Portugal	Christchurch	New Zealand
Chicago	United States	London	United Kingdom	Copenhagen	Denmark
Christchurch	New Zealand	Madrid	Spain	Cordoba	Argentina
Copenhagen	Denmark	Medellin	Colombia	Davao	Philippines
Cordoba	Argentina	Mendoza	Argentina	Delhi	India
Davao	Philippines	Rio de Janeiro	Brazil	Fairfield	United States
Delhi	India	San Lorenzo	Argentina	Ferreyra	Argentina
Dublin	Ireland	Santa Fe	Argentina	Frankfurt	Germany
Fairfield	United States	Santiago	Chile	Guangzhou	China

Sulphur dioxide		Dark matter		Suspended particles	
City	Country	City	Country	City	Country
Frankfurt	Germany	Sao Paulo	Brazil	Hamilton	Canada
Fray Louis Beltran	Argentina	Tehran	Iran	Harris County	United States
Glasgow	United Kingdom	Toulouse	France	Helsinki	Finland
Gourdon	France	Tucuman	Argentina	Hong Kong	Hong Kong
Guangzhou	China	Warsaw	Poland	Houston	United States
Hamilton	Canada	Wroclaw	Poland	Iligan City	Philippines
Harris County	United States			Jakarta	India
Helsinki	Finland			Karachi	Pakistan
Hong Kong	Hong Kong			Kuala Lumpur	Malaysia
Houston	United States			La Plata	Argentina
Jakarta	India			Lahore	Pakistan
Kuala Lumpur	Malaysia			Lisbon	Portugal
Lahore	Pakistan			Los Angeles	United States
Lima	Peru			Manila	Philippines
Lisbon	Portugal			Medellin	Colombia
London	United Kingdom			Melbourne	Australia
Los Angeles	United States			Mendoza	Argentina
Madrid	Spain			Montreal	Canada
Manila	Philippines			Nairobi	Kenya
Medellin	Colombia			New Delhi	India
Melbourne	Australia			New York	United States
Mendoza	Argentina			Osaka	Japan
Milan	Italy			Palpala	Argentina
Montreal	Canada			Rio de Janeiro	Brazil
Munchen	Germany			Santa Fe	Argentina
Nairobi	Kenya			Sao Paulo	Brazil
New Delhi	India			Shanghai	China
New York	United States			Shenyang	China

St. Ann	United States
St. Louis	United States
Sydney	Australia
Tehran	Iran
Tel Aviv	Israel
Tokyo	Japan
Toronto	Canada
Vancouver	Canada
Xian	China
Zagreb	Yugoslavia

Osaka	Japan
Rio de Janeiro	Brazil
San Lorenzo	Argentina
Santa Fe	Argentina
Santiago	Chile
Sao Paulo	Brazil
Seoul	Korea
Shanghai	China
Shenyang	China
St. Ann	United States
St. Louis	United States
Stockholm	Sweden
Sydney	Australia
Tehran	Iran
Tel Aviv	Israel
Tokyo	Japan
Toronto	Canada
Toulouse	France
Tucuman	Argentina
Vancouver	Canada
Warsaw	Poland
Wroclaw	Poland
Xian	China
Zagreb	Yugoslavia
Zurich	Switzerland

Notes

We are grateful to the Industrial Relations Section and International Finance Section of Princeton University, and the National Science Foundation for partial financial support. We thank Loren Baker, Kainan Tang, and Guillermo Frias for research assistance, and Drusilla Brown, Gardener Evans, and Greg Schoepfle for sharing their unpublished data. Joanne Gowa, Howard Gruenspecht, and Jeff Mackie-Mason provided helpful comments and discussion.

1. See Low and Safedi (1991), who cite several examples of writings that view open trade as detrimental to environmental protection.

2. See, for example, Gregory (1991), Kelly and Kamp (1991), National Wildlife Fedevation (1990), Leonard and Christensen (1991), and Ortman (1991).

3. A similar decomposition of the effects of economic growth on the output of pollution has been proposed by the Task Force on the Environment and the Internal Market (1990).

4. The GEMS data have been statistically analyzed by some environmental scientists (see World Health Organization [1984]), but they have neglected to use any economic variables in their exclusively bivariate analyses.

5. The GEMS data for 1977–1984 are published by the World Health Organization in the series *Air Quality in Selected Urban Areas*. Unpublished data for 1985–1988 have been kindly provided to us by Gardener Evans of the U.S. Environmental Protection Agency.

6. Lave and Seskin (1970) find, for example, that variation in SO_2 and population density together explain two-thirds of the variation in death from bronchitis in a sample of U.S. cities.

7. A few sites used nephelometric methods to measure suspended particles; i.e., they measured the light loss due to scattering when a light beam is passed through a sample of particle-laden air. This method gauges the mass of suspended particles, much as does the high-volume gravimetric method. Since the estimates are comparable in many cases, we pooled the observations from these two types of instruments, but included a dummy variable to allow for device-specific measurement differences.

8. Actually, SO_2 concentrations are never literally zero, but the machines are unable to detect very low levels of the gas.

9. We also estimated equations in which we entered per capita GDP in quadratic form. In general, the quadratic equations do not fit quite as well as the cubic equations, though in many cases the shape of the estimated relationship between income and pollution is found to be roughly the same.

10. Population densities were collected from several different sources. These sources and other details of our data set are available upon request.

11. We began our analysis with separate dummy variables for each year in our sample, but the estimates of thls model strongly suggested a simple, linear time trend.

12. However, we coded the desert dummy variable as zero for Cordoba, Argentina, in view of the fact that a mountain range lies between this city and the nearby desert. The regressions fit somewhat better with Cordoba treated this way, although none of our conclusions about the relationship of particulate pollution to GDP depends upon this designation.

13. The data on trade intensities were taken from the World Bank database.

14. That is, if μ_{ijt} is the total residual in the equation for some pollutant at site i in city j at time t, we assume that $\mu_{ijt} = \alpha_{jt} + \varepsilon_{ijt}$, where α_{jt} is the common-to-the-city component, ε_{ijt} is the idiosyncratic component, and $E(\alpha_{jt}\varepsilon_{ijt}) = 0$. Our estimation takes into account the unbalanced nature of this panel data set.

15. There are only two countries in our sample (the United States and Canada) with per capita incomes in excess of $16,000, so the fact that the estimated curves turn upward in this range probably should not be viewed as strong evidence for a renewed positive relationship between national product and SO_2 pollution at high income levels.

16. The Census survey did not include the apparel industry (SIC category 23). For these observations and four others with missing data, we inserted the average ratio of pollution abatement costs to value added for all manufacturing sectors included in the survey.

17. We note that the survey data on pollution abatement costs may give an underestimate of the average abatement cost in the U.S. industry. Absent from the survey are those firms that have exited the industry or moved their operations to Mexico or elsewhere. Conceivably, the potential (but not actual) producers that are missing from the survey sample may include some that ceased operations due to especially high, firm-specific costs of pollution abatement.

18. For twelve industries, this method gives a negative number as the estimate of the share of human capital. To ensure that our results were not sensitive to the choice of income for an unskilled worker, we also computed factor shares using the income level for unskilled workers ($10,819) that made the minimum share of human capital in our sample of industries equal to zero. The estimated import equations with these measures of factor shares look much the same as for our original measures.

19. The import figures and the effective tariff rates were provided to us by Greg Schoepfle of the U.S. Department of Labor. The tariff rates were estimated by dividing the total duties collected on imports from Mexico in a two-digit SIC industry by the total value of imports in the industry. Data on shipments, value added, employment, and payroll were taken from the N.B.E.R. trade and immigration data set (see Abowd, 1991). Since the trade data are classified according to the old (1972) SIC categories, we used manufacturing census data that were bridged to this classification scheme. The average income for a worker in the manufacturing sector with less than a high school education was calculated from the 1987 *Current Population Survey* by the authors. Injury rates by industry were taken from the Bureau of Labor Statistics publication, *Occupational Injuries and Illness in the United States by Industry*. In the few cases where an injury rate was not available for a

three-digit industry, we used instead the average injury rate for the applicable two-digit industry.

20. A simultaneity bias may exist here, insofar as many political-economic theories of tariff formation predict that high tariff rates will endogenously emerge in industries in which import penetration is great.

21. We note that INEGA withheld industry-level data for industries with sixteen or fewer maquiladora establishments. Thus our analysis treats as zero the maquiladora activity in sectors where some small amount of production may have taken place.

22. The following discussion is based on U.S. GAO (1991a).

23. The output data, which were provided to us by Drusilla Brown, are those that were used in the calibration of the BDS model. Since these data are reported on an ISIC basis, we were forced to reclassify some industries in order to make them compatible with the SIC-based TRI data.

References

Abowd, John M. 1991. "The NBER Immigration, Trade, and Labor Markets Data Files." In J. M. Abowd and R. B. Freeman, eds., *Immigration. Trade. and the Labor Market*. Chicago: The University of Chicago Press for the National Bureau of Economic Research.

Bennett, Burton G., Kretzschmar, Jan G., Akland, Gerald G., and de Koning, Henk W. 1985. "Urban Air Pollution Worldwide." *Environmental Science and Technology* 19:298–304.

Brown, Drusilla K., Deardorff, Alan V., and Stern, Robert M. 1991. "A North American Free Trade Agreement: Analytical Issues and a Computational Assessment." Mimeo. Institute of Public Policy Studies, University of Michigan.

Gregory, Michael. 1991. "Sustainable Development vs. Economic Growth: Environmental Protection as an Investment in the Future." Statement on Behalf of Arizona Toxics Information before the International Trade Commission, Hearing on Probable Economic Effect on U.S. Industries and Consumers of a Free Trade Agreement Between the United States and Mexico.

Harkness, Jon. 1978. "Factor Abundance and Comparative Advantage." *American Economic Review* 68:784–800.

Kelly, Mary E., and Kamp, Dick. 1991. "Mexico-U.S. Free Trade Negotiations and the Environment: Exploring the Issues." Mimeo. Texas Center for Policy Studies, Austin TX, and Border Ecology Project, Naco, AZ.

Kormondy, Edward J., ed. 1989. *International Handbook of Pollution Control*. New York and Westport, CT: Greenwood Press.

Krueger, Alan B., and Burton, John F., Jr. 1990. "The Employers' Costs of Workers' Compensation Insurance: Magnitudes, Determinants, and Public Policy." *Review of Economics and Statistics* 72:228–240.

Lave, Lester B., and Seskin, E. P. 1970. "Air Pollution and Human Health." *Science* 169:723–733.

Leonard, H. Jeffrey. 1988. *Pollution and the Struggle for World Product.* Cambridge: Cambridge University Press.

Leonard, Rodney E., and Christensen, Eric. 1991. "Economic Effects of a Free Trade Agreement between Mexico and the United States." Testimony on Behalf of Community Nutrition Institute before the International Trade Commission, Hearing on Docket No. 332–307.

Low, Patrick, and Safedi, Raed. 1991. "Trade Policy and Pollution." Mimeo. International Trade Division, World Bank.

McGuire, Martin C. 1982. "Regulation, Factor Rewards, and International Trade." *Journal of Public Economics* 17:335–354.

National Wildlife Federation. 1990. "Environmental Concerns Related to a United States-Mexico-Canada Free Trade Agreement." Mimeo. National Wildlife Federation, Washington, D.C.

New York Times. 1991. "Facing Environmental Issues." Sept. 22, Sec. 3:5.

Ortman, David E. 1991. "On a Comprehensive North American Trade Agreement." Testimony on Behalf of Friends of the Earth, National Wildlife Federation, and the Texas Center for Policy Studies before the Subcommittee on Trade, Committee on Ways and Means, U.S. House of Representatives.

Pethig, Rudiger. 1976. "Pollution, Welfare, and Environmental Policy in the Theory of Comparative Advantage." *Journal of Environmental Economics and Management* 2:160–169.

Schoepfle, Gregory K. 1991. "Implications for U.S. Employment of the Recent Growth in Mexican Maquiladoras." *Frontera Norte* 3:25–54.

Siebert, Horst. 1977. "Environmental Quality and the Gains from Trade." *Kyklos* 30:657–673.

Summers, Robert, and Heston, Alan. 1991. "The Penn World Table (Mark 5): An Expanded Set of International Comparisons, 1950–1988." *Quarterly Journal of Economics* 106:327–368.

Task Force on the Environment and the Internal Market. 1990. *1992: The Environmental Dimension.* Bonn: Economica Verlag.

The Economist. 1991. "Smog City." May 18:51.

Tobey, James A. 1990. "The Effects of Domestic Environmental Policies on Patterns of World Trade: An Empirical Test." *Kyklos* 43:191–209.

United States Department of Commerce. 1988. *Manufacturers' Pollution Abatement Capital Expenditures and Operating Costs.* Washington, D.C.: Bureau of the Census.

United States Environmental Protection Agency. 1982. *Air Quality Criteria for Particulate Matter and Sulfur Oxides.* Research Triangle Park, N.C.: U.S. EPA.

United States General Accounting Office. 1991a. "Toxic Chemicals: EPA's Toxic Release Inventory is Useful but Can be Improved." Report No. GAO/RCED-91-121, Washington, D.C.

United States General Accounting Office. 1991b. "U.S.-Mexico Trade: Information on Environmental Regulations and Enforcement." Report No. GAO/NSIAD-91-227, Washington, D.C.

United States General Accounting Office. 1991c. "U.S.-Mexico Trade: Some U.S. Wood Furniture Firms Relocated from Los Angeles Area to Mexico." Report No. GAO/NSIAD-91-191, Washington, D.C.

Walter, Ingo. 1982. "Environmentally Induced Industrial Relocation to Developing Countries." In S. J. Rubin and T. R. Graham, eds., *Environment and Trade*. New Jersey: Allanheld, Osmun, and Co.

World Health Organization. 1984. *Urban Air Pollution. 1973–1980*. Geneva: World Health Organization.

World Resources Institute. 1988. *World Resources: 1988–89*. New York: Basic Books.

Yohe, Gary W. 1979. "The Backward Incidence of Pollution Control—Some Comparative Statics in General Equilibrium." *Journal of Environmental and Economic Management* 6:187–198.

3   Wage Effects of a U.S.-Mexican Free Trade Agreement

Edward E. Leamer

New York Times, Wednesday, July 24, 1991:

Edith Cresson, Prime Minister of France, denied calling the Japanese "ants," but added, "I say they work like ants."

And she went on: "But we don't want to live like that. I mean, in the small flats, with two hours to go to your job an—we want to keep our social security, our holidays, and we want to live as human beings in the way that we've been always used to live."

1 Wage Equalization and Protection

The great difference in wages between workers in the advanced developed countries and workers everywhere else on the globe creates a major profit opportunity that has been driving much of the expansion of international commerce over the last several decades. This expansion of trade has largely eliminated the wage differences among a few countries, but the gap remains huge for many others, and the pressure for equalization in the future will surely be at least as strong as in the last decade. Actually, the remarkable increases in global economic integration that have been achieved in just the last several years seem likely to intensify the pressures for wage equalization.

The gains from this expansion of trade have been and will continue to be very unequally distributed among workers. Highly skilled workers in the advanced countries benefit from the integration of the world's labor market since they face relatively few foreign competitors. But our low-skilled workers face a sea of low-paid, low-skilled competitors around the world. This presents a severe policy dilemma for the developed countries of the world: Are we going to let our low-skilled workers continue to sink slowly in that sea? If not, what kind of lifeboat will we provide?

In some countries, those who lose from increased foreign competition are sufficiently compensated through private and public income redistribution that they do not insist on protection. In other countries, these relatively poor workers have little voice. But in countries like the United States with heterogeneous populations, weak private social insurance networks, and democratic political systems, trade protection is an important instrument for income redistribution and increased protectionism over the next several decades is a virtual certainty. Doesn't a U.S.-Mexican Free Trade Agreement take us in diametrically the opposite direction? Maybe, and maybe not.

The effect of a U.S.-Mexican free trade agreement on U.S. labor and capital depends on the size of Mexico. This size question can be accurately summarized by: "Who is the marginal supplier?" One possibility is that Mexico is small and Asia[1] remains the marginal supplier in the sense that any additional imports of labor-intensive goods come from Asia, not from Mexico. In that event, the product price inside the U.S. marketplace would equal the Asian price plus the U.S. tariff rate, and the effect of the agreement would only be a partial diversion of trade from Asia to Mexico with no substantial impact on the U.S. economy.

Another possibility is that Mexican supply is great enough to completely divert U.S. imports of some products away from Asia in favor of Mexico. Then Mexico is the marginal supplier and the protective effect of the U.S. tariff against Asian suppliers is at least partly undone. If Mexico is large enough to satisfy completely the U.S. demand for imports that would have occurred at the unprotected world market price, then U.S. protection would be completely undone by the agreement since the same product price would prevail in Asia, Mexico, and the United States, even though there is a tariff applicable against (the nonexistent) U.S. imports from Asia.

My answer to the question: "How big is Mexico?" is "BIG"—big enough to circumvent U.S. trade barriers that are designed to maintain wages of low-skilled workers. The Mexico of today is not that big, but the Mexico of the future in a free trade agreement with the United States will be much larger. One reason that Mexico will be larger is that *preferential access to the U.S. marketplace encourages the Mexicans to export all of their product to the protected U.S. market and to import for consumption from third sources.* This trade diversion effect by itself is enough to allow Mexico today to play a major role in the U.S. markets for some commodities. Future increases in productivity, accumulation of capital, high birth rates, and concentration on those labor-intensive sectors protected by the United States will greatly increase the potential Mexican exports to the United

States, enough, I argue, to greatly limit the ability of the United States to maintain wages of low-skilled workers by trade protection.

Except for the threat of anti-dumping (Palmeter 1991), current levels of U.S. trade barriers against Mexico and Asia are not very high except in a few products, particularly clothing and textiles, and these barriers are tentatively scheduled to be phased out over a ten-year period. If the NAFTA only meant the elimination of the few remaining barriers, it would have modest effects on the U.S. economy. But international agreements such as this one should not be evaluated in terms of the present levels of trade barriers, but rather in terms of the levels that might be put in place in the future. Canadian Prime Minister Brian Mulroney, commenting on the U.S.-Canadian Free Trade Agreement, put it this way: "Had it not been for the free trade agreement, we would have been dead as doornails in the American market in this hostile climate. What you have is a colossal volume of trade which is shielded from needless hostility."[2]

Let us thus understand that NAFTA is not an agreement that would be put in place today and undone tomorrow. If the Mexico of the future is as big as I argue, the NAFTA means that the United States will not be able to impose trade barriers to maintain wages of our low-skilled workers. *The real meaning of NAFTA to the United States is thus commitment: commitment to free trade, not just with Mexico, but with low-wage suppliers generally.* This would be a very serious commitment that would have the force of an international agreement. It would not be merely a politician announcing: "Read my lips: no new tariffs."

From the Mexican perspective, an FTA creates a windfall equal to the amount of the tariff revenue that would have been collected on U.S. imports if the imports came from third sources. Much of this revenue accrues not to the U.S. government but to third countries that administer the quota provisions of the multifiber agreement. [See Cline (1987), Banco Nacional de Mexico (1991), Botella et al. (1991), Erzan et al. (1989), Lande (1991).] *It is Hong Kong and Taiwan and Korea, not the United States, who will make the contributions to Mexico in support of the FTA.*

One (academic?) concern with an FTA from the Mexican perspective should be the indirect imposition of the U.S. structure of protection on Mexican manufacturing that would occur if Mexico sells a substantial portion of its output in United States markets. Protection that would raise wages in the U.S. can lower wages in Mexico, and an FTA can have the surprising effect of lowering Mexican wages. The reason for this surprising possibility is that the moderately capital-intensive commodities like textiles are in the labor-intensive segment of U.S. manufacturing, which tends to concentrate on more capital-intensive items, but these moderately capital-intensive goods are in the capital-intensive segment of Mexican production. Protection of textiles can raise wages in the United States and lower wages in Mexico.

This picture is not meant to apply the day after the agreement is signed. It could easily take a couple of uncertain decades for these effects to be fully felt. But we need to be forward looking. A free trade agreement is not likely to be signed one day and undone the next. Indeed, the commitment value of a free trade agreement is perhaps its greatest appeal from the standpoint of the United States. There are few institutions like this one that can commit a society to any course of action.

If, as I argue, an FTA prevents the United States from imposing trade barriers to maintain the wages of low-skilled workers, what effect will this have on wages? There is no way that this question can be answered with great precision. This paper presents a methodology for estimating the effect of further international integration on the earnings of U.S. productive factors. The component of the historical change in commodity prices that is associated with the commodity's labor intensity is extended into the future. Then these predicted relative price declines of labor-intensive products are mapped into the corresponding changes in factor earnings. One calculation of this type indicates that the annual earnings of $1,000 of capital would increase by $13, that the annual earnings of professional and technical workers would increase by $6,000, and the annual earnings of other workers would decline by $1,900. These seem like plausible numbers.

2 Wage Equalization Over The Last Several Decades

The dramatic shift in income distribution in the United States away from low-skilled workers in favor of high-skilled workers is the subject of a recent book provocatively titled *A Future of Lousy Jobs?* (Burtless 1990). Figures 3.1 and 3.2 are reproduced from Burtless's introduction. Figure 3.1 compares the wage growth at five different percentiles of the income distribution during two periods of time for men and women. During the earlier 1967–79 period, annual earnings of men grew at all percentiles, but the income distribution became more skewed because the growth rate of earnings was higher at the higher earnings percentiles. This income redistribution continued dramatically in the period 1979–87 because earnings at the 20th and 40th earnings percentiles actually declined. This shifting income profile is very consistent with the international wage equalization hypothe-

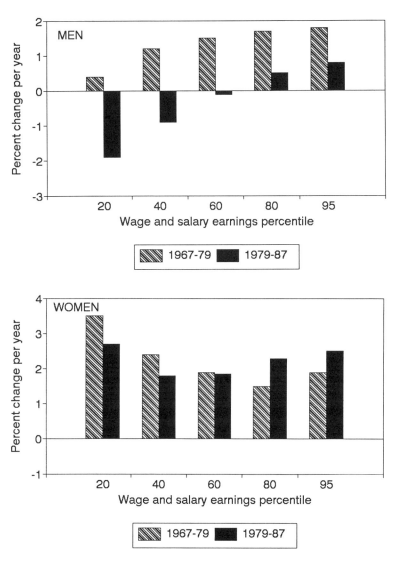

Figure 3.1
Growth of annual earnings at selected points in the earnings distribution

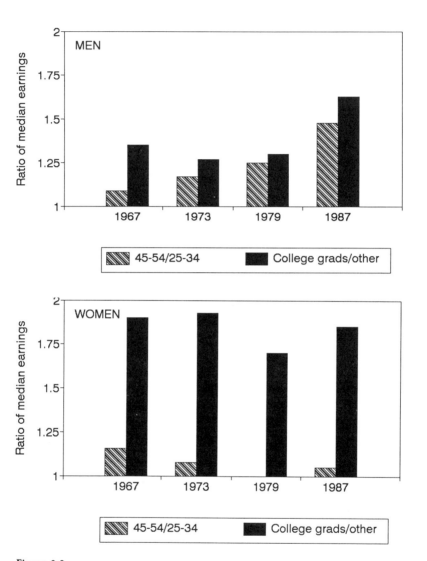

Figure 3.2
Trends in relative earnings by age and education, 1967–87

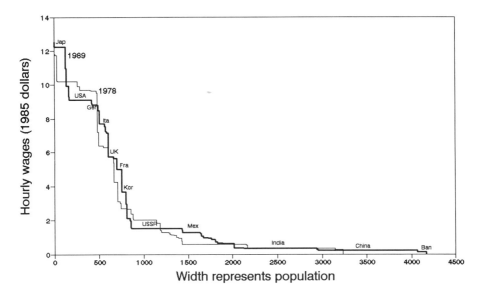

Figure 3.3
Industrial wages and populations, 1960 and 1978

sis discussed below, but the experience of women reported in the lower panel is substantially different and clearly requires another explanation.

Figure 3.2 indicates the relative earnings of workers by age and education from 1967 to 1987. When these bars are long, they indicate substantial income differences. For men, the effect of a college education on median earnings declined from 1967 to 1973, but shot up dramatically at the end of the period from 1979 to 1987. The effect of experience as measured by age rose substantially throughout the period. Again this is very consistent with the wage equalization hypothesis, but again the female data require a different explanation.

Blackburn, Bloom, and Freeman (1990) argue that a variety of demand and supply factors help explain this wage behavior, but "the most significant are changes in the industrial structure, declining rates of unionization and the fact that, after 1979, the number of college-educated young men entering the work force failed to keep pace with the rising demand for highly educated workers." The effects of the globalization of the labor market are not explicitly considered.

The next figures illustrate the magnitude of the force of international wage equalization. Figure 3.3 is a graph of wage rates and populations in 1960 and 1978 of about fifty countries that comprise roughly 75% of the

world's population and 85% of the world's GNP.[3] Each country is represented by a horizontal line segment with a length equal to the population
and a vertical placement equal to the industrial wage rate in 1985 dollars.
The area under a line segment thus represents the labor earnings (wages
times population), although this will be inaccurate if the industrial wage is
not adequately representative of wages in other sectors and/or if the ratio
of hours worked to population varies greatly across countries.

In viewing this graph and the next one, it is wise to keep in mind that
an international comparison of wage rates is fraught with difficulties. The
most important problem from the perspective of this study is that the skill
mix of workers in manufacturing varies greatly from country to country.
The wage equalization hypothesis applies to homogeneous workers. The
best, but unavailable, data would apply to skilled and unskilled workers
separately. An interesting theoretical possibility is that economic integration tends to equalize the wages of the unskilled workers, but tends to
drive apart the wages of the skilled workers.

The list of other problems with these data is very long, including the
following: (a) compensation packages and work rules vary greatly across
countries; (b) wage data from different countries apply to different units of
time (hourly, daily, weekly, monthly, annually,) which have to be somewhat arbitrarily standardized into hourly wages; and (c) wages are denomi-
nated in different currencies. These wage data are translated into a common
currency (dollars) using current exchange rates and then deflated by the
U.S. consumer price index to form a real wage series. This is intended to
answer the question, "If a producer wishes to sell in the U.S. marketplace,
where can the most inexpensive labor be found?" But the use of current
exchange rates causes a lot of volatility in these relative wage rates, which
could be reduced using purchasing power parity exchange rates. Another
very different question is, "Where is the best place for a worker to be
employed?" This would require a local price deflator.

Never mind all these problems; the main message is simple and clear:
There are vast differences around the world in the rates of labor compensation. Consider first the 1960 data in figure 3.3. The first horizontal line
segment for the 1960 data applies to the United States, with the highest
industrial wage of roughly $8 per hour and a population of roughly 200
million. As your eye moves down the graph, it passes over the United
Kingdom, with wages of about $6.50, and West Germany, with wages of
$2.10, and then moves on to India and then China, which have very low
wage rates and very large populations.

Think of this figure as if it were a reservoir of liquid with some very high levels and some very low levels. In the absence of dikes to maintain the difference in the levels, the liquid in the high spots would flow into the lower areas, eventually equalizing the level everywhere. This equalization produces lower wages for the high-wage countries and higher wages for the low-income countries.[4]

Wage equalization is a consequence of changes in the demand and supply of labor induced by the wage differences. The most direct force for wage equalization is labor migration from low-wage to high-wage areas. This labor migration reduces the supply of labor in the low-wage countries and raises the supply of labor in the high-wage countries. Other forces operate on the demand side. Migration of capital in the opposite direction of labor raises the demand for labor in the low-wage areas and reduces the demand in the high-wage areas. A more subtle reason for changes in the demand for labor are shifts in the composition of industrial output toward labor-intensive activities in the low-wage countries and toward capital-intensive activities in high-wage countries. The celebrated factor-price equalization theorem relies entirely on this third force and establishes conditions under which a shift in the composition of output is enough to bring about complete equalization of wages.[5] An essential condition of this theorem is that there are no barriers to trade that prevent prices of products from equalizing.

But of course there remain important economic barriers between these countries in the form of actual and threatened governmental measures that deter international commerce and migration of capital and labor. Even if all the governmental barriers were eliminated, including exchange risk, the process of wage equalization would not be instantaneous because there are also natural barriers including transportation costs and linguistic differences. The liquid of economics is molasses, not water. Regardless, none of these barriers is impermeable, and the greater the difference in the levels, the greater the force of profit opportunities to eliminate the difference.

Move your attention now to the data for 1978, the year in which the real U.S. industrial wage peaked. There are two obvious differences in the two years. The latter year has much higher wages in many countries, and also larger populations. These two changes seem to be stretching the figure along the two axes. But stretching alone will not make the 1960 figure look like the 1978 figure. The center needs to be pulled out. This is the change associated with the wage equalization process. This bulging of the curve is induced by the extraordinary real wage growth in Japan, West Germany, France, and Korea, but relatively less wage growth in the United States.

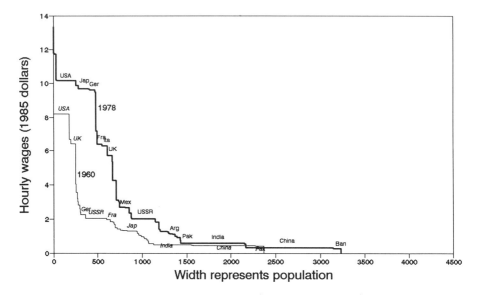

Figure 3.4
Industrial wages and populations, 1978 and 1989

Figure 3.4 shows what happened over the next decade, comparing 1978 with 1989. (Keep in mind that exchange rate gyrations can cause a lot of variability in these wage rates; in particular, an overvalued dollar will make wages in other countries seem low.) One obvious point about the second graph is that the eleven years from 1978 to 1989 did not offer nearly the wage growth of the nineteen years from 1960 to 1978. Keep in mind that these data do not refer to local standards of living, but only indicate that producers selling inside the United States didn't have to pay much more for labor regardless of where it was hired.

Although the 1978 and 1989 graphs are similar, there are some interesting differences. The U.S. and German wage rates declined and the Japanese wage rate increased, surpassing the U.S. figure by a considerable margin. Except for the Japanese figure, wage equalization is evident: wages of the high-wage countries declined somewhat, and wages in moderate-wage countries rose. This would be more clear if the French figure were higher. Notice also the further increases in population among the low-wage countries.

In summary, the force of wage equalization seems very much present for the 800 million people who live in countries that are "part of the game." Among these countries wage equalization has much farther to go, and we should expect continuing pressure on U.S. wage rates. Beyond this group of countries, there remains a vast number of people who have not experienced detectable economic improvement over the last three decades, including those in Latin America. If these countries become "part of the game," the downward pressure on wages in the high-wage countries will surely intensify.

The same kind of graphs are useful for examining the proposed NAFTA and comparing it with the European Economic Community (EEC) and the European Free Trade Agreement (EFTA). The data for the EEC countries, the EFTA countries, and the proposed NAFTA countries are displayed in figures 3.5, 3.6, and 3.7. France, West Germany; Italy, Belgium, the Netherlands, and Luxembourg formed the EEC in 1957. The United Kingdom, Ireland, and Denmark joined in 1973, Greece in 1981, and Spain and Portugal in 1986. There was a substantial wage difference between the United Kingdom and the other current members of the EEC in 1960. In 1978, the EEC seemed to divide into three groups: high wages in Denmark, Germany, Belgium, Luxembourg, and the Netherlands; intermediate wages in France, Italy, and the United Kingdom; and low wages in Ireland, Spain, Greece, and Portugal, the latter three not yet members. A considerable amount of wage equalization occurred between 1978 and 1989. Real wages in the high-wage countries fell, and real wages of the low-wage countries generally rose. If the French wage were adjusted upward, the EEC would have had a very uniform collection of wages, with the exceptions of Denmark on the high side and Greece and Portugal on the low side. The EFTA countries depicted in figure 3.6 exhibit relatively small wage differences and fairly uniform increases in real wages from 1960 to 1978. After 1978, there is also a very significant amount of convergence, with reductions in the real wages of the high-wage countries and increases in the real wages of the low-wage countries. The NAFTA data tell a very different story. The United States and Canada have wages that are very high compared with Mexico, and these differences are amplified by the decline in the Mexican wage.

The reason for looking at these figures is that the European experience may offer insights into the possible consequences of a NAFTA. Analogies with the EEC seem appropriate from the Mexican side, but not from the U.S. side. Mexico may sensibly look at Greece and Portugal to get an idea of the consequences of a NAFTA, as the wage gap is similar. Indeed, the Greek case is not suggestive of a very rapid improvement in wages. But the United States cannot look to the experience of the high-wage EEC countries because the entry of Greece, Portugal, Spain, and Ireland into the EEC

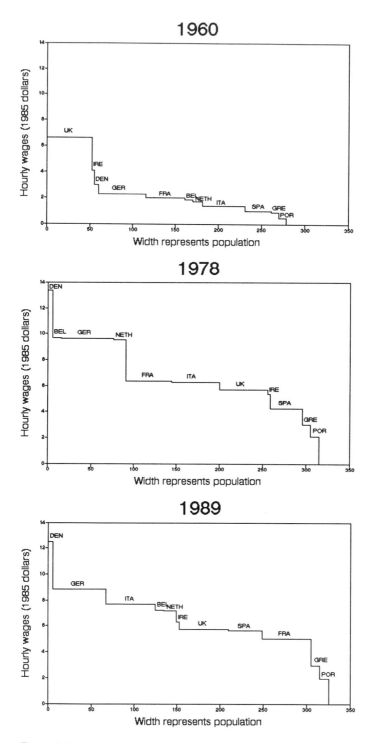

Figure 3.5
Industrial wages and populations, EEC

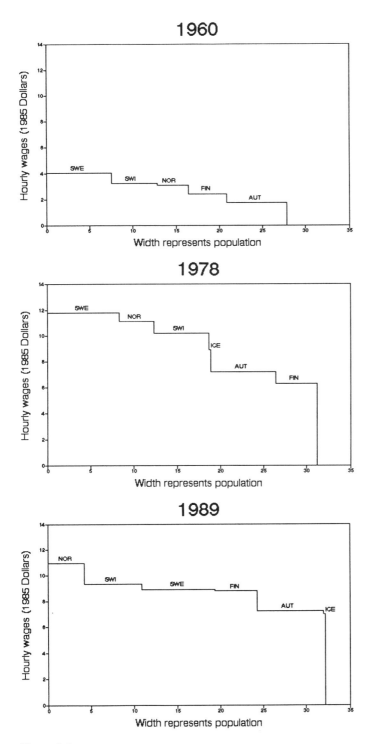

Figure 3.6
Industrial wages and populations, EFTA

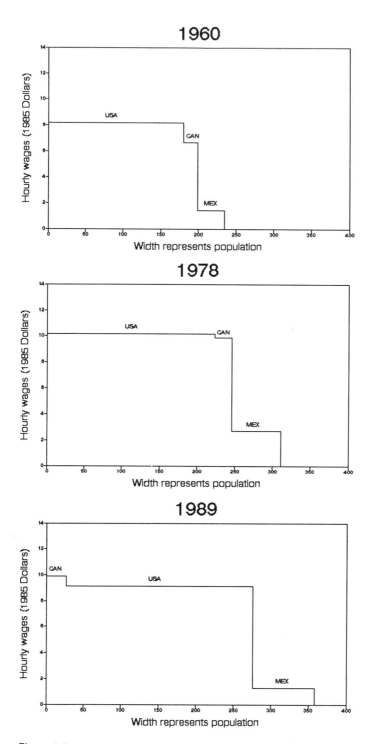

Figure 3.7
Industrial wages and populations, NAFTA

involve either smaller wage differences or smaller relative populations. Nonetheless, the evidence of wage convergence in both the EEC and EFTA is highly suggestive of what is in store for the United States.

I believe that in the absence of very substantial increases in trade barriers, real wages of low-skilled workers in the United States are virtually certain to decline over the next decade partly because of the forces of wage equalization. This is true regardless of the existence of a U.S.-Mexican free trade agreement. But an FTA seems likely at least to hasten the wage decline. If the effect of an FTA is to circumvent U.S. barriers against labor-intensive products that would otherwise be put in place, then an FTA will lower the eventual level of wages as well as increase the speed at which we converge on it.

3 Trends in the Trade Data

Reductions in barriers to international commerce release powerful forces that tend to eliminate differences in wages. One source of wage equalization comes from the adjustment in the pattern of production in accordance with comparative advantage. Low-wage countries concentrate production on labor-intensive goods, and high-wage countries concentrate on goods that use relatively little labor. This drives up the local demand for labor in the low-wage countries and drives down the local demand for labor in the high-wage countries. These changes in the demand for labor work to eliminate the wage difference.

In theory, wage differences can be, but need not be, completely eliminated if commodities move freely across borders. If they are not eliminated, there is an incentive for capital to flow from the high-wage to the low-wage countries. This flow of capital increases the relative supply of labor-intensive products and reduces their relative price. This change in relative prices of commodities in turn puts downward pressure on the wages in the high-wage countries.

This model of wage equalization is most accurately conveyed in a simple diagram that serves as a backdrop for an examination of the trends in the data that are discussed subsequently. Wage determination within the context of a simple general equilibrium model is depicted in figure 3.8. The axes are the labor and capital inputs. The four right angles represent unit *value* isoquants for three different sectors: machinery, which is the most capital intensive; textiles, which exhibits intermediate degree of capital intensity; and apparel, which is the most labor intensive. These unit value isoquants are combinations of capital and labor that are required to produce

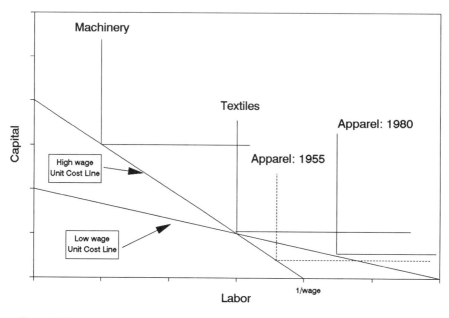

Figure 3.8
Isoquants and wage determination

a dollar's worth of output. These isoquants are drawn with right angles to indicate that the ratio of capital to labor is technologically fixed in each industry. This assumption of fixed input intensities is immaterial for almost every relevant aspect of the discussion that follows. Two different unit value isoquants are drawn for the apparel sector, one applicable to 1980 and one 1955. As illustrated, it takes more capital and labor to produce a dollar's worth of output in 1980 than in 1955, because of the reduction in the relative price of apparel, which I will argue is a consequence of economic integration.

Also on this figure are two unit isocost lines, that is, combinations of capital and labor that cost one dollar to employ. The equation for a unit isocost line is $1 = wL + rK$, where w is the wage rate and r is the rental price of capital. Using this equation and setting K to zero, we solve for $L = 1/w$. Thus the inverse of the wage is the intersection of the unit isocost line with the labor axis. Likewise, the intersection with the capital axis is the inverse of the rental rate of capital.

The isocost line beginning on the x-axis at the point indicated by 1/wage travels through the corner of the textile unit value isoquant and the corner of the machinery unit value isoquant. This line is the only unit isocost line that is compatible with the production of both machinery and textiles sold at world market prices. If this line falls below the unit isoquant, then costs of production exceed the value of the output and no output would be produced. If, on the other hand, the isocost line were to cross the unit isoquant, then the production costs would fall short of the product price, and the excess profits would attract resources into the sector, thereby either raising the factor prices or reducing the product prices, ultimately producing the required tangency condition.

The figure contains two isocost lines. One is compatible with the production of the more capital-intensive mix of commodities: machinery and textiles, and also apparel in 1955. The other unit isocost line selects the factor costs that are compatible with the production of a labor-intensive mix of commodities: textiles and apparel in 1980. This requires a lower wage rate and a higher return on capital. The choice between these two equilibria in 1980 depends on the relative supply of capital and labor. If a country's supply of factors falls in the cone swept out by the input mixes in machinery and textiles, then the high-wage equilibrium is selected and only textiles and machinery are produced. If capital is less abundant, the low-wage equilibrium is selected and only textiles and apparel are produced.

This model serves as an initial starting point for an examination of the data. In 1955 productive capacity outside the United States was rather small, and there were substantial barriers to international commerce that limited the economic transactions across borders. Accordingly, the United States produced economically all three products, including apparel. With the decline in trade barriers, and the rapid accumulation of capital outside the United States, there was a large increase in the worldwide supply of the labor-intensive product, apparel, which drove down the price of apparel and shifted the apparel unit value isoquant to its 1980 location. This new set of product prices separates countries into high-wage and low-wage groups. Assume that the United States lies in the high-wage cone and is suited to the production of the relatively capital-intensive goods: machinery and textiles. In the absence of protection, the United States would accordingly trade machinery for apparel. Textiles may be either exported or imported, depending on the demand for apparel and textiles relative to the U.S. productive capacity in machinery and textiles. Note that as yet there is no change in the U.S. wage rate. The only change from 1955 to 1980 is the departure of the apparel sector from the United States.

The story does not end here. As drawn, capital seeking the highest rate of return will locate in the low-wage countries. If countries are so scarce in

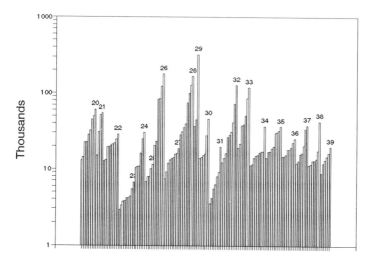

Figure 3.9
Capital per worker: Three-digit sectors

capital that their ratio of capital to labor is lower even than the apparel
ratio, then the increase in capital leads to an increase in the output of
apparel and no change in textile output. Once capital has accumulated
sufficiently that the ratio of capital available to labor supply exceeds the
ratio of capital to labor in the apparel sector, further increases in capital in
these low-wage countries leads to an increase in the supply of textiles and
a reduction of supply of apparel (the Rybczynski theorem). Changes in the
relative supply of textiles and apparel in turn induce changes in the price of
these goods. Changes of the price of apparel do not affect the level of U.S.
wages, since apparel is not produced. But a reduction in the price of textiles
shifts the textile unit isoquant to the northeast and does lower the wage
rate in the high-wage countries. Indeed, these supply changes and corresponding price changes continue until the difference in the wage rates is
eliminated.

This simple model sets the stage for an initial examination of the data.
What we are looking for are relative price declines of the labor-intensive
products, and a corresponding increase in imports and reduction of output.
These features could be studied in highly disaggregated data, but only with
some cost of confusion. An analysis of aggregates is much more memora-
ble. But the traditional aggregates were not formed to suit our purposes.
The kind of problem that is endemic in the SIC aggregates is illustrated in
figure 3.9, which indicates the capital per worker in each of the three-digit

sectors. This figure is formed by first sorting the three-digit sectors into the two-digit sectors, and then within each two-digit sector sorting by capital per worker in ascending order. Thus in this figure, each of the two-digit groups starts with a low capital-labor ratio and ascends to a peak, on which is placed the two-digit label. The message of this figure is dramatic: There are two labor-intensive two-digit sectors: 23 (apparel) and 31 (footwear). But SIC 31 has one sector that is rather capital intensive (tanning). Sectors 25 (furniture) and 27 (printing) have some labor-intensive three-digit sub-sectors, but also some fairly capital-intensive subsectors. The other two-digit sectors are very mixed, and none stands out as uniformly capital intensive. (Turn the figure upside down, if you like.)

Because of the apparent difficulties with the two-digit aggregates, I have opted instead to sort the three-digit sectors into nine categories separated by capital intensities of $15,000 per worker and $24,000 per worker, and separated by professional labor proportions of .11 and .17. (The professional category includes scientists and engineers and also managers; *Current Population Survey*, 1982). The full list of the three-digit categories is reported in table 3.1, which is sorted within each category by 1985 employment. The largest components of these aggregates are listed in table 3.2. Keep in mind that the names of these aggregates would be misleading if you were to take them to refer to types of commodities instead of the nature of production. Apparel and furniture are in the same class not because of the function they serve for consumers, but instead because they both use relatively little human capital and relatively little physical capital.

If you look at the detailed list of commodities, there will surely be features of this aggregation scheme that upset you, but there can be no scheme that is perfectly agreeable. In this case the highly unusual behavior of the price of computers calls out for some special treatment, and accordingly I have formed a tenth aggregate.

Various information about these ten aggregates is reported in table 3.3. Remember that we are looking for evidence of the wage equalization hypothesis, which is associated with a loss of comparative advantage in APPAREL and possibly the adjacent commodities in table 3.2, and a gain in comparative advantage in CHEMICALS and adjacent commodities. The data reported in table 3.3 seem quite compatible with this idea.

Prices
The history of prices over this period needs to make reference to three forces: (1) downward pressure on the prices of labor-intensive products

Table 3.1
Ten aggregates formed from three-digit SIC codes

SIC description	1985 capital	1985 emp	cap/ emp	% Prof	% Prof & Eng	% unsk
		(thous.)				
Apparel						
1 233 Women's and Misses' Outerwear	1188.1	354.7	3.35	0.052	0.055	0.047
1 201 Meat Products	4434.6	303.3	14.62	0.075	0.090	0.206
1 232 Men's and Boys' Furnishings	1189.4	272.2	4.37	0.052	0.055	0.047
1 251 Household Furniture	2176.8	271.7	8.01	0.077	0.088	0.077
1 205 Bakery Products	2757.1	208.8	13.20	0.082	0.088	0.102
1 243 Millwork, Plywood and Structural Members	2140.9	196.1	10.92	0.080	0.084	0.107
1 225 Knitting Mills	2466.5	192.7	12.80	0.066	0.066	0.066
1 314 Footwear, except Rubber	480.4	86.1	5.58	0.039	0.039	0.045
1 234 Women's and Children Undergarments	272.6	73.3	3.72	0.052	0.055	0.047
1 252 Office Furniture	789.6	68.3	11.56	0.077	0.088	0.077
1 254 Partitions and Fixtures	535.3	67.9	7.88	0.077	0.088	0.077
1 231 Men's and Boys' Suits and Clothes	272.7	64.9	4.20	0.052	0.055	0.047
1 236 Children's Outerwear	176.2	59.9	2.94	0.052	0.055	0.047
1 259 Miscellaneous Furniture and Fixtures	295.8	43.2	6.85	0.077	0.088	0.077
1 238 Miscellaneous Apparel and Accesories	177.1	42.5	4.17	0.052	0.055	0.047
1 326 Pottery and Related Products	474.6	33.5	14.17	0.000	0.087	0.174
1 244 Wood Containers	364.7	33	11.05	0.077	0.088	0.121
1 253 Public Building and Related Furniture	214.5	21.2	10.12	0.077	0.088	0.077
1 224 Narrow Fabric Mills	225	16.9	13.31	0.041	0.062	0.062
1 235 Hats, Caps, and Millinery	54.3	14.2	3.82	0.052	0.055	0.047
1 313 Boot and Shoe Cut Stock and Findings	43.1	5.4	7.98	0.039	0.039	0.045
1 237 Fur Goods	13.8	2.5	5.52	0.052	0.055	0.047
Printing						
2 275 Commerical Printing	6840.7	491.9	13.91	0.155	0.162	0.045
2 359 Misc Mach exc Electr, &3714 M V Parts	4045.4	284.2	14.23	0.116	0.157	0.028

2	239	Miscellaneous Fabricated Textile Products	1179.6	175	6.74	0.124	0.135	0.022
2	384	Medical Instruments and Supplies	1990.8	152.1	13.09	0.084	0.148	0.026
2	399	Miscellaneous Manufactures	1720.3	128.6	13.38	0.102	0.106	0.032
2	273	Books &2741 Misc Publishing	1640.3	114.3	14.35	0.155	0.162	0.045
2	347	Metal Services, N E C	1265	112.3	11.26	0.089	0.117	0.062
2	272	Periodicals	1139.2	95.8	11.89	0.155	0.162	0.045
2	278	Blankbooks and Bookbinding	562	61.2	9.18	0.155	0.162	0.045
2	279	Printing Trade Services	791.4	59.4	13.32	0.155	0.162	0.045
2	383	Optical Instruments and Lenses	602.4	53.2	11.32	0.084	0.148	0.026
2	274	Miscellaneous Publishing	388.7	52	7.48	0.155	0.162	0.045
2	391	Jewelry, Silverware and Plated Ware	418.8	47.1	8.89	0.102	0.106	0.032
2	396	Costume Jewelry and Notions	463.8	38.8	11.95	0.102	0.106	0.032
2	385	Ophthalmic Goods	294	24.9	11.81	0.084	0.148	0.026
2	317	Handbags and Personal Leather Goods	77.6	18.4	4.22	0.118	0.137	0.039
2	316	Luggage	82.3	13.1	6.28	0.118	0.137	0.039
2	393	Musical Instruments	177.9	12.1	14.70	0.102	0.106	0.032
2	302	Rubber and Plastic Footwear	167.2	12	13.93	0.091	0.125	0.091
2	328	Cut Stone and Stone Products	138.6	11.2	12.38	0.094	0.106	0.035
2	319	Leather Goods N E C	55.2	6	9.20	0.118	0.137	0.039
2	315	Leather Gloves and Mittens	12.3	3.5	3.51	0.118	0.137	0.039
2	303	Reclaimed Rubber	13	0.9	14.44	0.091	0.125	0.091
Rockets								
3	366	Communication Equipment	9865.7	672	14.68	0.119	0.226	0.024
3	344	Fabricated Structural Metal Products	5531.2	391.1	14.14	0.171	0.178	0.024
3	376	Guided Missiles, Space Vehicles, Parts	2826.7	217.8	12.98	0.188	0.572	0.014
3	382	Measuring and Controlling Devices	2975.4	217.1	13.71	0.135	0.213	0.021
3	364	Electric Lighting and Wiring Equipment	2458.3	164.2	14.97	0.093	0.192	0.029
3	348	Ordnance and Accesories, N E C	971.4	82.4	11.79	0.063	0.188	0.063
3	245	Wood Buildings and Mobile Homes	653.2	63	10.37	0.222	0.244	0.022
3	379	Miscellaneous Transportation Equipment	576.8	47.3	12.19	0.121	0.212	0.000
3	381	Engineering and Scientific Instruments	607.8	46.7	13.01	0.135	0.213	0.021

Table 3.1 (continued)

SIC description	1985 capital	1985 emp	cap/ emp	% Prof	% Prof & Eng	% unsk
Textiles						
4 203 Preserved Fruits and Vegetables	4951.8	221	22.41	0.078	0.099	0.156
4 265 Peperboard Containers and Boxes	3851.5	187.5	20.54	0.068	0.068	0.107
4 363 Household Appliances	2262.6	124.4	18.19	0.078	0.089	0.033
4 222 Weaving Mills, Synth &2262 Syn Finishing	2265.9	115	19.70	0.041	0.062	0.062
4 228 Yarn and Thread Mills &2269 Finishing NEC	2129.9	104.1	20.46	0.041	0.062	0.062
4 345 Screw Machine Products, Bolts, etc	1619.7	97.2	16.66	0.053	0.079	0.053
4 249 Miscellaneous Wood Products	1286.5	79.8	16.12	0.077	0.088	0.121
4 226 Textile Finishing, except Wool	1104.3	52.2	21.16	0.000	0.000	0.154
4 227 Floor Covering Mills	938.8	48.1	19.52	0.054	0.054	0.027
4 323 Products of Purchased Glass	691.2	42.7	16.19	0.034	0.034	0.148
4 311 Leather Tanning and Finishing	279	14.2	19.65	0.000	0.000	0.333
4 223 Weaving and Finishing Mills, Wool	288.5	13.1	22.02	0.041	0.062	0.062
Machinery						
5 307 Miscellaneous Plastics Products	8612.6	541.2	15.91	0.094	0.112	0.061
5 271 Newspapers	6475	411	15.75	0.125	0.134	0.013
5 349 Miscellaneous Fabricated Metal Products	4259.6	275.4	15.47	0.089	0.117	0.062
5 356 General Industrial Machinery	5360.7	269.4	19.90	0.116	0.157	0.028
5 358 Refrigeration and Service Machinery	3107.2	182.8	17.00	0.157	0.157	0.028
5 373 Ship and Boat Building and Repairing	2778.5	175.4	15.84	0.055	0.105	0.041
5 355 Special Industry Machinery	2869	166.1	17.27	0.116	0.157	0.028
5 209 Miscellaneous Foods and Kindred Products	3257.4	144.2	22.59	0.105	0.114	0.133
5 346 Metal Forgings and Stampings	2319.5	134.6	17.23	0.092	0.122	0.031
5 306 Fabricated Ruber Products N E C	1441.7	94.3	15.29	0.091	0.125	0.091
5 394 Toys and Sportings Goods	1448	73.9	19.59	0.109	0.130	0.011
5 276 Manifold Business Forms	878.2	54.2	16.20	0.155	0.162	0.045
5 343 Plumbing and Heating, except Electric	729.2	48	15.19	0.089	0.117	0.062

5	395	Pens, Pencils, Office and Art Supplies	453.6	27.5	16.49	0.102	0.106	0.032
5	277	Greeting Card Publishing	369.8	19.9	18.58	0.155	0.162	0.045
5	212	Cigars	60.2	4	15.05	0.139	0.139	0.056
Aircraft								
6	367	Electronic Component and Accessories	12444.1	558	22.30	0.093	0.192	0.029
6	372	Aircraft and Parts	8717.1	528.2	16.50	0.115	0.268	0.003
6	354	Metalworking Machinery	5022.9	264.4	19.00	0.139	0.179	0.023
6	264	Miscellaneous Converted Paper Products	4930.1	210.9	23.38	0.115	0.183	0.069
6	362	Electrical Industrial Apparatus	3491.1	178.9	19.51	0.093	0.192	0.029
6	369	Miscellaneous Electrical Equip and Suppl	2861.9	157	18.23	0.093	0.192	0.029
6	342	Cutlery, Handtools, and Hardware	2488.1	145.6	17.09	0.159	0.170	0.034
6	361	Electric Distributing Equipment	1451.6	93.4	15.54	0.093	0.192	0.029
6	336	Nonferrous Foundries	1589.2	82.6	19.24	0.152	0.209	0.078
6	339	Miscellaneous Primary Metal Products	617.9	28.5	21.68	0.099	0.174	0.066
6	387	Watches, Clocks and Watcheses	208.1	11.8	17.64	0.143	0.286	0.000
6	375	Motorcycles, Bicycles, and Parts	188.2	9.2	20.46	0.121	0.212	0.000
Steel								
7	331	Blast Furnace and Basic Steel Products	23969.6	278	86.22	0.052	0.077	0.093
7	242	Sawmills and Planing Mills	4131.2	164.7	25.08	0.080	0.084	0.107
7	332	Iron and Steel Foundries	5124.8	135.7	37.77	0.012	0.059	0.082
7	322	Glass and Glassware, Pressed or Blown	3310.2	80.1	41.33	0.034	0.034	0.148
7	241	Logging Camps and Logging Contractors	2299.3	76.3	30.13	0.061	0.076	0.053
7	221	Weaving Mills, Cotton &2261 Cot Finishing	1788.3	62.1	28.80	0.041	0.062	0.062
7	321	Flat Glass	1102.5	15.2	72.53	0.034	0.034	0.148

Table 3.1 (continued)

SIC description	1985 capital	1985 emp	cap/ emp	% Prof	% Prof & Eng	% unsk
Autos						
8 371 Motor Vehicles and Equipment	28540	751.5	37.98	0.075	0.143	0.029
8 353 Construction and Related Machinery	7389.8	229.2	32.24	0.096	0.136	0.032
8 208 Beverages	9112.2	183.4	49.68	0.138	0.159	0.097
8 327 Concrete, Gypsum, and Plaster Products	5415.2	173.3	31.25	0.126	0.126	0.101
8 202 Dairy Products	3896.5	137.6	28.32	0.108	0.108	0.144
8 262 Paper Mills, except Building Paper	11223.9	131.8	85.16	0.059	0.122	0.080
8 284 Soaps, Cleaners, and Toilet Goods	3850.7	123.4	31.21	0.114	0.148	0.068
8 329 Misc Nonmetallic Mineral Products	3018.3	107.1	28.18	0.094	0.106	0.035
8 204 Grain Mill Products	4442.4	99.2	44.78	0.145	0.169	0.084
8 386 Photographic Equipment and Supplies	4176	98.5	42.40	0.076	0.152	0.000
8 206 Sugar and Confectionery Products	2905.6	91.2	31.86	0.128	0.128	0.105
8 301 Tires and Inner Tubes	3248.3	70.3	46.21	0.047	0.109	0.109
8 285 Paints and Allied Products	1564.5	55.5	28.19	0.074	0.148	0.037
8 229 Miscellaneous Textile Goods	1336.3	54.1	24.70	0.138	0.138	0.069
8 263 Paperboard Mills	6699.5	53.9	124.29	0.059	0.122	0.080
8 341 Metal Cans and Shipping Containers	1903.4	52	36.60	0.089	0.117	0.062
8 211 Cigarettes	1942.4	35.5	54.72	0.139	0.139	0.056
8 325 Structural Clay Products	931.3	35.2	26.46	0.118	0.118	0.235
8 207 Fats and Oil	2061.8	33.8	61.00	0.105	0.114	0.133
8 374 Railroad Equipment	941.4	27.6	34.11	0.000	0.167	0.000
8 304 Rubber and Plastics Hose and Beltings	657.9	23.8	27.64	0.091	0.125	0.091
8 324 Cement, Hydraulic	2685.7	21.2	126.68	0.126	0.126	0.101
8 261 Pulp Mills	2873	16.3	176.26	0.059	0.122	0.080
8 214 Tobacco Stemming and Redrying	343.3	6.7	51.24	0.139	0.139	0.056
8 266 Building Paper and Board Mills	307.3	3.7	83.05	0.059	0.122	0.080
8 213 Chewing and Smoking Tobacco	91.8	3	30.60	0.139	0.139	0.056

Chemicals

	Code	Industry						
9	283	Drugs	6446.7	163.7	39.38	0.180	0.279	0.072
9	335	Nonferrous Rolling and Drawing	6368.2	163.7	38.90	0.128	0.193	0.072
9	282	Plastics Materials and Synthetics	12796.2	128.2	99.81	0.063	0.175	0.000
9	286	Industrial Organic Chemicals	20456.9	123.2	166.05	0.161	0.283	0.027
9	281	Industrial Inorganic Chemicals	7854.2	105	74.80	0.062	0.215	0.027
9	351	Engines and Turbines	3613.6	98.9	36.54	0.088	0.188	0.031
9	352	Farm and Garden Machinery	2758.6	89.4	30.86	0.148	0.313	0.050
9	291	Petroleum Refining	27682.7	85.7	323.02	0.161	0.283	0.035
9	289	Miscellaneous Chemical Products	2918.9	82.3	35.47	0.119	0.226	0.027
9	365	Radio and TV Receiving Equipment	1500.4	59.1	25.39	0.120	0.240	0.024
9	287	Agricultural Chemicals	5737.2	44.9	127.78	0.142	0.203	0.080
9	333	Primary Nonferrous Metals	4428.7	37.4	118.41	0.154	0.231	0.076
9	295	Paving and Roofing Materials	1064.4	29	36.70	0.132	0.196	0.231
9	334	Secondary Nonferrous Metals	809.6	16	50.60			0.074
9	299	Miscellaneous Petroleum and Coal Products	575.8	12.8	44.98	0.154	0.231	0.231

Computers

	Code	Industry						
**	357	Office and Computing Machines	12090.3	406.7	29.73	0.145	0.263	0.013

Total

			451763.1	17368.5	26.01			

	Industry						
1	*Apparel*	20743.1	2432.3	8.53	0.063	0.071	0.084
2	*Printing*	24066.5	1968	12.23	0.126	0.147	0.038
3	*Rockets*	26466.5	1901.6	13.92	0.139	0.241	0.024
4	*Textiles*	21669.7	1099.3	19.71	0.058	0.071	0.099
5	*Machinery*	44420.2	2621.9	16.94	0.103	0.129	0.045
6	*Aircraft*	44010.3	2268.5	19.40	0.113	0.208	0.028
7	*Steel*	41725.9	812.1	51.38	0.049	0.069	0.094
8	*Autos*	111558.5	2618.8	42.60	0.096	0.136	0.064
9	*Chemicals*	105012.1	1239.3	84.74	0.130	0.240	0.049
**	*Computers*	12090.3	406.7	29.73	0.145	0.263	0.013

Table 3.2
Principal elements of aggregates

	Skilled < 11%	11% < Skilled < 17%	17% < Skilled
K/L < 15,000	*Apparel* Food products Furniture Footwear	*Printing* Miscellaneous non-electrical machinery Medical instruments and supplies Optical instruments and lenses	*Rockets* Communication equipment Fabricated structural metal products Guided missiles Measuring and controlling devices
15,000 < K/L < 24,000	*Textiles* Paperboard Appliances	*Machinery* Miscellaneous food products Miscellaneous plastic products Miscellaneous fabricated metal products	*Aircraft* Electronic components and accessories Metalworking machinery Miscellaneous converted paper products
24,000 < K/L	*Steel* Sawmills Plaining Mills	*Autos* Dairy products Paper mill products Soaps Concrete	*Chemical* Nonferrous rolling and drawing Plastic materials and drawing Engines and turbines Farm and garden machinery Computers*

*Selected for special attention.

from foreign competition, (2) the oil price shock, and (3) the computer revolution. Prices rose on average by 142% from 1972 to 1985, but AP-PAREL prices rose by only 98%. Thus the relative price of APPAREL fell by about 44%. TEXTILE relative prices fell by about 22%; CHEMICALS relative prices grew by 80%, much of which is due to petroleum. The price of COMPUTERS fell tremendously in absolute terms as well as relatively.

Employment
Employment overall in manufacturing fell by 3%, but fell most substantially in all the sectors that use little human capital, including STEEL, which is physical capital intensive. This is exactly what we are looking for, but employment also fell in AUTOS and CHEMICALS, which is not compatible with the wage equalization hypothesis. These employment data are graphed in figure 3.10.

Trade
1972 U.S. imports and exports in manufacturing were roughly in balance at 7% of home production for imports and 5% for exports. An import boom in the early 1980s raised the import dependence ratio to 15% of home production by 1985. This import boom was only partly offset by increases of exports to 9% of home production.

The increased presence of foreigners in U.S. commerce was not uniform across all commodities. In 1972, using the net exports relative to output as a measure, the United States had a revealed comparative disadvantage in APPAREL, and STEEL and a comparative advantage in COMPUTERS and AIRCRAFT. From 1972 to 1985 the net trade balance as a percentage of home production deteriorated in many commodities, but most in APPAREL (13 points) and TEXTILES (14 points). These changes in trade are consistent with the wage equalization hypothesis that should be evidenced by a shift in comparative advantage away from labor-intensive manufactures.

The values of U.S. exports, imports, and apparent consumption in 1972 and 1985 are depicted in figures 3.11 and 3.12, with industries ordered by 1972 apparent consumption. Apparent consumption is defined as production plus imports minus exports. Since production data are used, not value added, the output of iron and steel, for example, is counted at least twice, once for its own industry and again as an input into other industries. As a result of this double counting, the sum of these output figures across industries is roughly twice the total manufacturing output.

Table 3.3
Aggregated data

Year	Industry	Labor	Capital	Output	Value added	Payroll	Imports	Exports	Consump.
1972	Apparel	2946.9	17625.4	93463.1	36103.3	18696.4	5757.0	1171.1	98103.0
1972	Textiles	1317.7	18690.4	48615.5	21529.7	9760.9	1829.0	1204.5	49240.1
1972	Steel	1317.2	45835.5	51132.1	24278.7	12600.3	5079.0	2067.9	54143.2
1972	Printing	1626.1	15213.1	44600.7	27035.1	13445.3	2866.0	1498.4	45968.3
1972	Machinery	2435.1	31972.0	78965.1	44407.0	21161.8	3498.0	4702.5	77760.6
1972	Autos	3020.2	77047.3	199120.1	82287.1	30807.4	14321.0	11772.1	201669.0
1972	Rockets	1647.8	16660.3	53503.6	29784.1	16185.3	1389.0	2881.4	52011.3
1972	Aircraft	1969.9	29381.7	63130.6	36895.4	19195.4	4011.0	6990.0	60151.6
1972	Chemicals	1411.2	76226.2	109474.0	43914.3	14660.5	10625.0	7204.6	112894.4
1972	Computers	208.5	3315.6	8604.9	4904.4	2277.5	951.0	1776.7	7779.2
1972	TOTAL	17900.6	331967.5	750609.7	351142.1	158790.8	50326	41215.11	759720.6
1985	Apparel	2432.3	20743.1	201034.1	81735.7	35552.2	40570.0	4792.5	236811.6
1985	Textiles	1099.3	21669.7	124873.5	51757.2	20148.4	22792.0	3850.7	143814.9
1985	Steel	812.1	41725.9	95730.5	37944.5	19274.6	16453.0	4337.6	107845.9
1985	Printing	1968.0	24066.5	154447.4	92742.6	39421.0	22792.0	8633.8	168605.6
1985	Machinery	2621.9	44420.2	243173.0	131292.7	54332.8	23810.0	15380.9	251602.1
1985	Autos	2618.8	111558.5	557846.3	219296.0	70649.7	86541.0	41288.2	603099.1
1985	Rockets	1901.6	26466.5	181953.1	105753.3	48992.8	12949.0	13695.4	181206.8
1985	Aircraft	2268.5	44010.3	225254.0	126154.6	56508.2	33335.0	45758.7	212830.3
1985	Chemicals	1239.3	105012.1	415516.1	117310.0	35328.2	66174.0	39329.8	442360.3
1985	Computers	406.7	12090.3	62221.4	27331.4	12090.7	13713.0	15568.8	60365.6
1985	TOTAL	17386.5	451763.1	2262049	991317.9	392298.6	339129	192636.3	*********
Rates of growth, 1972–1985 (percent) Changes: 1972–1985									
	Apparel	−17.5	17.7	115.1	126.4	90.2	604.7	329.0	390.8
	Textiles	−16.6	15.9	156.9	140.4	106.4	1146.1	219.7	1083.3
	Steel	−38.3	−9.0	87.2	56.3	53.0	223.9	109.8	201.4
	Printing	21.0	58.2	246.3	243.0	193.2	695.3	476.2	465.3
	Machinery	7.7	38.9	207.9	195.7	156.7	580.7	227.1	561.5
	Autos	−13.3	44.8	180.2	166.5	129.3	504.3	250.7	433.7
	Rockets	15.4	58.9	240.1	255.1	202.7	832.3	375.3	697.0
	Aircraft	15.2	49.8	256.8	241.9	194.4	731.1	554.6	433.3
	Chemicals	−12.2	37.8	279.6	167.1	141.0	522.8	445.9	356.5
	Computers	95.1	264.6	623.1	457.3	430.9	1342.0	776.3	1188.8
	TOTAL	−3.0	36.1	201.4	182.3	147.1	573.9	367.4	407.8

Table 3.3 (continued)

Price	Value added, real	Output real	Capital/ emp	Value/ emp	Payroll/ labor	Imports/ output	Exports/ output	Net Exp/ output
1.0	36106.3	93463.1	6.0	12.3	6.3	0.06	0.01	−0.05
1.0	21529.7	48615.5	14.2	16.3	7.4	0.04	0.02	−0.01
1.0	24278.7	51132.1	34.8	18.4	9.6	0.10	0.04	−0.06
1.0	27035.1	44600.7	9.4	16.6	8.3	0.06	0.03	−0.03
1.0	44407.0	78965.1	13.1	18.2	8.7	0.04	0.06	0.02
1.0	82287.1	199120.1	25.5	27.2	10.2	0.07	0.06	−0.01
1.0	29784.1	53503.6	10.1	18.1	9.8	0.03	0.05	0.03
1.0	36895.4	63130.6	14.9	18.7	9.7	0.06	0.11	0.05
1.0	43914.3	109474.0	54.0	31.1	10.4	0.10	0.07	−0.03
1.0	4904.4	8604.9	15.9	23.5	10.9	0.11	0.21	0.10
1.0	351142.1	750609.7	18.5	19.6	8.9	0.07	0.05	−0.01
1.98	41329.4	101652.2	8.5	33.6	14.6	0.20	0.02	−0.18
2.20	23540.7	56796.1	19.7	47.1	18.3	0.18	0.03	−0.15
2.56	14824.8	37401.6	51.4	46.7	23.7	0.17	0.05	−0.13
2.31	40135.7	66839.4	12.2	47.1	20.0	0.15	0.06	−0.09
2.52	52066.8	96435.3	16.9	50.1	20.7	0.10	0.06	−0.03
2.32	94698.4	240894.4	42.6	83.7	27.0	0.16	0.07	−0.08
2.23	47455.5	81649.2	13.9	55.6	25.8	0.07	0.08	0.00
2.23	56618.9	101095.3	19.4	55.6	24.9	0.15	0.20	0.06
3.23	36358.0	128781.5	84.7	94.7	28.5	0.16	0.09	−0.06
0.14	197974.6	450699.9	29.7	67.2	29.7	0.22	0.25	0.03
2.4	605003	1362245	26.0	57.1	22.6	0.15	0.09	−0.06
97.8	14.5	8.8	42.6	174.3	130.4	0.14	0.01	−0.13
119.9	9.3	16.8	39.0	188.2	147.4	0.14	0.01	−0.14
156.0	−38.9	−26.9	47.7	153.5	148.1	0.07	0.00	−0.07
131.1	48.5	49.9	30.7	183.4	142.3	0.08	0.02	−0.06
152.2	17.2	22.1	29.0	174.6	138.5	0.05	0.00	−0.05
131.6	15.1	21.0	67.0	207.3	164.5	0.08	0.01	−0.07
122.8	59.3	52.6	37.7	207.7	162.3	0.05	0.02	−0.02
122.8	53.5	60.1	30.1	196.9	155.6	0.08	0.09	0.01
222.7	−17.2	17.6	56.9	204.2	174.4	0.06	0.03	−0.03
−86.2	3936.7	5137.7	86.9	185.7	172.2	0.11	0.04	−0.07
141.9	72.3	81.5	40.3	191.0	154.6	0.08	0.03	−0.05

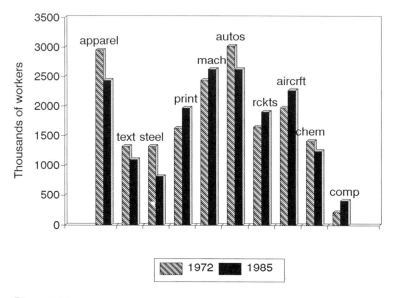

Figure 3.10
U.S. employment: aggregates

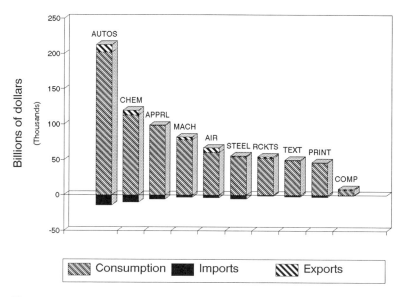

Figure 3.11
1972 apparent consumption and trade

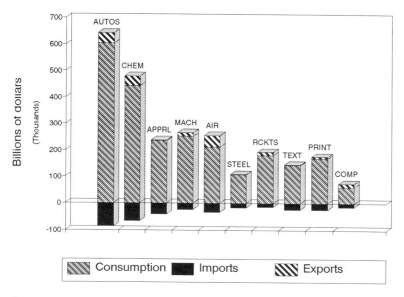

Figure 3.12
1985 apparent consumption and trade

A number of observations may be made about these figures:

1. The 1972 data indicate a low level of trade dependence. The level of trade dependence increases markedly by 1985, more on the import side than the export side. There were big increases in imports of AUTOS and APPAREL.

2. Exports and imports seem to offset each other. In other words, the volume of intra-industry trade seems high. The exceptions are APPAREL and TEXTILES, which have very low levels of exports.

3. The 1985 data indicate some important changes in the size of these industries. If there were no change, the size of the bars would fall off smoothly in 1985, as they do in 1972. But the relative decline of AP-PAREL, STEEL, and TEXTILES is apparent in this figure. This is associated with the relative decline of the prices of APPAREL and TEXTILES, but the STEEL sector seems to have suffered from a shift of consumption toward other products, COMPUTERS being one example.

Figures 3.11 and 3.12 indicate clearly the relative size of the industries, but are less clear about the role of trade in each of the sectors. Figures 3.13 and 3.14 have the reverse character: they indicate nothing about the size

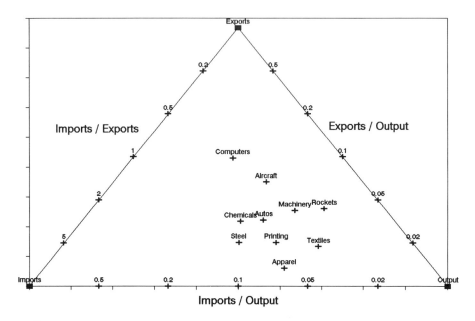

Figure 3.13
U.S. imports, exports, and production: 1972

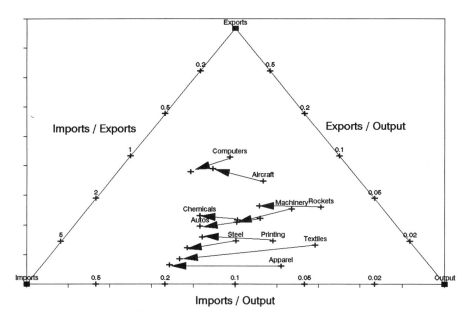

Figure 3.14
U.S. imports, exports, and production: 1972 and 1985

of the sectors, but do illustrate clearly the role of international trade in each sector. These triangular figures depict for each industry three ratios: exports/production, imports/production, and imports/exports. The scales for these ratios are placed along the three edges of the triangle. For example, in the 1972 figure on the edge labelled imports/exports, find the number 1, indicating that imports and exports are exactly in balance. Trace a straight line from this point directly toward the vertex labeled "OUTPUT." On every point along this straight line the ratio of imports to exports is exactly one. The AUTOS point and the TEXTILES point are slightly below this line, indicating that imports are just slightly larger than exports. Check it out in figure 3.13. Now let your eye move from the number 1 on the Import/Export edge to the number 5, where imports are five times exports. Again in your mind trace a straight line from this number 5 directly toward the OUTPUT vertex. On every point along this line the ratio of imports to exports is five. You found the APPAREL point on this line, and this sector accordingly has imports that are five times exports. By drawing two more straight lines through the APPAREL point toward the other two vertices, you can read from this figure that the ratio of imports to production in APPAREL was about .06 and the ratio of exports to production is less than .02.

Figure 3.14 contains data for both 1972 and 1985, with arrows connecting the industries. These arrows all point generally in the direction of the IMPORTS vertex, a reflection of the import boom that afflicted every sector. Using the imaginary lines drawn through the OUTPUT vertex and the Imports/Exports = 1 point, we can locate the sectors in which the United States had a revealed comparative advantage in both years, in the sense of having exports exceeding imports. These sectors are computers, aircraft, and rockets.

The big difference between the two years is the very noticeable shift of all the points toward the import vertex in 1985. None of the arrows is pointing directly at or below the imports vertex, which means that the ratio of exports to output of every sector is increasing, but not nearly as much as the ratio of imports to output. The one sector that best resisted this tendency was aircraft, which has an arrow pointing almost directly at the Imports/Exports = 1 point. This direction of movement could come about with no change in production, but an equal absolute increase in imports and exports.

I had hoped that this figure would indicate some points shifting toward the import vertex and others shifting toward the export vertex as the

United States has increased its international commerce and adjusted to its newly defined comparative advantage. The shift toward the import vertex of the labor-intensive sectors, apparel and textiles, is very evident, but the export shift is not. The overvaluation of the dollar in 1985 thus seriously masks the sectors toward which U.S. comparative advantage is shifting. I would expect figures applicable to more recent data to reveal a very different pattern, with some sectors moving clearly in the direction of the export vertex as the problem with the overvaluation of the dollar cures itself.

The bottom line, though, is that the trade data offer substantial support to the simple model of wage equalization through international commerce.

4 An FTA in the Two-Factor Heckscher-Ohlin Model

A two-factor, three-good model of wage equalization has been presented in the previous section. Here this model is used to discuss the possible consequences of an FTA. In this discussion it is assumed that international prices of these products are given, that the United States' factor supplies are in the high-wage cone, and that Mexico, which is labor abundant, is in the low-wage cone. Thus in the absence of protection there would be no apparel output in the United States and no machinery output in Mexico. Incidentally, this is not suggested as conforming exactly with the facts, because transport costs, economies of scale, and immobile inputs all contribute to maintaining an industry that otherwise would be unprofitable. This theory is presented as establishing a tendency. All that is being said is that, in the absence of protection, there are economic pressures in the United States to move the production of labor-intensive products to foreign locations.

Protection that raises the price of a product shifts a unit isoquant in toward the origin because smaller amounts of capital and labor are required to produce a unit value of output. Figure 3.15 illustrates the effect of the protective structure of the United States, which is assumed to protect the labor-intensive sectors, textiles, and apparel. The wage rate in this protected equilibrium, wage*, is higher than the wage rate prevailing in the high-wage country, wage. Indeed, that is the intent of the protection: to raise the wage rate.

This figure is offered as indication of the current state of U.S. manufacturing. Product prices in the labor-intensive sectors have fallen relative to the prices in the capital-intensive sectors, and wages accordingly have begun to decline. This decline is resisted by protection in the labor-intensive

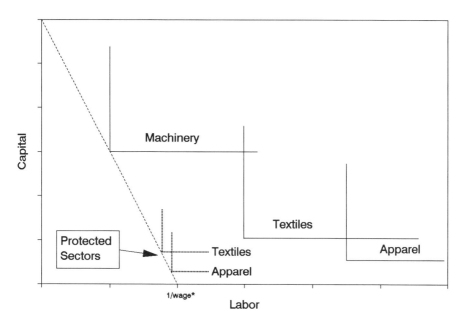

Figure 3.15
U.S. isoquants

sectors. Data on 1983 tariffs and nontariff barriers are reported in table 3.4, which includes the three-digit commodities for which tariff averages are highest. The NTB column indicates the percent of imports that were covered by a nontariff barrier. This is disaggregated into barriers that aim at maintaining internal prices (PRIC), quantitative restrictions (QUAN), health and safety regulations (HLTH), and threats (THR). As has been assumed in this discussion, the protection rates are highest for a variety of clothing items and other labor-intensive products. Textiles seem more subject to nontariff barriers, principally the Multi-Fibre Agreement.

Figure 3.16 illustrates the effect of protection in Mexico. Here it is assumed that the machinery sector has been protected (at least until 1986 when Mexico joined the GATT) as part of an import-substitution strategy. Incidentally, because machinery is an input into the other two sectors, protection that raises the price of machinery increases the capital input requirements in the other two sectors, which shifts their unit value isoquants vertically upward. Also, because textiles is an input into apparel production, protection of textiles reduces the value added in apparel and this shifts the apparel unit value isoquant away from the origin. These complex linkages between sectors are ignored in this discussion.

Table 3.4
Revealed comparative advantage and trade barriers: 1983 (sorted by tariff average)

SIC3	DESCR	S/C	M/C	X/C	M/S	X/S	TAR	NTB	PRIC	QUAN	HLTH	THR
302	Rubber footwear	.67	.34	.01	.50	.02	.42	.04				.04
223	Wool	.88	.13	.01	.15	.01	.32	.09				.09
236	Kids outerwear	.90	.16	.05	.17	.06	.25	.09		.01		.08
232	Male furnish.	.85	.16	.01	.19	.01	.25	.09		.61		.04
234	Female underwr.	.95	.09	.03	.09	.03	.24	.65				.08
233	Female outerwr.	.79	.21		.27	.01	.24	.08				.08
231	Male suits	.79	.22		.28	.01	.23	.07				.07
211	Cigarettes	1.10		.10		.09	.22	1.00	1.00			
225	Knitting	1.00		.01		.01	.22	.40	.08	.39		.01
325	Clay prod.	.94	.10	.04	.11	.04	.19	.13				.11
222	Syn. Wear. and Finish	.97	.06	.03	.06	.03	.17	.59	.34	.08		.51
315	Leather gloves	.76	.28	.04	.37	.05	.17					
316	Luggage	.81	.22	.03	.28	.04	.16	.01				.01
203	Canned fruit	.98	.04	.03	.04	.03	.15	.45	.45			.22
317	Handbags	.54	.47	.01	.87	.01	.15	.25	.23			.02
396	Costume jewel.	.87	.18	.05	.20	.05	.14					
322	Glassware	.95	.07	.02	.08	.02	.13					
228	Yarn, thread	.99	.02	.01	.02	.01	.12	.56	.20	.50		.07
239	Misc. fabr. text.	.98	.05	.03	.05	.03	.12	.48	.03	.36		.14
326	Pottery	.71	.36	.08	.51	.11	.12	.03	.03			
224	Narrow fabric	1.05	.04	.09	.04	.08	.11	.49	.12	.49		
395	Pens, pencils	.98	.08	.07	.08	.07	.11	.24		.24		
221	Cot. Weav. and Finish	.93	.10	.03	.11	.04	.11	.84	.03	.71		.13
206	Confectionery	.92	.10	.02	.11	.02	.11	.63	.60	.62		
235	Hats	.81	.21	.02	.26	.03	.11	.59		.55		.04
238	Misc. apparel	.74	.27	.01	.37	.02	.11	.23	.04	.13		
213	Tobacco	.68	.36	.03	.53	.05	.11					.09

Note: M = Imp, X = Exp, S = Ship, C = Cons

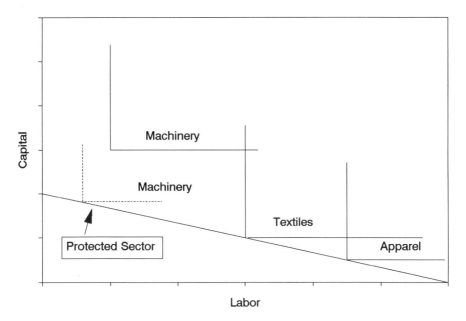

Figure 3.16
Mexican isoquants

4.1 A U.S.-Mexican Free Trade Agreement: Capital Immobile

The two-factor general equilibrium model depicted in these figures is a useful point of departure for considering the consequences of a Mexican-U.S. Free Trade Agreement. We can suppose that the United States is capital abundant and has factor supplies that make it suited to production of the relatively capital-intensive mix of commodities, machinery, and textiles. Mexico, on the other hand, is labor abundant and is suited to the labor-intensive mix of products: textiles and apparel. What can we expect if Mexico and the United States form a Free Trade Agreement? There are several possibilities depending on the mobility of capital and the effect that the agreement will have on product prices in Mexico and in the United States. First, assume that capital is immobile.

Before discussing the general equilibrium effects, it is useful to begin with the partial equilibrium depicted in figures 3.17 and 3.18 which convey the important message that the effect of the FTA on the United States depends critically on the economic size of Mexico.[6] Figure 3.17 indicates the effect of a FTA when the form of the U.S. protection is a tariff. In this figure the world price and the U.S. protected price are illustrated with

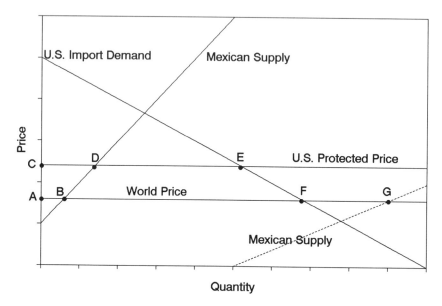

Figure 3.17
Trade diversion and an FTA: Tariffs

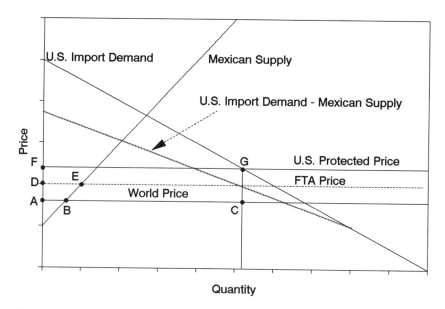

Figure 3.18
Trade diversion and an FTA: Quotas

horizontal lines. The downward-sloping curve is the U.S. import demand, and the two upward-sloping lines are alternative Mexican supply curves. If Mexico is small and has the supply curve close to the vertical axis, then prior to the establishment of the FTA Mexican production would be *AB* and U.S. import demand would be *CE*. A portion of the Mexican supply would go to satisfying home demand and, if there is any left over, the rest might find its way to the U.S. market. After the FTA, all the Mexican output is sold at the high U.S. prices, and Mexican demand is satisfied at the world price from third sources. The Mexican supply to the U.S. market increases to *CD*, which crowds out third-country exports to the United States. The total trade diversion is between *CD* and *CD* − *AB*, the latter figure applicable if all the Mexican product were sold in the U.S. market prior to the FTA. The facts are that very little of Mexican product is currently sold in the United States, and the larger figure *CD* seems applicable. On the other hand, the simple diagram includes no transportation and marketing costs, which would encourage home sales and would prevent all the Mexican product from being sold in the United States.

If this first supply curve is applicable, then the FTA would not affect the prices at which goods sell inside the United States. But now move the Mexican supply to the right. At some point it will intersect the U.S. demand at the point *E* where all U.S. import demand is satisfied from Mexican sources. Further increases in Mexican supply will drive down the U.S. internal price. If the Mexican supply curve goes through the point *F* on the U.S. import demand curve, then the world price would prevail in the U.S. markets. Further increases in Mexican supply would not cause further reductions in the U.S. price because Mexican suppliers would not sell at any price lower than the one prevailing in the world market. The dashed line in the lower right of figure 3.17 illustrates this case. Total Mexican supply is *AG*. The amount *AF* is sold in the U.S. market at world prices, and the remainder *FG* is sold partly at home and partly in third markets. From this figure we derive the following important conclusion: *If Mexico is large enough that it can completely satisfy incipient import demand of the United States that would occur at world market prices. then an FTA would completely dismantle U.S. protection.*

A substantially different description applies to the quota case illustrated in figure 3.18. Here the quota is assumed to be quantity *FG*, and prices inside the U.S. market are adjusted so that import supply and import demand are equalized. This quota level is selected to create an initial equilibrium equivalent to the tariff equilibrium depicted in figure 3.17. With the formation of the FTA; the equivalence of the quota and tariff breaks down.

The smallest amount of Mexican supply supplements the quota-restricted imports and puts downward pressure on U.S. prices. The FTA price D can be found in figure 3.18 by defining U.S. import demand net of Mexican supply and then selecting a U.S. price that equates net demand to the quota level. This import price is lower than the U.S. protected price, even though Mexico is too small to satisfy total U.S. import demand. Note that by moving the Mexican supply to the right, one may conclude that the U.S. price reverts to the unprotected world market price if Mexican supply is enough to make up the difference between the U.S. import demand that would occur at the world price and the quota level of imports. In the extreme, if the quota level is zero, then we revert to the tariff conclusion: The world price prevails if Mexico is large enough to satisfy completely U.S. import demand at the world market price.

The product price changes that are implied by these partial equilibrium models can be mapped into wage changes using the simple general equilibrium model illustrated in figures 3.15 and 3.16. The following discussion applies when the barrier is a tariff, in which case an FTA may leave U.S. prices unchanged. Keep in mind that it is assumed that the apparel sector in the United States would not exist at world prices, and accordingly the incipient import demand is equal to the total U.S. demand.

Case 1
Mexican production is too small in apparel and textiles to satisfy fully the U.S. import demand. The United States fully protects the apparel industry.

United States: Since both textiles and apparel are imported from third sources, the prevailing prices in the United States are the world market prices, adjusted upward by the U.S. level of protection. This is the case of pure trade diversion: supply of textiles and apparel from third countries is displaced by Mexican supply, but there is no change in U.S. prices or the composition of U.S. output. The United States loses the tariff revenue on displaced imports that now come from Mexico instead of third sources.

Mexico: Wages in the United States and Mexico equalize at the high U.S. level. The high Mexican wages force Mexican producers to use an excessively capital-intensive method of production. Protection of the apparel sector in the United States requires a relatively high tariff on apparel compared with textiles. This relatively high apparel price induces Mexican producers to specialize excessively in apparel. All Mexican production of apparel and textiles is sold in the United States at the high prices. Textiles

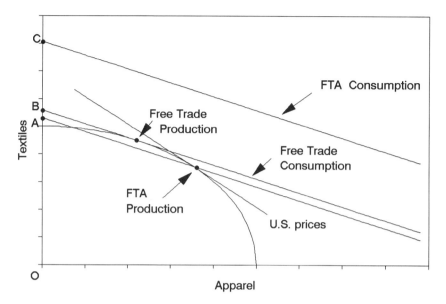

Figure 3.19
Mexican production possibilities: The effect of an FTA

and apparel for consumption in Mexico are imported from the rest of the world at low prices. These are prevented from transshipment into the United States, although leakages may occur.

Important aspects of this case are illustrated in figure 3.19. The curved line in the figure represents the Mexican production possibilities of textiles and apparel. Free trade production is found by maximizing the value of output at world prices. This maximization selects the indicated production point defined where the production possibilities curve is tangent to a straight line, with slope equal to world relative prices. This line then defines the free trade consumption possibilities on the assumption that trade is balanced (value of production = value of consumption).

A free trade agreement that raises the relative price of apparel induces a shift of output in favor of apparel. *More dramatically. the agreement creates a balanced trade consumption line that is entirely above the free trade line if both markets are protected by the United States.*[7]

The amount *AB* measures the welfare loss caused by the excessive specialization by Mexico in the production of apparel. The amount *BC* is a pure transfer to Mexico. It is the difference between the value of Mexican free trade production in the U.S. market and in the world market. If the difference between U.S. internal prices and world prices were entirely due to U.S. tariffs, then the U.S. government, in effect, would turn over the tariff revenues to Mexican producers who distribute the proceeds to Mexican labor and capital by bidding up the prices of inputs to U.S. levels. The amount of this tariff loss is AC. But much of the implicit tariff revenue is collected by third-country suppliers in the form of quota rents. These third-country suppliers accordingly are forced to effect a substantial portion of the transfer amount AC to Mexico. *It is Taiwan, Hong Kong, and other beneficiaries of the Multi-Fibre Agreement that will pay for the U.S.-Mexican Free Trade Agreement.*

Case 2
Mexican production is enough to satisfy fully the U.S. import demand for the labor-intensive product apparel, but not for textiles.

United States: The price of apparel falls below the protected price because imports come entirely from Mexico. The apparel sector disappears because it is cheaper to produce apparel in Mexico, but wages remain at the high protected level.

Mexico: The price of apparel for Mexican producers is somewhere between the pre-FTA U.S. protected price and the low world market price. The textile price for Mexican producers is the high U.S. protected price. These goods prices require Mexican wages to be lower than U.S. wages. If the Mexican supply is enough to push the price of apparel down to the world market price or close to it, then Mexico ends up with lower wages than it would have without the FTA, because by joining the FTA Mexico ends up protecting textiles.

The message here is an important one: *Protection in the United States that is intended to maintain the wages of U.S. workers may make Mexican workers worse off,* if there is a free trade agreement. The reason for this contradictory outcome is that the product mixes differ greatly in Mexico and the United States. Textiles and iron and steel, which are in the labor-intensive wing of U.S. production, are in the capital-intensive wing of Mexican production. Thus protection of textiles and iron and steel drives up the demand for labor in the United States as the output mix shifts away from the most capital-intensive sectors such as chemicals. But the same protection in Mexico drives down the demand for labor as the output mix is shifted away from the most labor-intensive sectors such as apparel and footwear.

Case 3
Mexican production is enough to satisfy fully the U.S. import demand at the protected prices for both apparel and textiles.

United States: Both the price of apparel and the price of textiles fall below the protected price, because U.S. imports come entirely from Mexico. The prices end up between the protected prices and the unprotected prices, depending on U.S. import demand and Mexican production. The U.S. apparel sector disappears because it is cheaper to produce in Mexico. The wage in the United States falls with the price of textiles.

Mexico: The relative price of textiles to apparel may be either lower or higher than the free trade relative price, and consequently wages in Mexico may be either higher or lower.

   In both of these cases I take it as given that the U.S. machinery sector is large enough to satisfy the total Mexican demand. Competition with U.S. suppliers accordingly will drive out of business the protected capital-intensive sectors in Mexico and the internal price of these reverts to the unprotected price. This "trade creation" is accompanied by a shift of resources into the more labor-intensive sectors where they are more productive. The level of Mexican GNP accordingly rises. Figure 3.19 is misleading in that it does not indicate the efficiency gain from shutting down the capital-intensive sectors.

Case 4
Mexican production is enough to satisfy fully the U.S. import demand for textiles, but not for apparel.
   Left as an exercise.

5 A Three-Factor Model with Mobile Capital

The discussion in the previous section has been based on the assumption that the accumulation and location of capital is not affected by a free trade agreement. But it is highly likely that the rate of capital accumulation in Mexico would increase if a serious agreement were put in place. Some of this additional capital would come from increased Mexican savings, some from the United States, and some from third countries that will find Mexico a useful location for gaining access to the U.S. market.

   The preceding discussion is easily amended to allow capital mobility. In the two-factor, three-good model, an increase of capital in Mexico shifts production in favor of the moderately capital-intensive sectors, textiles. A standard trade result, the Rybczynski theorem, suggests that the size of the labor-intensive sector, apparel, shrinks absolutely as well as relatively with this increase in capital. Likewise, a reduction in capital in the United States shifts output from machinery toward textiles. This paradoxical result seems worth repeating for emphasis: An FTA accompanied by capital mobility from the United States shifts the structure of U.S. production toward the U.S. labor-intensive sectors (textiles, for example).

If this model with only two factors is used as a guide, the capital flow into Mexico continues until Mexico adopts the high wages and low capital costs of the United States. This can occur only when Mexico and the United States have the same product mix. The complete equalization of wages from capital mobility is a necessary implication of a two-factor model. But a three factor model discussed in Leamer (1987) offers some richer alternatives. One three-factor model with high-skilled and low-skilled workers as well as capital is illustrated in figure 3.20. This triangular figure allows one to display the three factor ratios at the same time, each along a different side of the triangle. Each vertex of the triangle is labeled with one of the three factors. The ratio of capital to low-skilled labor,

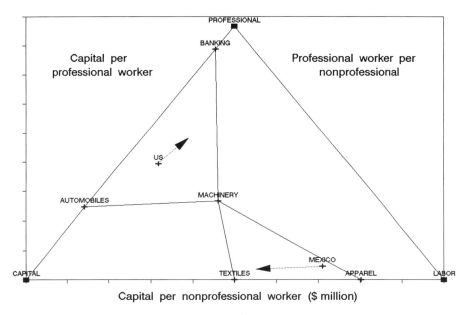

Figure 3.20
Three-factor triangle

for example, is scaled along the bottom side of the triangle connecting the capital and labor vertex. Points closer to the labor vertex are labor intensive; points closer to the capital vertex are more capital intensive. As drawn, therefore, textiles is more capital intensive than apparel. The capital/low-skilled labor ratio of any other point in the triangle can be found by drawing a line that begins at the "professional" vertex and extends to the bottom of the triangle through the point. For example, an imaginary line from the professional vertex through the machinery point intersects the bottom of the triangle to the left of the textile point. This means that the capital per low-skilled ratio in machinery is higher than in textiles. The textile and apparel points lie on the bottom of the triangle, indicating that they use no professional workers as inputs. Automobiles and banking lie on the left edge of the triangle, indicating that they use no low-skilled workers. If this isn't clear, pause a minute to get it straight, because these triangular diagrams will prove extremely useful.

There are five different industrial sectors illustrated in this figure. The labels and locations of these industries in the triangle are suggestive, not exact. For example, the banking sector stands for an array of financial and other professional services produced with professional labor, very little physical capital, and very little unskilled labor. The machinery point is connected to the other commodities to divide the figure into "cones of diversification." The United States, which is relatively well endowed with physical capital and professional workers, lies in the cone with banking, automobiles, and machinery vertices. Mexico lies in the more labor-intensive cone with apparel, textiles, and machinery vertices.

The factor price equalization theorem implies that factor prices are constant within a cone of diversification. To get a partial handle on how factor prices change between cones, we can trace lines from one cone to another in the direction of one of the factor vertices. For example, it is possible to go from the U.S. cone into the Mexican cone on a straight line to the labor vertex. This movement toward the labor vertex represents an increase in the supply of unskilled labor, and accordingly the wage rate must either fall or stay the same (result of Samuelson). This implies that wages of low-skilled workers are lower in the Mexican cone than in the U.S. cone. The ordering of the other factor returns is not clear because it is impossible to trace a line from one cone to the other straight toward either the capital vertex or the professional vertex. If the machinery point were a little to the right, with a capital/skilled labor ratio less than textiles, a line can be drawn from the Mexican cone and U.S. cone straight at the professional vertex. This increase in the professional work force would imply that the wages of professionals were lower in the United States than in Mexico. But as the figure is drawn, there is no necessary relationship between Mexican and U.S. capital returns or wages of professionals. If, as seems to be the case, the price of banking services is high enough, the wages of professionals would be higher in the United States than in Mexico. Because both types of labor would then command higher wages in the United States, and because both Mexico and the United States produce machinery, the third factor, capital, has to be cheaper in the United States than in Mexico. If that is the case, there is an incentive for capital to migrate from the United States to Mexico; this migration is illustrated by the arrows in the figure, Mexico toward the capital vertex and the United States away. This migration leaves unchanged the returns to capital until the product mix changes, that is, until either the United States or Mexico gets to the edge of its cone. If Mexico is small enough and close enough to its edge, then it will be the first to exit a cone. In this case the apparel sector disappears from Mexico and the textile sector grows. The corresponding capital outflow from the United States leaves unchanged the returns to factors, but does shrink the automobiles sector and expands the banking sector. If the capital flow is great enough, the United States may lose its automobiles sector. Thus the capital flows induced by an FTA put pressure on those sectors in the United States that use large amounts of capital and relatively small amounts of professional and unskilled labor. In Mexico, the pressure is put on the most labor-intensive products.

Evidence

Reality is a great deal more complicated than figure 3.20 suggests, but, I would argue, the main ideas underlying the figure carry a ring of truth. The sectors in the United States that will fare well use relatively large amounts of high-skilled labor, which is abundant in the United States but scarce in Mexico. Figure 3.21 displays the industrial characteristics of the ten commodity aggregates that were earlier discussed. Figure 3.22 displays the resource supplies of a set of countries for which there exist ILO data on the proportion of the labor force in the "professional" category, and also capital stock figures (1982) formed by accumulating and discounting investment flows. The Mexican and U.S. resource supply points have been placed in the industrial characteristics triangle, figure 3.21. In your mind transfer the other countries into the diagram for industrial characteristics. It appears that as countries accumulate human and physical capital, they seem initially to follow a very similar path through the thicket of commodities beginning

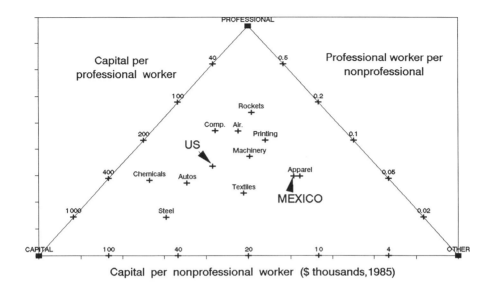

Figure 3.21
Industrial characteristics of the nine aggregates

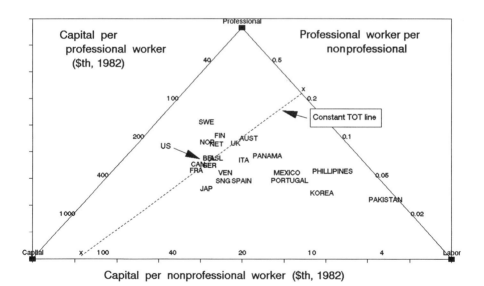

Figure 3.22
Resource supplies

at the labor vertex and passing very close to the apparel point. Here the development paths may diverge. Some countries like Singapore and Japan accumulate physical capital relatively rapidly and have resource mixes more suited to steel and autos than to aircraft and computers. Other countries like Austria and Sweden place relatively heavy investments in human capital and have resource supplies more suited to machinery, printing, and aircraft.

If the theory is taken literally with respect to this set of commodities, we would divide figure 3.21 into a set of triangular "cones of diversification" by connecting the commodity points with lines. Production would concentrate exclusively on the three commodities that surround the resource supply point. The way that this diagram would be divided into cones of diversification depends on product prices, so much so that there are product prices that support any division. If you increase sufficiently the price of a commodity, its point insists on connecting to as many other points as possible, for then the commodity is produced over the greatest range of factor endowments.

Unless apparel is very expensive, it will be separated from the U.S. point by at least one of these lines, and absent protection would not be produced in the United States. If technological change and price movements have made textiles a high-profit sector, the United States would lie in a cone formed from the chemicals, machinery, and textiles points, or from chemicals, aircraft, and textiles. Other prices would place the United States in cones not including textiles as a vertex, and the U.S. would not be producing textiles absent protection.

Real production patterns do not conform with the extreme implications of the model, but they do conform in the sense that production concentrates on those products that use inputs in ratios similar to their supply. As the Mexican factor supplies are very close to the input mix in apparel, liberalization of the Mexican economy should induce a concentration of production on these labor-intensive products including certain food products, furniture, and footwear. Capital accumulation would take Mexico directly toward the textile point and would be accompanied by a shift out of apparel and into textiles and household appliances. The relative supply of human capital to unskilled labor is not likely to increase in Mexico for some time, and we should not be expecting much production of machinery or certainly aircraft and rockets.

It is unlikely that the capital flows associated with an FTA would alter the location of the U.S. resource point very much, and therefore would have little effect on U.S. comparative advantage. But Mexican production of apparel and textiles will make it difficult for the United States to protect these sectors, and the United States will be forced to adjust out of apparel and possibly out of textiles in the longer run. A liberalized Mexico would import more of those products that are intensive in skilled labor and very intensive in capital: steel, chemicals, and aircraft (including metalworking machinery and electrical machinery). U.S. manufacturers are well positioned to satisfy this new Mexican demand.

6 Wages and Employment in a Multisectoral Model

Is international competition causing the fall in the real wages of low-skilled workers?[8] More specifically, is the wage decline related to three features of the international commerce of the United States: (1) the increased level of international trade as a percentage of GNP, (2) the large trade deficit that the United States has had during the 1980s and/or (3) the shift in the commodity composition of trade, especially the increased imports of labor-intensive products?

The literature on the relationship between trade and wages that has come out of the labor economics tradition has focused on the trade deficit as the cause of the fall in the wages.[9] This literature has three basic problems. First, the trade deficit is a temporary phenomenon, but the intensity

Table 3.5
Notation

Exogenous variables:	
Factor supplies	v
Product prices	p. $P = \mathrm{diag}\{p\}$
Taste/technology	t
Trade surplus	B
Total expenditure	Y
Endogenous variables:	
Factor prices	w
Input intensities	A
Inverse intensities	$E = A^{-1}$
Production	q
Consumption	C
Net exports	T
Consumption shares	$\alpha(p)$
Subscripts	
h	traded goods produced at home
f	traded goods not produced at home
n	nontraded goods

Table 3.6
The Heckscher-Ohlin Samuelson model

I. Full fixed set of traded commodities	
Equilibrium conditions	
Cost minimization	$A = f(w, t)$
Zero profits	$w = E'_h p_h$
Factor market equilibrium	$A_h q_h = v$
Uneconomic products	$p_f < A'_f w$
Equilibrium equations	
Factor price equalization	$w = w(p_h, t)$
Production	$q_h = E_h v$
GNP	$\text{GNP} = p'_h E_h v$
Total expenditure	$Y = \text{GNP} = B$
Consumption	$C = P^{-1} \alpha(p) Y,$
Net exports	$T_h = E_h v - P_h^{-1} \alpha_h(p) Y,$
	$T_f = E_f v - P_f^{-1} \alpha_f(p) Y,$

II. Incomplete, fixed set of traded commodities (one nontraded good); fixed input intensities

Definition	
Inverse intensities	$E' = A'^{-1} = [E_h, E_N]$
Equilibrium conditions	
Zero profits	$w = E_h p_h + E_N p_N$
Factor market equilibrium	$A_h q_h + A_N q_N = v$
Equilibrium equations	
Factor prices	$w = E_h p_h + E_N [\alpha_N/(1 - \alpha_N)](p'_h q_h - B)/q_N$
Traded goods output	$q_h = E'_h v,$
Nontraded goods output	$q_N = E'_N v$
Nontraded goods prices	$p_N = [\alpha_N/(1 - \alpha_N)](p'_h q_h - B)/q_N$
GNP	$\text{GNP} = p'_h q_h + p'_N q_N$

of interest in the wage decline reflects the concern that the decline is permanent and will not disappear if the deficit improves. Second, the word "cause" makes an implicit reference to a hypothetical change in the system, but the counterfactual implicit in pointing to the trade deficit as the "cause" of the wage decline is quite unclear. Exactly what change in the economy is imagined that would jointly affect the deficit and also the level of wages? Is it increased barriers against imports? Is it a reduction of government expenditure? Is it looser monetary policy? Do these all have the same effect on wages? The third problem is related to the second: these calculations lack a clear theoretical foundation.

A clear theoretical foundation for computing the effects of international competition on the labor market can be provided by the general equilibrium model commonly employed in international economics, which links wages with product prices through the "Stolper-Samuelson" functions: the derivatives of factor prices with respect to product prices. Thus, according to this model, the path by which international competition affects wages goes first through product prices. Changes in international trade that are not accompanied by product price changes leave the returns to factors unchanged. In particular, an overvalued exchange rate that would be associated with a trade deficit increases the demand for tradeables and therefore the level of imports, but need not have any impact on the levels of factor prices. Factor migration may also have no affect on wages. The potential affect on wages of an increase in the labor force may be fully dissipated by a shift in the product mix in favor of commodities that use labor intensively.

If this model is taken as a guide, the empirical evidence of the link between trade and wages needs to be established in two steps. One step is the estimation of the Stolper-Samuelson equations that map product prices into wages. The other step isolates those changes in product prices that can be attributed to relevant changes in the international markets.

The data that might be used to estimate the Stolper-Samuelson functions has three components of variability: country, commodity, and time. None of these is likely to reveal much about the Stolper-Samuelson functions. Cross-industry comparisons of wages and prices cannot be used to estimate these functions because an explicit assumption of the model is that factors are mobile across sectors and command the same returns. Cross-country comparisons are not likely to be fruitful because differences in internal product prices and wages are too small and measured with too much error to be very informative. Cross-time comparisons probably do not get at the long-run aspect of the model, and when they do, they are subject to the criticism that the Stolper-Samuelson mapping depends on the technology that cannot be taken as constant for long stretches of time.

Though the prospects for direct estimation of the Stolper-Samuelson effects $(\partial w/\partial p)$ seem small, it is possible to obtain estimates of the Rybczynski effects $(\partial q/\partial v)$ that link output levels (q) with resource supplies (v). The enterprise is then saved by the duality between the Stolper-Samuelson and the Rybczynski effects, $(\partial w/\partial p) = (\partial q/\partial v)$. The Rybczynski derivatives can be estimated by regressing output levels of particular industries on country factor supplies at one point in time. For example, the cross-country variation of the output of textiles might be explained by the country's supplies of college graduates, high-school graduates, and less-than-high-school graduates. If each extra high-school graduate is associated with $700 additional dollars of textile output, then the duality result implies that a reduction in the price of textiles by 10% lowers the wages of the high-school graduates by 700 × .1 = $70 per year ($pdq/dv = pdw/dp$).

Once we have estimated the Stolper-Samuelson derivatives, we still must link the changes in relative product prices to events in the international marketplace. One phenomenon that I wish to emphasize is the substantial global integration that has greatly increased the access of producers to low-wage labor in other countries. We can use the zero-profit conditions to get a handle on the effects that access to low-wage labor is likely to have on product prices. A zero-profit condition applicable to commodity k is $p_k = A'_k w$. Logarithmic differentiation of this pricing equation, holding fixed the technology A_k, produces an expression for the percentage change in price: $dp_k/p_k = H'_k\{dw_i/w_i\}$, where H is a vector of input shares $(w_i A_{ki}/p_k)$ and $\{dw_i/w_i\}$ is a vector of percentage changes in factor costs. This points to the estimation of a cross-commodity regression with the price change over some interval of time as the dependent variable and input shares as the explanatory variables:

$$\Delta p_k/p_k = \sum_i \beta_i^*(\text{input share})_{ik}.$$

In this equation β_i represents the change in the factor costs. Using this equation, we can ask what would prices have been if the low-cost alternative labor supply were not available. The answer is prices would have been higher by $-\beta^*$(low-skilled labor share). Left out of this equation are the effects of technological improvements on the input intensities. The regression analysis is based implicitly on the assumption that the cross industry variability of rates of technological improvements are independent of the input shares; for example, there is no tendency for technological improvements to be concentrated in capital-intensive sectors. The obvious association between research inputs and technological improvements can be accommodated by including scientists as one of the input categories.

6.1 Estimates Using OECD Data

Ideally, one would estimate a Heckscher-Ohlin model using data from a long list of countries. Important sensitivity questions would be studied, especially looking for evidence of substantial nonlinearities that would suggest defects in the structure of the model. Unfortunately, data are very limited. The best data set that includes levels of output has been compiled by the OECD and includes the structure of production (ISIC) for only thirteen countries. A fairly simple model is therefore estimated with these limited data. The factor supplies that are used as explanatory variables are the level of the capital stock, the number of professional workers (ILO classification), and the number of others classified as "economically active." The variability of these resources is not as great as one might hope, as can be seen by looking at figure 3.22, restricting attention to the OECD countries. But data on the composition of output of countries like Korea, the Philippines, and Pakistan are not available.

Estimates using 1972 and 1985 data are reported in tables 3.7 and 3.8. Commodities are sorted according to the sign patterns of the coefficients. Comparative advantage of the first group of products, wood products and footwear, comes from the abundance of nonprofessional workers; comparative disadvantage comes from the abundance of capital and professional workers.

Many of these coefficients seem pretty much what one would expect from the data on industrial characteristics, figure 3.21. Textiles and iron and steel are located in countries that are abundant in capital and nonprofessional workers. Motor vehicles use capital and professional workers. But there are some surprises. There is a large group of commodities that have all positive coefficients, fewer in 1985 than 1972. The Rybczynski theorem suggests that there will be at least one negative coefficient. The all-positives finding might lead one to question the applicability of the Rybczynski theorem to this multicommodity setting. It might suggest, for example, economies of scale. Alternatively, the finding might be dismissed as due to sampling uncertainty: there is no commodity that has all three t-values larger than one.

Another observation about these tables is that there are some commodities with very low R^2's. These measures of fit do not include the scale effect since they come from a regression with output divided by capital as the dependent variables. Thus one should not expect the R^2's to be very high. But the model is virtually informationless regarding the location of production of several of the commodities. It does do a pretty good job for many of the labor-intensive products including footwear (1985), leather products, textiles, and apparel.

These limited data cannot yield precise detailed conclusions about the determinants of production patterns, but they do suggest pretty clearly that resource supplies do matter. The substantial difference in Mexican and U.S. capital/labor ratios thus seems to be an important aspect of an FTA.

Table 3.7
Regression coefficients ordered by sign pattern (year = 1972)
Model: $Q = \alpha + \beta_1 CAPITAL + \beta_2 PROF + \beta_3 OTHER + \varepsilon CAPITAL$

ISIC	Name	β_1	β_2	β_3	α	R^2	Adj. R^2
		$(-)$	$(-)$	$(+)$			
321	Wood prod	-8.09	-837.78	419.11	248241	0.29	0.05
324	Footwear	-0.74	-269.22	72.31	15685	0.43	0.18
		$(-)$	$(+)$	$(-)$			
3411	Pulp, pape	-8.13	1626.78	-54.02	825276	0.54	0.38
341	Paper, pro	-6.16	2042.31	-9.02	825402	0.57	0.40
		$(-)$	$(+)$	$(+)$			
323	Leather, p	-29.68	1525.23	210.32	87686	0.82	0.74
361	Pottery, c	-25.62	1524.79	164.32	-54949	0.93	0.89
314	Tobacco	-15.60	1222.86	131.22	-142477	0.85	0.81
342	Print., pu	-15.16	3479.34	11.15	-196246	0.75	0.67
3513	Synth. res	-7.55	682.89	113.76	-66456	0.55	0.36
354	Petrol. pr	-2.10	294.15	16.73	536	0.23	-0.03
381	Metal pro	-1.95	3129.31	118.59	-589598	0.68	0.58
		$(+)$	$(-)$	$(+)$			
3211	Spinning	5.68	-795.57	240.36	-110647	0.74	0.65
369	Oth. non-m	3.44	-370.12	147.04	26713	0.51	0.30
356	Plastic p	1.97	-122.72	102.22	-64985	0.61	0.49
332	Furniture	1.49	-28.34	78.49	-76014	0.59	0.46
321	Textiles	9.24	-403.89	309.50	-225065	0.70	0.59
362	Glas, prod	3.35	-22.76	16.07	-31413	0.13	-0.17
371	Iron, stee	26.80	-1563.28	334.46	-134884	0.66	0.06
384	Trnsprt e	56.40	-1602.62	273.48	-1010459		0.54
		$(+)$	$(+)$	$(-)$			
372	Non-ferro	2.81	6733.97	-581.51	-221896	0.47	0.29
311	Food	38.01	3303.44	-133.42	341287	0.42	0.23
3843	Motor veh	44.74	675.23	-12.75	-948633	0.61	0.49
3841	Shipbuild	4.63	25.32	-5.38	337369	0.53	0.35
		$(+)$	$(+)$	$(+)$			
3522	Drugs, med	5.49	117.54	0.52	-115753	0.43	0.24
353	Petr. refi	14.95	453.41	11.23	-220161	0.17	-0.11
3511	Basic che	1.98	1117.94	19.74	-169910	0.45	0.27
390	Oth. indus	0.74	335.27	25.20	-117752	0.55	0.41
355	Rubber pr	2.02	326.55	27.05	-137558	0.88	0.84
322	Wearing a	9.37	214.68	29.90	-83580	0.24	-0.02
3825	Office, co	1.60	105.91	33.52	-128672	0.76	0.66
385	Professio	1.56	336.92	34.88	-179476	0.64	0.52
352	Oth. chemi	10.08	321.50	96.22	-236320	0.66	0.54
313	Beverages	0.35	469.46	111.94	-176174	0.59	0.43
3832	Radio, TV	2.53	613.99	117.85	-312534	0.55	0.40
351	Indust. ch	0.26	1539.21	138.14	-247149	0.63	0.48
382	Machinery	2.44	3542.31	171.00	-865329	0.63	0.50
383	Electr. ma	10.98	1330.76	217.08	-565868	0.68	0.58
3	Manufactu	54.90	28961.17	2518.99	-4138238	0.92	0.89

Number of observation = 13
PROF and OTHER in thousands; CAPITAL in millions

Table 3.8
Regression coefficients ordered by sign pattern (year = 1985)
Model: $Q = \alpha + \beta_1 CAPITAL + \beta_2 PROF + \beta_3 OTHER + \varepsilon CAPITAL$

ISIC	Name	β_1	β_2	β_3	α	R^2	Adj. R^2
		$(-)$	$(-)$	$(+)$			
331	Wood prod	−19.63	−1179.88	1315.46	1793842	0.32	0.07
324	Footwear	−3.22	−349.45	221.31	192865	0.62	0.49
		$(-)$	$(+)$	$(+)$			
314	Tobacco	−3.03	440.58	205.27	−256285	0.44	0.26
323	Leather, p	−19.31	518.91	663.43	776642	0.72	0.63
361	Pottery, c	−14.48	805.61	511.49	−68518	0.71	0.61
3411	Pulp, pape	−16.07	2890.80	142.66	3013741	0.51	0.35
341	Paper, pro	−13.37	4281.70	98.59	2838333	0.47	0.24
		$(+)$	$(-)$	$(+)$			
384	Trnsprt e	44.38	−4711.07	1113.15	−3000106	0.64	0.52
321	Textiles	1.66	−1757.23	777.55	−26687	0.66	0.54
3211	Spinning	0.51	−1210.63	486.22	−98777	0.70	0.58
371	Iron, stee	0.36	−939.78	1009.14	129386	0.51	0.35
369	Oth. non-m	1.73	−937.97	355.84	521637	0.32	0.09
356	Plastic p	8.84	−770.00	161.56	−371382	0.45	0.27
3511	Basic che	8.74	−587.87	363.47	−236813	0.28	0.01
322	Wearing a	0.13	−552.95	364.55	−25011	0.58	0.44
332	Furniture	1.18	−518.46	240.74	−318	0.55	0.40
3841	Shipbuild	2.82	−478.39	50.94	829769	0.51	0.33
351	Indust. ch	13.30	−394.42	562.84	−99974	0.16	−0.12
362	Glas, prod	2.05	−108.60	55.31	−67403	0.37	0.14
3513	Synth. res	2.31	−91.01	186.94	291780	0.10	−0.20
390	Oth. indus	2.16	−42.78	111.21	−310450	0.51	0.35
355	Rubber pr	2.10	−10.31	109.53	−273416	0.76	0.65
		$(+)$	$(+)$	$(-)$			
372	Non-ferro	24.51	11527.13	−2195.47	−2291449	0.68	0.58
3843	Motor veh	48.93	1120.31	−343.79	−3764712	0.51	0.35
381	Metal pro	26.04	2013.33	−302.45	−1609393	0.34	0.09
3522	Drugs, med	5.63	430.90	−43.22	−551458	0.40	0.17
385	Professio	6.67	413.73	−10.44	−828237	0.42	0.23
342	Print., pu	3.23	2649.06	−3.06	−1011	0.35	0.13
		$(+)$	$(+)$	$(+)$			
3825	Office, co	3.86	499.04	11.46	−674013	0.34	0.12
354	Petrol. pr	0.63	282.35	19.49	−75236	0.15	−0.16
353	Petr. refi	21.05	4111.58	39.41	−1522410	0.13	−0.16
382	Machinery	19.02	3882.94	149.54	−2333022	0.36	0.15
3832	Radio, TV	12.34	246.33	154.77	−1371870	0.33	0.10
352	Oth. chemi	10.79	466.54	199.56	−958392	0.60	0.46
313	Beverages	1.42	304.43	243.37	−401458	0.47	0.30
311	Food prod	22.99	1380.94	525.69	−941338	0.20	−0.06
383	Electr. ma	17.51	472.06	525.93	−1945206	0.39	0.17
3	Manufactu	164.32	18822.08	6853.62	−8645906	0.40	0.20

Number of observations = 13
PROF and OTHER in thousands; CAPITAL in millions

7 Estimates of the Effects of an FTA

7.1 How Big Is Mexico?

As argued in section 4, the effects on the United States of a free trade agreement depend critically on the impact that Mexican sales will have in the U.S. product markets. Is Mexico so small that the agreement will hardly be felt in the Unite States? Or is Mexico large enough to substantially decrease the relative prices of labor-intensive products in the United States? Specifically, if Mexico is large enough to supply all of U.S. imports, then U.S. tariff barriers are at least partially circumvented, and an FTA would tend to push U.S. internal prices down to the foreign price level. If Mexican supply is enough to satisfy all U.S. import demand that would occur at the international prices, then trade barriers, tariffs or quotas, would be completely undone by an FTA.

Table 3.9 contains information that helps to answer the question: How big is Mexico? The first column labeled (la) reports the ratio of 1984 U.S. imports from Mexico divided by total U.S. imports in that commodity class.[10] For example, the largest ratio of Mexican to total imports was 9% for ISIC 369, other nonmetallic mineral manufactures. The next largest was 8% for glass and for electrical machinery. Remember the critical number is 100%: If the form of protection is a tariff, unless Mexico is large enough to satisfy U.S. import demand, an FTA diverts trade but does not have any effect on U.S. prices.

Based on these figures, it seems unlikely that Mexico could export enough to have much of an effect on the U.S. markets. Certainly, with import shares of less than 10%, we would not expect the U.S. markets to be much affected by a free trade agreement. But there are five counter-arguments to that viewpoint. First, a free trade agreement that has high barriers into the United States against third-source imports creates an incentive for Mexico to export all of its product to the United States and to import from third sources for domestic needs. Second, the liberalization of the Mexican markets that has been occurring since the country joined GATT in 1985 is likely to be accompanied by substantial productivity increases, a trend that would probably be accentuated by a free trade agreement (Clague (1991)). Third, liberalization should induce greater specialization of Mexican production in commodities that are suited to the country's comparative advantage, namely the labor-intensive sectors. Fourth, an FTA encourages concentration of production on those products against which the United States has relatively high protection. Fifth, a free trade agree-

Table 3.9
Mexican 1984 trade and output: Actual and three hypotheticals

ISIC		(1a)	Mexican output/ U.S. imports				Mexican output/ U.S. output				Mexican output/ U.S. apparent cons.			
			(2a)	(2b)	(2c)	(2d)	(3a)	(3b)	(3c)	(3d)	(4a)	(4b)	(4c)	(4d)
3513	Synth. res	0.04	1.06	2.67	3.13	3.39	0.56	1.41	1.64	1.78	1.51	3.81	4.46	4.83
369	Oth. non-m	0.09	1.37	5.02	5.45	4.12	0.64	2.34	2.54	1.92	0.55	2.00	2.18	1.64
361	Pottery, c	0.02	0.38	8.22	3.65	3.06	0.25	5.31	2.36	1.98	0.16	3.37	1.50	1.26
323	Leather, p	0.01	0.45	7.86	3.27	1.77	0.19	3.32	1.38	0.75	0.14	2.52	1.05	0.57
324	Footwear	0.02	0.25	0.93	0.64	0.79	2.42	8.97	6.21	7.62	0.23	0.86	0.60	0.73
331	Wood prod	0.02	0.31	5.41	3.85	6.80	0.04	0.74	0.52	0.92	0.04	0.67	0.48	0.84
371	Iron, stee	0.02	0.59	2.38	2.40	2.09	0.09	0.37	0.37	0.32	0.08	0.33	0.33	0.29
321	Textiles	0.02	1.07	3.20	3.33	3.22	0.08	0.24	0.25	0.24	0.08	0.23	0.24	0.23
314	Tobacco	0.06	8.37	51.7	39	13.1	0.05	0.29	0.22	0.07	0.05	0.31	0.23	0.08
332	Furniture	0.05	0.28	1.77	1.93	1.15	0.04	0.23	0.25	0.15	0.03	0.21	0.23	0.13
3511	Basic che	0.05	0.40	1.19	1.60	1.15	0.06	0.16	0.22	0.16	0.06	0.17	0.22	0.16
351	Indust. ch	0.04	0.49	1.29	1.70	1.43	0.06	0.15	0.20	0.17	0.06	0.16	0.21	0.17
313	Beverages	0.03	1.24	1.98	2.15	0.90	0.12	0.19	0.21	0.09	0.11	0.18	0.19	0.08
3841	Shipbuild	0.03	0.12	2.68	4.23	3.03	0.01	0.12	0.18	0.13	0.01	0.12	0.18	0.13
362	Glas, prod	0.08	0.60	1.23	1.84	1.63	0.06	0.12	0.18	0.16	0.06	0.12	0.17	0.15
355	Rubber pr	0.01	0.52	0.91	1.16	1.18	0.08	0.14	0.17	0.18	0.07	0.12	0.16	0.16
356	Platstic p	0.02	0.53	1.81	3.22	1.90	0.03	0.09	0.16	0.10	0.03	0.09	0.16	0.09
311	Food	0.04	1.45	1.69	2.36	1.96	0.10	0.11	0.16	0.13	0.09	0.11	0.15	0.13
384	Trnsprt e	0.02	0.10	0.46	0.76	0.48	0.02	0.09	0.15	0.10	0.02	0.09	0.14	0.09
352	Oth. chemi	0.01	1.27	2.05	3.18	2.45	0.06	0.09	0.14	0.11	0.06	0.09	0.14	0.11
322	Wearing a	0.02	0.14	0.56	0.56	0.44	0.05	0.19	0.19	0.15	0.04	0.14	0.14	0.11
383	Electr. ma	0.08	0.08	0.47	0.66	0.55	0.02	0.10	0.14	0.11	0.01	0.09	0.13	0.10
354	Petrol. pr	0.03	0.89	1.80	2.20	0.91	0.05	0.10	0.13	0.05	0.05	0.10	0.12	0.05
390	Oth. indus	0.01	0.09	0.24	0.31	0.25	0.05	0.13	0.17	0.14	0.04	0.09	0.12	0.10

Table 3.9 (continued)

ISIC		(1a)	Mexican output/ U.S. imports				Mexican output/ U.S. output				Mexican output/ U.S. apparent cons.			
			(2a)	(2b)	(2c)	(2d)	(3a)	(3b)	(3c)	(3d)	(4a)	(4b)	(4c)	(4d)
353	Petr. refi	0.05	0.29	0.65	1.07	1.19	0.03	0.08	0.12	0.14	0.03	0.07	0.11	0.13
3522	Drugs, med	0.01	0.78	0.42	1.72	0.23	0.05	0.03	0.11	0.01	0.05	0.03	0.11	0.02
382	Machinery	0.02	0.08	0.47	0.73	0.74	0.01	0.07	0.10	0.11	0.01	0.07	0.11	0.11
3843	Motor veh	0.02	0.11	0.06	0.44	0.43	0.03	0.01	0.11	0.11	0.02	0.01	0.10	0.09
381	Metal pro	0.03	0.29	0.17	1.21	0.90	0.02	0.01	0.10	0.07	0.02	0.01	0.09	0.07
385	Professio	0.03	0.07	0.22	0.62	0.23	0.01	0.03	0.09	0.03	0.01	0.03	0.09	0.03
3832	Radio, TV	0.06	0.05	0.25	0.44	0.29	0.01	0.06	0.10	0.07	0.01	0.05	0.09	0.06
342	Print., pu	0.01	1.56	4.88	5.94	4.13	0.02	0.06	0.07	0.05	0.02	0.06	0.07	0.05
3825	Office, co	0.02	0.02	0.14	0.28	0.06	0.00	0.03	0.06	0.01	0.00	0.03	0.06	0.01
341	Paper, pro	0.02	0.30	1.32	0.62	0.71	0.02	0.11	0.05	0.06	0.02	0.10	0.05	0.06
3411	Pulp, pape	0.03	11.4	57.5	11.2	23.9	0.03	0.17	0.03	0.07	0.03	0.18	0.03	0.07
372	Non-ferro	0.05	0.12	0.00	0.00	0.00	0.02	0.00	0.00	0.00	0.02	0.00	0.00	0.00

Scenarios:
(1) U.S. imports from Mexico/Total U.S. imports
(a) Actual data
(b) Using regression with Mexican factor supplies
(c) Using regression with Mexican labor and augmented capital
(d) Using Italian productivity

ment is likely to attract capital to Mexico from the United States and from third countries.

These five observations raise a host of complicated questions, but it is possible to draw tentative conclusions about some of them. Consider first the trade-diverting aspect of a free trade agreement on the extreme assumption that all Mexican production is sold in the U.S. market and displaces imports from other developing countries. The second column of table 3.9, labeled (2a), reports the ratio of total Mexican output to U.S. imports. Now we get quite a few numbers approaching and exceeding one, among them textiles, food, beverages, and printing and publishing. But in several of the labor-intensive sectors including apparel, shoes, and leather, current Mexican production is well below the level of U.S. imports. For that matter, the composition of U.S. imports of textiles, for example, is very different from the current composition of the output of Mexican producers, and no simple substitution is going to occur. Thus the Mexico of today seems not large enough to have a major impact on commodity prices inside the United States. If we didn't expect Mexico to change much as a result of trade liberalization and a free trade agreement, the image of a gnat and an elephant seems pretty accurate. But presumably the intent of an FTA is to render a major change in Mexican production and trade. One way to get an idea of where this may take Mexico is to use the model of production discussed in section 6. This model is estimated with data from thirteen OECD countries and explains the level of output of each of these ISIC categories as functions of the countries' supplies of capital and professional and nonprofessional labor. We can use the model to predict what Mexican trade would be like if Mexico became like these countries, not in the sense of having the same structure of trade, but rather in the sense of having the same relationship between trade and resource supplies. Of course, this assumption is suspect for two reasons. First, the model is estimated with data from industrialized OECD countries, and the estimates may not properly be extended in factor space as far as is necessary to include Mexico. (Nonlinearities are probably important.) Second, the model ignores the pressure to concentrate production on those sectors for which U.S. protection is highest. With those caveats in mind, we may forge ahead.

In table 3.9, the actual data are reported in columns labeled (a). The columns labeled (b), (c), and (d) refer to three different ways to project Mexican production after liberalization. The first (b) inserts Mexican supplies of capital and high-skilled and low-skilled labor into the regression reported in table 3.8. The second (b) uses the same regressions, but augments Mexican capital to close half of the gap between the U.S. and

Mexican capital per worker. The third hypothetical (d) uses Italian productivity and Mexican labor. These are found by taking the Italian output data and multiplying by the ratio of Mexican total labor to Italian total labor. Italy is one of the thirteen countries that are used to estimate the model—indeed, is the one with the lowest capital per worker. The point of this third series is to remind us that the regression-based prediction is based on analogies between Mexico and the OECD countries. Roughly speaking, Mexico is viewed as similar to the capital-scarce OECD countries, with adjustments for the greater scarcity of capital. As it turns out, there is a great difference between the actual columns (a) and the hypothetical columns (b), (c), and (d), but relatively little difference between the three hypothetical columns. Thus the principal effect embodied in the three hypotheticals is the increase in total factor productivity that we hope will come from liberalization. Minor adjustments to the way the model is estimated or to the assumed level of capital seem to matter little in comparison with this gain in total factor productivity.

The columns in table 3.9 are arranged into four subgroups, each reporting a different ratio: (1) U.S. imports from Mexico/total U.S. imports, (2) Mexican output/U.S. imports, (3) Mexican output/U.S. output, (4) Mexican output/U.S. apparent consumption, defined as output plus imports minus exports. The effect of Mexican production on U.S. tariff-protected prices begins to take hold when Mexico is large enough to satisfy ,current U.S. import demand, that is, when the ratios in columns (2) exceed one. U.S. protectionism would be completely undone if the ratios in columns (4) exceed one, since then Mexican production is enough to satisfy total U.S. consumption, and therefore more than enough to satisfy imports at international prices. Because imports at world market prices would surely be less than total consumption, the full circumvention of U.S. protectionism would occur at import levels considerably below consumption, the exact value requiring a more detailed study of U.S. demand and supply.

The industries are sorted by the numbers in column (4c), representing the Mexico of the future, with more capital and much higher total factor productivity. There are the three-digit sectors with ratios of hypothetical Mexican production to U.S. consumption in excess of one: other nonmetallic mineral manufactures, pottery, and leather. Note that capital accumulation tends to reduce Mexican output in both pottery and leather, but for all three counterfactuals, these numbers exceed one and are the only ones that do.

Although there are few ratios of Mexican output to U.S. consumption that exceed one, there are many ratios of Mexican output to U.S. imports that do. Take textiles, for example: the projected level of Mexican output of textiles is over three times current U.S. imports, but only 23% of U.S. consumption. These numbers suggest that Mexico is large enough to partially undo the Multi-Fibre Agreement, but maybe not so large as to completely eliminate its effects. It depends on whether, free of the constraints of the Multi-Fibre Agreement, U.S. imports would be more than 23% of consumption. If yes, then Mexico would not be large enough to completely undo the effect of the agreement. But this discussion has not dealt at all with the incentive for Mexico to concentrate production on sectors that the U.S. protects, which would of course make Mexico seem larger. Another comment that should be made is that the data that have been used to project Mexican output come from an OECD experiment that is afflicted by trade barriers. In particular, the output levels in the OECD countries in apparel and textiles are presumably higher than they would be absent the Multi-Fibre Agreement. This makes us project too much output for Mexico in these sectors. On the other hand, the simple linear model that has been estimated does not adequately account for the concentration of production on a different mix of commodities in non-OECD countries with lower levels of capital per worker.

How big is Mexico? Even with all this waffling, a pretty clear image emerges: big enough for the United States to be concerned.

7.2 How Much Will This Affect Wages?

In this section, I provide an answer to the following question: What was the redistributive effect of the decline in the relative prices of labor-intensive products over the period 1972–1985? Through a (tortured?) chain of logic, I argue that the answer to this question is the same as the answer to: What will be the redistributive effect of a free trade agreement with Mexico? These questions have the same answer for the following reasons/conjectures (1) As has been argued, a future Mexico is big enough to undue U.S. protection of labor-intensive products, and, therefore, an FTA amounts to a commitment to free trade more generally; and (2) absent the free trade agreement, the forces of protectionism in the United States will win the day, and the United States will erect barriers that prevent redistribution away from low-skilled workers. Thus (1) and (2) imply that an FTA amounts implicitly to the *future elimination* of trade barriers against imports from labor-abundant countries. Furthermore, I assume that the intensity of competition in labor-intensive products over the next decade will be about the same over the last decade. Thus in the absence of trade barriers, we can expect to see about the same redistributive affect in the next decade as in the last.

What I do in this section is to carry out the steps that are discussed in section 6, first to form predictions about the probable changes in commodity prices that would occur without major interventions in international commerce, and then to link these hypothetical price changes with changes in factor costs using the duality between the Stolper-Samuelson effects and the Rybczynski effects. Details of these calculations are saved for an appendix. The results are reported in table 3.10

Table 3.10 contains three scenarios differing in the assumed changes in relative prices. Actual price changes over the period 1972–1985 are used for one set of calculations. A second set of calculations use the component of the 1972–85 price change that is correlated with capital intensity. This component is argued to be associated with foreign competition, and projected into the future, particularly if the Mexican-U.S. FTA is put in place. Under this scenario, the relative price of labor-intensive goods is assumed to fall and that of capital-intensive goods to rise. The scenario $m = 1$ is based on the assumption that future foreign competition is like the 1972–85 history. The third set of price changes, labeled $m = 5$ in the

Table 3.10
Earnings changes induced by relative price changes (actual price changes, 1972–1985, and price changes correlated with capital intensities)

		Per unit change in earnings					
		Petroleum included			Petroleum excluded		
	1982	Actual	$m = 1$	$m = 5$	Actual	$m = 1$	$m = 5$
Capital (1982$)	3516,184 b	1.1%	1.3%	6.7%	−0.6%	0.3%	1.3%
Man. and sci.	17311 th	7843	6077	30384	983	1919	9596
Other workers	99856 th	−2262	−1862	−9312	19	−465	−2323
		Total change in earnings ($billions)					
Capital (1982$)		38.7	47.1	235.6	−20.7	9.1	45.7
Man. and sci.		135.8	105.2	526.0	17.0	33.2	166.1
Other workers		−225.9	−186.0	−929.9	1.9	−46.4	−232.0
TOTAL		−51.4	−33.7	−168.3	−1.8	−4.0	−20.1

DATA

GNP	3988.91 b
Population	238 m
GNP/pop	16.69 th
Capital/worker	30.01002 th
Capital/pop	14.71207 th

table, amplify the $m = 1$ price changes by a factor of five. This would represent a very substantial increase in the intensity of competition.

As it turns out, these calculations depend greatly on whether or not petroleum refining is included. The two petroleum sectors have relative price increases of 305% and 47%, and almost everything else has a relative price decline. These extreme numbers are primarily a consequence of the big increase in the price of an intermediate input (crude petroleum), and they do not generate an increase in the demand for capital in the refining sectors. A model that includes intermediate prices implies that our calculations require "value-added" prices, not output prices.[11] In the absence of the proper adjustments to deal with intermediate inputs, I provide the calculations with and without the petroleum sector included.

The actual and hypothetical relative price changes excluding refining are reported in table 3.11, where you can see that the $m = 1$ scenario has

Table 3.11
Difference between the change in price 1972–85 and the weighted average (W/o Petroleum)

ISIC			$m = 0.5$	$m = 1$ (percentages)	$m = 5$	Weights	Sj
311	Food produc	FOOD	−2.1	−4.2	−21.0	0.110	0.185
313	Berverages	BEV	5.1	10.2	51.2	0.021	0.036
314	Tobacco	TOB	0.8	1.7	8.3	0.010	0.017
321	Textiles	TEXT	−5.6	−11.2	−55.8	0.036	0.061
322	Wearing app	APP	−11.5	−23.0	−115.1	0.019	0.032
323	Leather, prd	LEA	−9.8	−19.7	−98.5	0.005	0.009
324	Footwear	SHOE	−10.5	−21.0	−105.0	0.003	0.004
331	Wood produc	WOOD	−6.7	−13.4	−66.8	0.027	0.045
332	Furniture	FURN	−9.7	−19.5	−97.3	0.013	0.022
341	Paper, prod.	PAPR	18.1	36.3	181.4	0.040	0.068
342	Print., publ	PRNT	−8.1	−16.2	−80.8	0.043	0.073
351	Indust. chem	CHEM	14.3	28.5	142.7	0.066	0.111
352	Oth. chemic.	O. Ch	13.0	26.0	130.1	0.043	0.072
355	Rubber prod	RUBB	−4.9	−9.7	−48.7	0.010	0.018
356	Plastic prd	PLAS	23.4	46.8	233.8	0.026	0.043
361	Pottery, chn	POT	−5.6	−11.1	−55.7	0.005	0.008
362	Glas, produc	GLSS	2.8	5.6	28.2	0.007	0.012
369	Oth. non-met	OTH	5.1	10.2	51.0	0.015	0.026
371	Iron, steel	IRON	9.6	19.2	96.1	0.056	0.094
372	Non-ferrous	N-FR	5.2	10.3	51.5	0.029	0.048
381	Metal prod.	MET	−6.7	−13.4	−66.8	0.065	0.109
382	Machinery	MACH	−4.1	−8.2	−41.2	0.104	0.176
383	Electr. mach	ELEC	−5.8	−11.7	−58.5	0.082	0.139
384	Trnsprt equ	TRAN	−5.2	−10.3	−51.6	0.130	0.220
385	Profession.	PROF	−6.6	−13.1	−65.7	0.022	0.038
390	Oth. industr	OTH	−7.8	−15.6	−78.1	0.012	0.021

apparel declining by 23% and plastics increasing by 47%. These relative price declines of labor-intensive manufactures are mapped into the changes in wages and capital earnings displayed in table 3.10. Focusing on the $m = 1$ column under the "petroleum excluded" heading, the numbers indicate that as a consequence of these changes in product prices, the return on capital rose by 3%, the annual earnings of high-skilled workers rose by $1,919 and the annual earnings of other workers declined by $465. Below these numbers are the corresponding changes in total income, using the factor supplies that are indicated in the first column. Thus the relative price decline of labor-intensive manufactures over the 1972–85 period is estimated to have reduced the earnings of low-skilled workers by $46.4 billion and to have increased the earnings of capital by $9.1 billion and high-skilled workers by $33.2 billion.

The sum of these total changes in earnings is $-$4.0 billion which might make one conclude erroneously that trade is not beneficial overall. This is incorrect for two reasons. First, it confuses the static gains from trade with the effect of terms of trade changes. The economic theorems that establish the collective gains from trade do not imply that any changes in the prices of goods will make a country better off. Quite the opposite, a deterioration of the terms of trade because of more intense foreign competition will surely make a country worse off. Specifically, the numbers in the upper panel of table 3.10 would have indicated an overall gain if the United States had been less abundant in low-skilled workers compared with capital and high-skilled workers. If, for example, we had 1 million more managers and scientists and 1 million fewer other workers, then the $2.7 billion loss in earnings would have been adjusted upward by $(1,919 + 465) \times 1m =$ $2.384 billion. There is a message here: *We are getting ourselves in trouble in the international marketplace because we have too few scientists and managers, and too little capital. We need to invest more in both physical and human capital if we are to benefit collectively from the increasingly intense international competition in the markets for labor-intensive goods.*

The factor price changes of .3%, 1,919, $-$465 can be used to separate countries that gain as a result of a reduction in the prices of labor-intensive goods from countries that lose. Denoting the supplies of capital, scientists, and other labor by K, H, and L, the countries that gain can be separated from those that lose by the line $0 = .003K + 1,919H - 465L$. This line is labeled "Constant TOT line" in figure 3.22; countries with factor supplies to the left gain, countries to the right lose. Thus according to these calculations, the skill-abundant Nordic countries of Sweden, Finland, Norway, and also the Netherlands benefit from these product price changes. Most of the other developed countries lie pretty much on the no-change line. The other countries, including Japan (in 1985) had insufficient supplies of physical and human capital to benefit from these hypothetical factor price changes.

So what if these changes in prices are making us collectively worse off? Does that mean that we can offset this effect by closing our borders? Quite the contrary. Here the static welfare theorems do come into play: The imposition of trade barriers in response to deteriorating terms of trade surely makes us all even worse off. Trade is beneficial, that's for sure. But the level of the benefits can fall (or rise) over time.

There is a second concern with the numbers reported in table 3.10 The hypothetical change under study is a rather large change in relative prices normalized to keep the average manufacturing price unchanged (see table 3.11). This doesn't keep constant the cost of any particular consumption basket; in particular, it makes no reference to the prices of nontraded goods and services. Deteriorating earnings in the traded goods sector reduces the demand for nontradeables and lowers their price, thereby somewhat offsetting the reductions in money income reported in table 3.10.

My guess is that the rate of decline in the relative price of labor-intensive manufactures is likely to increase and these figures in the $m = 1$ column that are based on historical changes from 1972 to 1985 need to be adjusted upward. The $m = 5$ column is probably pretty extreme, allowing relative price changes that are five times as large as occurred from 1972–1985. The induced changes in factor earnings are five times as great.

The $m = 1$ scenario uses only the component of price changes that is associated with capital intensity. The redistributive effect of the actual price changes are also indicated in table 3.10. Excluding petroleum, the method estimates a decline in the return to physical capital, and increases to both earnings of both kinds of labor, more to skilled than to unskilled. I am inclined to attach less meaning to these figures, since the calculations make use of the assumption that none of the product price changes are due to technological change, which seems to me to be an inappropriate assumption in a period including the first stages of the computer revolution. I am more inclined to associate the component of the price changes correlated with capital intensity to things other than technological change, in particular to international competition.

Finally, it should be clearly understood that the numbers in table 3.10 are highly uncertain. The labor categories are much too aggregated. The experiment implicit in the OECD cross-country data set is very weak. Furthermore, the precise economic theory that underlies these computations is uncompelling and lacks external validation. Nonetheless, I would argue that the numbers are in the right ballpark, and at least they serve to focus attention on the important fact that everyone need not benefit from increased international commerce Indeed, if the reason for the expansion of international commerce is increased access to low-wage unskilled foreign labor, it is virtually certain that our low-skilled workers will have their earnings reduced. Reductions in annual earnings over the next decade on the order of $1000 seem very plausible.

Appendix

To determine the historical relationship between price changes and capital intensity, I have estimated the following equation using the NBER data Abowd (1991) for the period 1972 to 1985:

$$\%\Delta(\text{price})_i = \alpha + \theta \, (\text{capital/worker})_i.$$

I assume that the component of variability of price that is correlated with capital intensity is associated with foreign competition, and therefore I use the following equation to project the continuing effect of foreign competition on prices:

$$\text{Projected } \%\Delta(\text{price}_i) = m\theta \, (\text{capital/worker})_i.$$

Here the multiplier m is one if the intensity of foreign competition is similar to the period 1972 to 1985 and greater than one if the competition is more intense.

Next we need to adjust these figures to maintain the overall level of prices so that we are dealing with price relatives only. To do this, an index weighted by output value is formed:

$$I = \sum_i \%\Delta(\text{price})_i p_i Q_i / \sum_i p_i Q_i.$$

Then the predicted price change is

$$\pi_i = m\theta \, (\text{capital/worker})_i - I.$$

These predictions are at the three-digit SIC level of commodities. These need to be concorded to the two-digit ISIC to get to predicted price changes for each two-digit ISIC class.

For each two-digit ISIC sector (indexed by i) table 3.7 has estimated an equation of the form

$$Q_i = \alpha_i + \beta_{1i}\text{CAPITAL} + \beta_{2i}\text{PROF} + \beta_{3i}\text{OTHER}.$$

For output of services we have a similar expression.

$$NONTRADED = \alpha + \gamma_1 CAPITAL + \gamma_2 PROF + \gamma_3 OTHER.$$

Now define the consumption share

$s_i = $ (total output of sector i over all thirteen OECD countries)/
     (total GNP $-$ total service GNP).

Then according to the model discussed in section 6, the induced changes in factor rewards are:

$\sum_i \pi_i (\beta_{1i} + \gamma_1 s_i) = $ change in CAPITAL real earnings

$\sum_i \pi_i (\beta_{2i} + \gamma_2 s_i) = $ change in PROF real earnings

$\sum_i \pi_i (\beta_{3i} + \gamma_3 s_i) = $ change in OTHER real earnings

Notes

This paper has been written with the able assistance of Raul Orozco, Luis Ibarra, and Luis Hernandez. Helpful comments were provided by participants at a seminar at the Federal Reserve Board of Governors.

1. "Asia" here refers to other low-wage suppliers. Most low-wage products currently come from Asia, but the Caribbean and Latin America may be more important in the future.

2. *Financial Times*, March 9, 1992, p. 1.

3. The actual population shares in 1960, 1978, and 1989 are 78.7, 75.6, and 74.1. The GNP shares in 1978 and 1987 are 84.0 and 86.3. Excluded are Africa, Eastern Europe, Brazil, and Indonesia. Adjusting the figures for these other countries and regions is straightforward.

4. Physical liquids do not expand as they flow to eliminate differences in levels, but economic systems are different. The processes that work to eliminate wage differences also tend to raise world labor income and thereby to offset but not eliminate the wage reductions in the higher-wage Countries.

5. See, for example, Leamer (1984), chapter 1.

6. Discussion like this can be found in McCulloch and Pinera (1977); the authors offer a partial equilibrium treatment of the tariff case. Gardner and Kimbrough (1990) do the general equilibrium case. See also Vousden (1990).

7. This FTA consumption line is found from the Mexican budget constraint:

Value of production = Value of consumption

$$p_{A,US} q_A^* + p_{T,US} p_T^* = p_A c_A + p_T c_T,$$

where $p_{A,US}$ and $p_{T,US}$ are the high prices prevailing in the protected U.S. market, p_A and p_T are the (external) prices applicable to the consumption choices, q_A^* and q_T^* are the production levels after the FTA, and c_A and c_T are the consumption levels. This budget constraint can be rewritten as

$$c_T = (p_{A,US}q_A^* + p_{T,US}q_T^* - p_A c_A)/p_T$$
$$= (p_{A,US}q_A^* + p_{T,US}q_T^*)/p_T - (p_A/p_T)c_A.$$

This compares with the free-trade consumption line

$$c_T = (p_A q_A + p_T q_T)/p_T - (p_A/p_T)c_A,$$

where the production levels without the asterisks refer to free trade outputs. These two lines and a third parallel line through the FTA production point are depicted in figure 3.19. The differences in these lines, measured along the textile axis, are the line segments AB and BC. These are just the differences in the intercepts which can be expressed as

AB: $(q_A - q_A^*)(p_A/p_T) + (q_T - q_T^*)$

BC: $\tau_A(p_A/p_T)q_A + \tau_T q_T$

AC: $\tau_A(p_A/p_T)q_A^* + \tau_T q_T^*,$

where τ is the U.S. tariff level (plus tariff equivalents of the MFA), $(p_{US} - p)/p$.

8. This is a condensed version of this section. The fuller version formally lays out a Heckscher-Ohlin-Samuelson model with nontraded goods and with and without a full complement of traded goods. The algebra of these models is presented in tables 3.5 and 3.6.

9. See, for example, Borjas, Freeman, and Katz (1991) or Freeman and Katz (1991).

10. The year 1984 was selected here because of data limitations in Mexican 1985 information on production.

11. The equations in tables 3.5 and 3.6 need to be modified to allow for intermediate inputs in the following way. Let final output be $f = q - Bq$, where Bq are the intermediate products used to produce output q. Retain the relationship between outputs and inputs, $q = A^{-1}v$. Then the relationship between final output and factor supplies v is $A(I - B)^{-1}f = v$, which has the Stolper-Samuelson dual: $w' = A^{-1}(I - B)p$. Note that the cross-section regressions of outputs on inputs yield estimates of the relationships $q = A^{-1}v$, but the Stolper-Samuelson equations require not A^{-1} but $A^{-1}(I - B)$, Alternatively, instead of using output prices p, one could use value added prices $(I - B)p$ in the calculations.

References

Abowd, John M., eds. 1991. *Immigration, Trade, and the Labor Market.* New York: National Bureau of Economic Research.

Banco Nacional de Mexico. (1991). "The Textile Industry." *Review of the Economic Situation of Mexico* LXVII: 249–255.

Blackburn, McKinley L., Bloom, David E., and Freeman, Richard B. 1990. "The Declining Economic Position of Less Skilled American Men," in *A Future of Lousy Jobs?: The Changing Structure of U.S. Wages,* ed. Gary Burtless. Washington, D.C.: The Brookings Institution, 31–76.

Borjas, George J., Freeman, Richard B., and Katz, Lawrence F. 1991. "On the Labor Market Effects of Immigration and Trade." NBER Working Paper No. 3761.

Botella C., Ovidio, Garcia C., Enrique, and Giral B., Jose. 1991. "Textiles: The Mexican Perspective," in *U.S.-Mexican Industrial Integration: The Road to Free Trade*, eds. Sidney Weintraub, Luis Rubio F., and Alan D. Jones. Boulder, CO: Westview Press, 193–220.

Burtless, Gary, ed. 1990. *A Future of Lousy Jobs?*. Washington, D.C.: The Brookings Institution.

Clague, Christopher K. 1991. "Factor proportions, relative efficiency and developing countries' trade." *Journal of Development Economics* 35:357–380.

Cline, William. 1987. *The Future of World Trade in Textiles and Apparel*. Washington, D.C.: Institute for International Economics.

Erzan, Refik, Goto, Junichi, and Holmes, Paula. 1989. "Effects of the MFA on Developing Countries' Trade." Institute for International Economic Studies, Stockholm, Seminar Paper No. 449, September.

Freeman, Richard B., and Katz, Lawrence. 1991. "Industrial Wage and Employment Determination in an Open Economy," in *Immigration. Trade. and the Labor Market*, eds. John. M. Abowd and Richard B. Freeman. New York: National Bureau of Economic Research, 235–260.

Gardner, Grant W., and Kimbrough, Kent P. 1990. "The Economics of Country-Specific Tariffs." *International Economic Review*, Vol. 31, No. 3, (August):575–588.

Lande, Stephen. 1991. "Textiles: U.S. Perspective," in *U.S.-Mexican Industrial Integration: The Road to Free Trade*, eds. Sidney Weintraub, Luis Rubio F., and Alan D. Jones. Boulder, CO: Westview Press, 221–248.

Leamer, Edward E. 1984, *Sources of International Comparative Advantage: Theory and Evidence*, Cambridge, MA: MIT Press.

Leamer, Edward E. 1987. "Paths of Development in the Three-Factor N-Good General Equilibrium Model." *Journal of Political Economy* 961–999.

McCulloch, Rachel, and Pinera, Jose. 1977. "Trade as Aid: The Political Economy of Tariff Preferences for Developing Countries." *American Economic Review* 67 (December), 959–967.

Palmeter, N. David. 1991. "The Rhetoric and Reality of US Anti-Dumping Law." *The World Economy* 14:19–36.

Vousden, Neil. 1990. *The Economics of Trade Protection*, Cambridge: Cambridge University Press.

II

Regional and Local Production and Employment Effects

4

Some Favorable Impacts of a U.S.-Mexico Free Trade Agreement on U.S. Urban Employment

J. Vernon Henderson

Trade liberalization with Mexico has already dramatically increased U.S. exports to Mexico of a number of manufactured products. A Free Trade Agreement (FTA) would enhance those exports by further lowering tariffs and nontariff trade barriers and by solidifying the current gains from trade liberalization. In some industries, the export increases would be large enough to affect U.S. domestic employment levels and prices significantly.

The gains or losses for any industry depend on the specifics of the current trade situation, as well as the specifics of a FTA. With respect to the latter, there is the issue of how successful a FTA will be in eliminating nontariff barriers to trade such as licensing restrictions, irrelevant inspections, and unnecessary specifications for product standardization. There is a second issue of how a FTA deals with third-country trade. For apparel and textiles, the hope is that demand by Mexican-based apparel manufacturers for textiles will help prop up the U.S. textile industry. But unless textile imports from Asia are restricted, an FTA could severely hurt U.S. textile manufacturers. Mexican manufactured apparel produced with Asian cloth would hurt not only the U.S. apparel industry, but also the textile industry.

Apart from the specifics of an FTA, the nature of Mexican import demand is also critical. For products such as computers, telecommunications equipment, capital goods (machinery), and certain instruments, the demand for U.S. products is for consumption by Mexican firms and consumers. The U.S. gains for these industries have no direct repercussions on other U.S. industries, except through regular price and employment general equilibrium effects. However, many products involve compatible trade, where a strong Mexican sector is being matched with a strong U.S. sector, at the expense of both countries' corresponding weak sectors. In the textile-apparel example, a U.S. textile boom based on a Mexican apparel boom could diminish the U.S. apparel industry, as it loses out to imports from

Mexico (made with U.S. cloth). Overall, the United States may gain from compatible trade, but specific subsectors will lose. The story for electronic components played out in the maquiladoras is similar. Many U.S. firms will gain from increased component production, but some assembly operations will suffer, as U.S. parts and components are shipped back and forth across the border for labor-intensive stages of production.

Although these changes are typically viewed at the national level, their impacts are very localized. For example, one industry that has already been significantly affected is electronic components. Yet this industry has non-negligible employment (over 250 workers) in only about 40% of U.S. metropolitan areas, and local employment over 3,500 workers in only 19 of the over 300 metropolitan areas. Of those 19 metropolitan areas, 37% are in the West, compared to only 18% of all U.S. metro areas (and 20% of the population) being in the West. As a second example, textile and apparel production are usually concentrated in different places. So textile towns may gain from an FTA, whereas apparel towns will lose out.

This chapter examines the impacts of an FTA on urban employment in a number of key industries that will be favorably affected by an FTA: textiles, plastics, instruments, machinery, and electrical machinery. The three-digit computer, electronic components, communications equipment, and medical instrument industries are examined separately as well. The industries chosen represent major exports to Mexico that have already benefited from trade liberalization and that are viewed as likely benefi-ciaries of an FTA (see ITC 1990a, 1990b, 1989, and INFORUM 1990).

To assess the impacts of an FTA on urban employment requires an assessment of the national impacts of an FTA on domestic prices, of differ-ential price impacts across regions, and of which cities will be affected and by what order of magnitude. This chapter is not concerned with the exact national magnitude of export changes from an FTA, but rather on the spatial distribution of those changes for different industries. It analyzes those spatial impacts based on a plausible scenario for the national impacts of combined trade liberalization and an FTA. For example, the Lift model of the INFORUM (1990) report projects an approximate tripling of exports of textiles, electronic components, communications equipment, and com-puters from 1988 to 1995, due to the relaxation of trade constraints. For industries such as plastics, and electrical distribution equipment and appara-tus, it predicts even larger impacts. The differential in responses depends not only on the differences in current trade barriers for different prod-ucts, but also on assumptions about compatible trade and third-country responses.

Given these types of magnitudes of export changes, we can calculate approximate impacts on national prices, based on plausible values of domestic demand elasticities and on both plausible and estimated values of supply elasticities. In general, increased exports result in increased demand for U.S. domestic production. As production increases, relative domestic prices of exported products rise (along the national supply curve). These price increases affect domestic demand negatively, dampening the supply expansion. However, a critical feature of spatial impacts involves differential regional impacts. Products from areas closer to Mexico have lower transport costs and are cheaper to export to Mexico. The impact on domestic prices of export expansion will differ by region. I estimate the relevant elasticities for different industries, based on state export patterns to Mexico, to obtain different regional price impacts and potential supply responses.

Within a region, production of any product is concentrated in a handful of cities. For any product the immediate effect of a price rise and supply response is confined to cities producing the product. This study focuses on those cities. This impact will differ absolutely by city according to the relative importance of the industry in that city, but it may also differ relatively by city, according to other urban characteristics. In particular, I will estimate some interactive or multiplier effects for certain industries. For example, in a particular city, output of electronic components may be spurred because of direct Mexican demand for those components, and also because an FTA increases local production of components used in production of computers and instruments which outputs are also spurred by an FTA.

For some products with really large production increases, cities previously not producing the product may start doing so. The estimation allows for calculation of these effects, but previous work (Henderson, 1993) indicates that they tend to be fairly small. However, these effects do not include long-term regional locational shifts that might be induced by an FTA. That would require a more comprehensive examination of how mobility differs by industry, as well as an assessment of long-term regional shifts in employment composition.

Industrial Location and Its Determinants

In this section I examine where certain U.S. industries are located. I specify a model of where industries locate and what their scale of operation is in cities in which they are found. Then I present some econometric results on the determinants of industrial location, and on the elasticities of industrial employment responses to increased product demand. I focus on two-digit industries of textiles, machinery, electrical machinery, and instruments. I also explore the interrelationships of high-tech industries, such as computers, electronic components, and communications equipment; and examine other three-digit industries such as plastics.

Current Spatial Concentration of U.S. Industry

Where is industry currently concentrated in the United States? There are two measures of concentration: absolute employment levels and relative employment levels. In table 4.1, for each two-digit industry and some subcomponents, we list the handful of metropolitan areas where employment has its largest absolute values and then the handful of cities where it has the greatest relative concentration. For the latter, we list the cities for which industry employment share in the local area exceeds a critical percentage. Consider machinery in Los Angeles-Long Beach. Although we have chosen the primary metropolitan area (of over 8 million) rather than the consolidated metropolitan area (of over 13 million), employment in machinery of 64,000 is only about 1.5% of its over 4 million workers. A 20% increase in its 64,000 workers only represents a 0.3% increase in total L.A. employment due to the direct impact of machinery expansion. Even allowing for a multiplier effect in the service sector of 2 or 3 only raises the total L.A. employment expansion to just under 1%. A 20% machinery employment increase is simply swallowed up in the overall environment. However, in Rockford, Illinois, where machinery accounts for 10% of the work force, a 20% increase in machinery employment directly increases city employment by 2%. With a multiplier of 2 or 3 on other local employment, machinery expansion has a noticeable impact on the local community.

For machinery, electrical machinery, and instruments, in general the cities with large absolute employments are among the country's largest metropolitan areas. Note this particular set of industrial metropolitan areas — Chicago, Detroit, Los Angeles, Boston, Philadelphia, Phoenix, and Dallas —does exclude a number of other large metropolitan areas such as New York City, San Francisco, Miami, Houston, and Washington. Employment in manufacturing is large in certain metropolitan areas because these areas are very large. In contrast, metropolitan areas where particular industries dominate the employment scene tend to be much smaller, with the exception of San Jose with its concentration of high-tech industries.

Table 4.1

Machinery	*Machinery*
Employment greater than 20,000	Employment share greater than 7.5%
Houston TX	Hagerstown MD
Anaheim Santa-Ann CA	Boulder-Longmont CO
Los Angeles-Long Beach CA	Davenport-Rock Island IL
San Jose CA	Decator IL (10%)
Chicago IL	Peoria IL
Detroit MI	Rockford IL (10%)
Minneapolis-St. Paul MN	Waterloo-Cedar Falls IA (10%)
Cleveland OH	Benton Harbor MI
Dayton-Springfield OH	Muskegon MI
Milwaukee WI	Rochester MN (10%)
Hartford-New Britain CN	La Crosse WI
Boston-Lowell MA	Poughkeepsie NY (15%)
Philadelphia PA	
Computers	*Computers*
Employment greater than 10,000	Employment share greater than 5%
(Phoenix AZ (9200))	San Jose CA (10%)
Austin TX	Boulder-Longmont CO
(Boulder-Longmont CO (9500))	Rochester MN (10%)
Anaheim-Santa Ana CA	Poughkeepsie (10%)
San Jose CA	
Minneapolis-St. Paul MN	
Boston-Lowell MA	
Poughkeepsie NY	
Electrical machinery	*Electrical machinery*
Employment greater than 20,000	Employment share greater than 7.5%
Phoenix AZ	Fort Smith AZ
Dallas TX	Melbourne-Titusville FA (10%)
Anaheim-Santa Ana CA	San Jose CA (10%)
Los Angeles-Long Beach CA	Anderson IN (15%)
San Jose CA	Bloomington IN (15%)
Chicago IL	Binghamton NY (10%)
Milwaukee-Racine WI	Poughkeepski (15%)
Boston-Lowell MA	
Salem-Glocester MA (Essex County)	
Nassau-Suffolk NY	
New York NY	
Philadelphia PA	

Table 4.1 (continued)

Communications equipment	*Electronic components*
Employment greater than 7,500	Employment share greater than 10,000
Dallas TX	Phoenix AZ
Oklahoma City OK	Dallas TX
Los Angeles CA	Anaheim-Santa Ana CA
San Jose CA	Los Angeles CA
Chicago IL	San Jose CA
Boston-Lowell MA	Chicago IL
Philadelphia PA	Boston-Lowell MA
Instruments	*Instruments*
Employment greater than 20,000	Employment share greater than 7.5%
Baltimore MD	Boulder-Longmont CO
Dallas TX	Rochester NY (10%)
Anaheim-Santa Ana CA	
Los Angeles-Long Beach CA	
San Jose CA	
Chicago IL	
Minneapolis-St Paul MN	
Boston-Lowell MA	
Nassau-Suffolk NY	
Rochester NY	
Philadelphia PA	
Textiles	*Textiles*
Employment greater than 10,000	Employment share greater than 7.5%
Burlington NC	Dothan AL (10%)
Charlotte-Gasonia NC	Burlington NC (10%)
Fayetteville NC	Charlotte-Gastonia NC
Greensboro-Winston NC	Hickory NC (10%)
Greenville-Spartanburg SC	Anderson SC (10%)
Chattanooga TN	Greenville-Spartanburg SC (10%)
Los Angeles CA	Danville VA (10%)
Plastics	*Plastics*
Employment greater than 10,000	Employment share greater than 5%
Anaheim-Santa Ana CA	Iowa City IA
Los Angeles-Long Beach CA	Sheboygan WI
San Diego CA	
Chicago IL	
Philadelphia PA	

For textiles, we have a more traditional picture, where little manufacturing of textiles occurs in large cities (except L.A.). Large employment numbers accompany high concentrations, both in smaller metro areas. That traditional picture applies to industries such as pulp and paper, automobiles, and tobacco, which are not covered in this study.

A Model of Industrial Location

How do we model the extent of employment in a particular industry in a particular city? In this section, a simple model underlying the reduced-form equations to be estimated is presented. The model of industrial location is based on Henderson (1988) and Henderson (1993), and is related to empirical location work by Carlton (1985) and Lee (1989). Firms in a city j in a particular industry have a profit function

$$\Pi_j = \Pi(A_j, s_j, \varepsilon_j), \tag{1}$$

where A_j is a vector of arguments such as input prices, local population, and the scale of operations of any related industries that might affect local demand for the product or supply conditions for the product. Local population could, for example, be one measure of the size of the local market for the product. The size of related industries also could enhance demand or affect production conditions. For example, for electronic components, the existence of a local computer or instruments industry might increase demand for locally produced electronic components and provide positive externalities for the functioning of local specialized labor markets or for information flows among high-tech firms.

s_j is a measure of the local scale of this industry, which has an impact in two opposing ways. Presuming that there are localization economies of scale, a larger local industry positively affects individual firm profits, as the production environment improves. However, a larger local scale means there is more and more of the product to sell in the local market area, which may negatively affect the (unobserved) output price. Finally, in equation (1), ε_j is an error term.

A particular industry in a local area also faces a supply of potential firms, or entrepreneurs. The local supply of entrepreneurs to the industry is a function of a vector of arguments, Z_j, which could include local population, costs of living, or the scale of related industries that might supply competent entrepreneurs. Thus we have the inverse supply relationship

$$\Pi = \tilde{\Pi}(Z_j, s_j, u_j), \tag{2}$$

where, as local scale s_j rises, per firm profits must rise to attract more entrepreneurs to this industry from other activities or locations.

The scale of local operations is determined by the intersection of the "demand" ($\Pi(\cdot)$) and "supply" ($\tilde{\Pi}(\cdot)$) functions of local entrepreneurs. Equating and solving for s_j we get a reduced-form equation of the form

$$s_j = s(A_j, Z_j, e_j). \tag{3}$$

Equation (3) forms the basic estimating equation. e_j is a combination of u_j and ε_j.

A complication particularly for three-digit industries is that not all, or perhaps even most cities have positive employment. Whether or not a city has the industry depends on whether at some minimal scale, $\bar{s}_j$, the profits the industry can provide $\Pi(A_j, \bar{s}_j)$ are sufficient (i.e., exceed $\tilde{\Pi}(Z_j, \bar{s}_j)$). There are several ways to model minimum scale, $\bar{s}_j$ (Henderson, 1993) but, regardless, a discrete choice criterion emerges where the probability that a city has the industry is the

$$Prob(\Pi(A_j, \bar{s}_j, \varepsilon_j) > \tilde{\Pi}(Z_j, \bar{s}_j, u_j))$$

$$= Prob(m(A_j, Z_j) > \tilde{e}_j). \tag{4}$$

$m(\cdot)$ is a reduced-form function with a different shape from $s(\cdot)$ in (3), and an error term $\tilde{e}_j$, combining u_j and ε_j.

The specification and estimation method for either (3) or (4) must be tailored to the data. To see how and why we turn to the data.

Data

The basic data are from the *1987 Census of Manufacturers, Geographic Area Statistics, Table 6*. These tables give two-, three-, and four-digit industry information by Metropolitan Statistical Area (MSA) on employment and other economic data. The unit of observation is the MSA and, in the case of consolidated metropolitan area, we use the Primary Metropolitan Statistical Area (PMSA) as the unit of observation. , So New York is broken into Bergen-Passaic, Bridgeport-Stamford-Norwalk-Danbury, Jersey City, Middlesex-Somerset-Hunterdow, Monmouth-Ocean, Nassau-Suffolk, New York City, Newark, and Orange County. The manufacturing data are supplemented with data from the 1986 State and Metropolitan Area data book on urban characteristics such as population, wages, education, housing, etc. In addition, there are data on locational aspects of cities.

The manufacturing data are censored in two respects. First, if industry employment is less than 250 employees, zero employment is reported.

Second, if disclosure is a problem because, for example, only one or two major firms dominate the industry locally, the employment data are reported in interval form and the rest of the economic data are suppressed. Unfortunately, the upper interval for these observations is open-ended beyond a modest employment level of 2,500. To fill in this gap in our information, for observations with open-ended employment, we turned to the 1987 County Business Patterns data. This data tends to be less strictly censored and the employment intervals are much more extensive. The upper open-ended interval, for example, starts at 100,000. By filling in the gaps, almost all upper open intervals were replaced by either point estimates or fairly narrow intervals.

The major econometric problem posed by the censoring concerns whether, for any MSA, a zero for employment is a zero or is 1–249 workers. If no zeros truly exist, all cities have a positive s_j value in (3) but some (those under 250) are censored. A natural form to estimate equation (3) is then a Tobit, where every city has the same $s(\cdot)$ function, but numbers below 250 are not disclosed. However, if many zeros are true zeros, then there is a discrete-continuous choice problem. Then the model must be estimated by a two-step process. In this case, for all MSA's I estimate the $m(\cdot)$ function in equation (4), by Probit. This yields a discrete choice criterion for whether the industry is found in a particular city, or not. Then for cities with the industry I estimate the $s(\cdot)$ function in (3), including a Mill's ratio correction factor for selectivity bias.

For our major two-digit durable goods industries, 58% to 90% of urban areas register industry employment over 250. I take the position that all cities have some employment in the machinery, electrical machinery, and instruments industries. I also include plastics in that category. I am assuming every city has, say, at least one small workshop employing five to ten people turning out small-scale, perhaps special-order, products in those industries. For those industries we estimate equation (3) only, by Tobit. For our three-digit industries and for textiles, that assumption stretches reality too far. We know from other detailed employment data (County Business Patterns and Population Census) that employment in these industries truly is zero in some cities. Moreover, in our data only 18% to 35% of cities register employment above 250. So I estimate a reduced-form Probit equation determining whether or not the MSA registers employment (the $m(\cdot)$ function), and then an OLS equation for those that register employment (the $s(\cdot)$ function).

Among the explanatory variables determining employment in an industry in a locality are employment in related industries, such as all other manufacturing and major other interactive industries. For example, employment in electronic components tends to be closely associated with employment in computers and instruments and vice versa. This immediately raises simultaneously issues. For many of the equations I present both simple Tobit or OLS estimates, and some type of two-stage estimates, where in the second stage potential endogenous explanatory variables are replaced by predicted values from first-stage reduced-form equations.

Variable List

For each industry, there is a standard list of variables common to all industries. These are average wages of production workers, percent of the adult population with medium schooling (high school or some college) and higher schooling (at least one college degree), metropolitan area population, and locational variables such as the region, whether the city is a port, whether the city is a PMSA that is part of a larger consolidated metropolitan area, and distance from the metro area to the nearest of Rand McNally's thirty primary urban market centers in 1990.

Next, for each industry in each locality there is a set of specific variables related to that industry. These include a total of all-other-manufacturing employment in the locality, an index of diversity of all other manufacturing employment, and employment in particular closely related industries. For a given city population, increased all-other-manufacturing employment may represent a demand base for the product, a supply of potential entrepreneurs, or some type of general communications—labor market external economy of scale benefit. The diversity index is a variant of the Hirschman-Herfindahl index, where, in each MSA for any industry, I sum the employment shares of each other two-digit industry in total all-other-manufacturing employment. An increase in the index reflects higher concentration or specialization in the city. Given nineteen other two-digit industries, the lowest value of the index in a city is 0.053 (for each industry having an equal share) and the highest is 1.0 (for all other employment in one industry). The issue concerns whether industries thrive in a manufacturing environment that is very diverse, as opposed to very narrow. Employment in related manufacturing provides either a demand or input base, and a source of external economies of scale.

Empirical Results: Location Model

The discussion of results is divided into three parts, by groups of industries. The first part covers the two-digit industries in the sample: machinery, electrical machinery, instruments, and textiles. The second part examines the interaction among related high-tech three-digit industries. The third examines remaining three-digit industries. For industries that are wide-spread, we estimate a Tobit equation, with both a simple version and a version attempting to account for simultaneity issues. For industries that are not widespread, we estimate a combined discrete-continuous choice model, using a two-stage Heckman procedure. Additionally, we investigate issues of simultaneity.

For any industry, the discussion of all results contains three components: price variables, location variables, and variables describing the scale of the city, of its manufacturing, and of it related industries. Price variables are critical to inferring supply elasticities. Except in Probit specifications, the dependent variable is the log of industry employment in the MSA. Wage and other employment explanatory variables are also transformed into logs. The specifications represent first-order approximations to the general $s(\cdot)$ and $m(\cdot)$ functions.

Two-Digit Industries

The results for machinery, electrical machinery, instruments, and textiles are presented in table 4.2. The sample size is 313 MSA's and PMSA's in 1986. The explanatory power of the model in the (not reported) OLS estimates of starting values for the Tobit is high for the different industries in cross-section analysis with an R^2 ranging from .62 to .71.

The two-stage Tobit treats the 1987 measure of all-other-manufacturing and the 1987 diversity index calculated from the 1987 Census of Manufacturers as endogenous variables, using first-stage OLS estimates as replacements.[1] Only for machinery does controlling for endogeneity appear to have a really profound effect. This is not surprising, given that machinery is the largest and most widespread manufacturing industry, with the greatest potential to influence all-other-manufacturing employment. However, going to two-stage estimates does have one consistent impact—to reduce or turn negative the population scale term and to increase the all-other-manufacturing scale term. This suggests that employment in an industry is positively correlated with both city size and all-other-manufacturing. However, controlling properly for manufacturing scale, larger urban size is a detriment, raising land costs and congestion. In contrast, controlling for urban size, more all-other-manufacturing improves the environment for any particular manufacturing industry. An improved environment could reflect an increased local demand base for the product and external effects

Table 4.2
Two-digit industry employment (t-statistics in parentheses)

	Machinery		Electrical machinery		Instruments	
	Tobit	Two-stage Tobit	Tobit	Two-stage Tobit	Tobit	Two-stage Tobit
Log (1982 manu. wage)	−.189 (.63)	−.921 (2.93)	−1.526 (3.85)	−1.609 (4.05)	−2.130 (4.53)	−2.106 (4.26)
% medium education (1980)	3.381 (2.88)	4.71 (4.10)	3.366 (2.21)	4.028 (2.71)	4.882 (2.87)	5.438 (3.21)
% high education (1980)	3.081 (3.03)	2.159 (2.42)	7.247 (5.47)	7.932 (6.40)	7.684 (5.10)	8.07 (5.33)
Distance to nat'l. bus. center	−.052 (2.33)	−.039 (1.96)	−.066 (1.85)	−.052 (1.52)	−.089 (1.82)	−.076 (1.55)
Port dummy	−.346 (2.72)	−.302 (2.67)	−.292 (1.83)	−.247 (1.64)	.384 (2.16)	.419 (2.37)
Consolidated metro area dummy	.209 (1.22)	.095 (.61)	.336 (1.73)	.239 (1.31)	.442 (2.09)	.394 (1.89)
N.C. region dummy	.594 (3.57)	.512 (3.49)	−.197 (.91)	−.420 (2.01)	.046 (.19)	−.076 (.31)
NE region dummy	.401 (2.54)	.282 (1.99)	.159 (.82)	.003 (.02)	.523 (2.45)	.455 (2.18)
West region dummy	−.224 (1.23)	−.245 (1.40)	−.381 (1.59)	−.355 (1.55)	.162 (.60)	.188 (.70)
Log (1984) metro area population	.480 (4.30)	−.023 (.20)	.023 (.17)	−.415 (2.87)	.121 (.85)	−.147 (.93)
Log (all other 1987 manu.)	.560 (6.43)	1.336 (8.45)	.860 (6.80)	1.291 (8.56)	.841 (6.51)	1.090 (6.85)
Diversity index (1987)	−1.286 (2.59)	3.426 (2.36)	−2.351 (3.22)	−1.903 (1.36)	−1.341 (1.71)	−1.584 (1.05)
Constant	−5.167 (3.17)	−8.524 (4.84)	−9.587 (4.55)	−9.111 (4.02)	−14.984 (5.91)	−14.353 (5.21)
N	313	313	313	313	313	313
R^2 (based on OLS)	.71		.62		.66	

Table 4.2 (continued)

	Textiles	
	OLS (corrected for censoring)	Probit
Log (wage)	−2.592 (3.76)	−1.647 (2.71)
% medium education	−7.748 (3.02)	−5.961 (2.78)
% high education	−8.330 (3.63)	−2.722 (1.134)
Distance to national business center	−.0003 (.003)	−.066 (1.86)
Port dummy	.014	−.032
Consolidated metropolitan area dummy	−.157 (.73)	−.148 (.52)
N.C. region dummy	−.406 (1.13)	.476 (1.52)
West region dummy	−.024 (.085)	1.072 (3.59)
West region dummy	.186	.352
Log (metropolitan area population)	−.257 (1.53)	.026 (.13)
Log (all other manu. employ)	.917 (4.64)	.347 (1.83)
Diversity index	1.373 (1.40)	
Inverse: Mill's ratio	.431 (1.04)	
Log (apparel employ)		.419 (3.08)
Log (ind. price for electricity		−.332 (1.71)
Constant		−5.157 (1.73)
N	313	109
% predicted correctly		84%
R^2	.58	

in labor markets or information flows among industrial sectors enhancing technology choices.

In the presentation of results, we focus on the two-stage Tobit results for machinery, electrical machinery, and instruments. For textiles, we focus on the OLS results, although the Probit results are also instructive. The Mill's ratio coefficient suggests a weak case for selectivity bias in textiles. For textiles, the standard errors underlying the t-statistics are correctly calculated. The two-stage Tobit standard errors are uncorrected.

Price Effects
Controlling for labor force quality, higher wages levels result in lower employment, the expected price effect. For durable goods industries, labor force quality improvements, as measured by educational attainment of the population, raise employment. These could reflect direct productivity benefits in the industry, an externality in the environment, or an improved supply of potential entrepreneurs. However, having an improved work force is detrimental for textiles, an effect that is robust. That may result from the nature of the work, and the use of a more heavily immigrant work force.

The wage effects are critical to our analyses of price and supply elasticity effects. An FTA would work to raise product prices to domestic producers, stimulating price. A critical issue concerns the supply response to increased output. We don't observe output price differences in the data. The only reliably observed price with a robust, consistent effect is the local wage rate in manufacturing.[2] From the estimating equation, we may directly calculate

$$\frac{d \log L_{ij}}{d \log w_j} = b_{1i} \tag{5}$$

where L_{ij} is employment in industry i in metro area j, and b_{1i} is the estimated coefficient on the wage variable for industry i. For the four industries reported in table 4.2, the b_{1i} coefficients range from $-.921$ to -2.592.

How do we make use of these coefficients? They allow us to get a ballpark figure on supply elasticities. From a $\hat{b}_{1i}$, for any particular functional form for technology an output price effect on employment may be inferred from equation (5). So, for example, for a Cobb-Douglas production function and corresponding profit function, the output price effect would be

$$\frac{d \log L_{ij}}{d \log q_{ij}} = -\hat{b}_{1i}/\alpha_i \tag{6}$$

q_{ij} is the price of product i in city j. α_i is labor's share in product i. Labor's share (in total value of production, not value added) is typically 0.2 to 0.3. So for a value of, say 0.25, the employment response to an output price increase is four times the response to a wage decrease. Even though the wage effect on employment includes input substitution effects, the overall output price effect is generally much larger than the effect of an input price decrease, because the latter only affects the costs of one input. To be approximately equivalent we would have to decrease the costs of all inputs by the same fraction that output price increases.

If inputs are less substitutable than in a Cobb-Douglas form, less of the employment expansion from a wage change is due to substitution and more to output effects. Therefore in moving from (5) to (6) we would blow the response in (5) up by *less*, in calculating the response to an output price change (since (5) already captures more of output responses). For example, for a simple decreasing returns to scale CES production function where the elasticity of substitution is 0.6, the multiple drops from 4 to under 2.[3]

Equations (5) and (6) are based on simple log linear forms, where the wage-employment elasticities are assumed to be the same in each city. I experimented with nonlinear forms in Tobit estimation (but not two-stage), adding a wage squared term and interacting wage with all continuous variables. The supply elasticities at the mean of explanatory variables are about the same as in the linear form. However, controlling for price, with location and population variables set at the mean, for cities with a one standard deviation increase in the manufacturing employment variables listed, the elasticities in machinery and electrical machinery increase (by about 50%), while that in instruments falls somewhat.

Location Effects
Locational effects include access to the nearest Rand-McNally market center. Increased distance to a market lowers employment consistently, reflecting the expected negative transport cost effect. Being a port (including a Great Lake port) has inconsistent impacts by industry, negatively affecting machinery and electrical machinery. While one-third of MSA's are ports, they are more oriented to producing traded services, which may account for the inconsistent effects in manufacturing. Except for textiles, being in a PMSA (18% of the sample) within a consolidated metro area helps employment. Presumably some type of urbanization economies arise from being in a larger labor market.

Regional dummies, relative to the South, are mixed. The North Central [NC] and Northeast [NE] regions are traditional machinery centers, while the South appears to have an advantage in electrical machinery. Textiles are particularly interesting, with the NC and NE having positive impacts on whether a city has textiles or not (Probit), but negative in terms of the level of employment (OLS) compared to the South. Employment today is centered in the South, but the NE and also the NC have remnants of the former textile giants of the 1850–1945 period, scattered throughout the various metropolitan areas.

Scale Effects
Especially when corrected for endogeneity, as noted earlier, all-other-manufacturing contributes positively to own industry employment, while urban population contributes negatively. The diversity index for all-other industries is a measure exploring whether environments that are more specialized are better than ones that are more diverse. Higher values of the diversity index imply increased specialization (in other activities), so a positive coefficient indicates the own industry thrives in a less diverse environment. In trying to deal with simultaneity, this variable demonstrated some modest instability, but generally the coefficients are significant and results consistent across the choice of instrumental variables. Machinery and textiles thrive in less diverse environments, while instruments and electrical machinery thrive in more diverse environments. Machinery switches sign (a robust effect with respect to choice of instruments) when accounting for simultaneity. This suggests that, while machinery employment may be positively correlated with more diverse environments, in fact properly controlling for simultaneity with scale, machinery employment is enhanced in a more specialized environment.

Related Industries
Employment in electrical machinery, instruments, and textiles all appear to be a further enhanced by the presence and scale of particular related industries. For example, a city is more likely to have textiles in the Probit equation, if it has apparel. However, the level of apparel employment does not appear to affect the level of textile employment, in the OLS equation in cities having textiles. Again, historical locational linkages between apparel and textiles may be surfacing in the Probit results.

In ordinary Tobit estimates, electrical machinery employment strongly benefits from either increased instruments or increased computer employment. Instruments employment in turn benefits from electrical machinery

Table 4.3
Interrelationship among electrical machinery, instruments, and computers*

	Electrical machinery		Instruments	
	Ordinary Tobit	Two-stage Tobit	Ordinary Tobit	Two-stage Tobit
Log (all other employ.)	.281 (3.06)	1.319 (2.94)	.381 (2.78)	.865 (1.35)
Log (instrument employ.)	.351 (5.30)	1.086 (3.26)		
Log (electrical mach. employ.)			.407 (5.02)	−.272 (1.20)
Log (computer employ.)	.205 (3.29)	−.820 (2.13)	.157 (2.07)	.415 (1.21)

*t-statistics for two-stage estimates are based on estimates of standard errors that are not consistent.

and computer employment. Clearly simultaneity is an issue here, and ordinary Tobit estimates are inappropriate. Unfortunately, two-stage estimates are not very robust, in terms of choice of instrumental variables or precise specification. I report just the employment results for these specifications in table 4.3. For the electrical machinery equation, after accounting for simultaneity, the positive impact of instruments employment appears to persist, but the computer impact is reversed. For the instruments equation, the computer impact persists, but the electrical machinery impact is reversed. Taken together, these results suggest that instruments employment benefits electrical machinery employment (derived demand), but not vice versa. Given these results and the difficulty in controlling for simultaneity, we decided to look more intensively at these high-tech industry interrelationships, by focusing on the three-digit level. This allows us to detail the interactions, for more finely defined industries.

High-Tech Industries

The results for some three-digit high-tech industries are given in table 4.4 We picked two subcomponents of electrical machinery—communications equipment and electronic components—as well as computers and medical equipment. We present simple Probit estimates of the $m(\cdot)$ function in (4) and OLS estimates of the $s(\cdot)$ function in (3), corrected for selectivity bias.[4]

The price and location variables perform similarly to those in table 4.2. We shortened the list for the $s(\cdot)$ function to accommodate the smaller

Table 4.4
High-tech industries

	Communications		Electrical components		Computers	
	OLS	Probit	OLS	Probit	OLS	Probit
Log (wage)	−1.284	−1.959	−1.130	−1.628	−.015	−.942
	(1.53)	(3.00)	(2.32)	(2.90)	(.02)	(1.35)
% medium	1.457	2.000	3.744	2.738	8.215	5.175
education (1980)	(.61)	(.87)	(2.13)	(1.35)	(1.94)	(1.99)
% high	2.152	5.378	2.151	4.773	13.527	8.524
education (1980)	(.79)	(2.45)	(1.21)	(2.36)	(3.20)	(3.67)
Distance to nat'l	−.038	−.041	−.084	−.061	.035	−.068
bus. center	(.51)	(.83)	(1.54)	(1.20)	(.31)	(.82)
Port dummy		−.012		.139		−.116
		(.05)		(.62)		(.46)
Consolidated metro		.051		.588		−.209
area dummy		(.18)		(1.92)		(.68)
N.C. region	−.163	.133	−.158	−.246	−.897	−.343
dummy	(.53)	(.40)	.66	(.81)	(1.83)	(.95)
NE region dummy	−.709	−.177	.317	.250	−.416	.058
	(2.70)	(.61)	(1.62)	(.93)	(1.10)	(.19)
West region	−.597	.321	.337	.199	−.656	.075
dummy	(2.02)	(.93)	(1.44)	(.60)	(1.30)	(.20)
Log (all other	−.284	.362	.080	.339	−.279	.186
manufact.)	(1.13)	(1.65)	(.48)	(1.87)	(.65)	(.70)
Log (instrument	.546	.260	.359	.363	.339	.340
employ)	(4.63)	(2.13)	(3.94)	(3.03)	(1.76)	(2.61)
Dummy: (comput.		.295		.194		
industry)		(1.22)		(.776)		
Log (computer	.198		.320			
employ)	(2.28)		(5.01)			
Log (population)	.521	.222	.222	.232	.575	.346
	(2.66)	(1.05)	(1.70)	(1.16)	(1.81)	(1.53)
Log (other			.025	−.168		
electrical mach.)			(.38)	(1.81)		
Log (electrical					.575	.187
mach.)					(3.06)	(1.52)
Inverse Mill's	.761		.912		1.722	
ratio	(1.70)		(3.13)		(3.03)	
Constant	−8.853	−13.461	−8.624	−11.615	−10.826	−11.690
	(1.67)	(3.71)	(2.76)	(3.74)	(1.64)	(3.06)
R^2/% predicted	.54	83%	.72	80%	.43	88%
correctly						
N	95	313	139	313	102	313

Table 4.4 (continued)

| | Medical instruments and supplies | |
	OLS	Probit
Log (wage)	−.918	−.886
	(2.04)	(1.47)
% medium	1.791	−3.298
education	(1.05)	(1.51)
% high	2.578	2.713
education	(1.65)	(1.35)
Distance to national	.006	−.065
business center	(.12)	(.85)
Port dummy		.299
		(1.28)
Consolidated		.011
metropolitan area dummy		(1.28)
N.C. region	.230	.316
dummy	(1.11)	(.98)
NE region	.530	.222
dummy	(3.01)	(.79)
West region	.670	−.089
dummy	(2.75)	(.25)
Log (metropolitan	−.042	.511
area population)	(.31)	(2.32)
Log (all other	.681	.484
manufacturing)	(4.05)	(2.41)
Log (all other	.013	.153
instruments)	(.26)	(1.42)
Inverse Mill's ratio	.415	
	(1.51)	
Constant	−7.449	−6.665
	(2.33)	(2.51)
N	313	119
% predicted correctly/R^2	85%	.50

sample size. The scale variables for these high-tech industries are different, however. These industries appear to benefit from being in larger cities, but they do not benefit from more all-other-manufacturing, in contrast to their two-digit counterparts. Under any attempts to correct for endogeneity of RHS variables, this phenomenon persisted.

To deal with simultaneity among these high-tech industries, I first isolated communications and electronic components, because they are small industries, which might benefit through externalities or market demand from the scale of two larger industries—computers and overall instruments —which arguably we could treat as exogenous in employment levels to the smaller industries. (I also tried some two-stage estimations, which had little impact on the interactive industry coefficient.)[5]

The communications industry appears to benefit from instrument and computers employment. An FTA would directly stimulate communications, but the industry would benefit also indirectly through, say, increased instrument employment. If the direct stimulation to instruments expands its local employment by 10%, the indirect impact on communications is 6% from table 4.4 ($.55 \times .10 \times 100\%$). Electronic components also indirectly benefits from instruments and computer employment. There will be further feedback effects as well, if the induced expansion in communications or electronic components themselves stimulate instruments employment. These feedback effects are generally small. In the current case, in fact, overall electrical machinery employment has an uncertain impact on instruments (see table 4.3).

Not surprisingly, both instruments and electrical machinery stimulate computers employment. Using two-stage estimates to correct for endogeneity, however, these effects are statistically weak. For medical instruments, other specific manufacturing industries had no effects except for employment in other instrument industries.

In table 4.5, we list the MSA's with over 40,000 workers in electronic components, computers, communications equipment, and instruments. Additional towns where employment in these industries exceeds 10% of the work force include Boulder-Longmont, CO, Melbourne-Titusville, FA, and Rochester, MN. For metropolitan areas, containing significant employment in various high-tech industries, an FTA will have strong interactive effects. In the absence of fully efficient estimation procedures, the numbers in tables 4.3 and 4.4 must be regarded as preliminary, but they give an order of magnitude.

For example, if total instruments employment in a locality expands directly by 5% from an FTA, electronics, communications, and computers

Table 4.5
High-tech towns

Over 40,000 workers	
Phoenix AZ	Chicago IL
Dallas TX	Minneapolis-St. Paul MN
Anaheim-Santa Ana CA	Boston-Lowell MA
San Jose CA	Nassau-Suffolk NY
	Rochester NY
	Philadelphia PA

will each expand by 1.8%, 2.7%, and 1.7%, respectively, due to instrument expansion alone. If each of these four sectors employs 10,000 workers, the overall expansion from the instruments component of an FTA is over 1,100 jobs. Moreover, if an FTA has a direct 5% impact on each of these sectors, then while the direct employment effects total 2,000, the first-round indirect effects could raise the total to 3,500. This last calculation adds to the 2,000 direct jobs, the indirect impacts of a 5% employment expansion of computers and instruments on communications and electronic components, of a 5% employment expansion in instruments and electrical machinery on computers, and of a 5% employment expansion in computers and electrical machinery on instruments. Adding in interactive impacts can readily double the initial direct effects of an FTA among the relevant industries, especially if one accounts for further multiplier effects.

Other Three-Digit Industries

In Table 4.6, we report results for plastics and electrical industrial machinery. They are not especially surprising, and we do not comment on them separately.

Impacts on Exports and Domestic Prices of an FTA

National Impact of an FTA

This study adopts U.S. export expansion scenarios consistent with the observed expansion since 1988 due to Mexican trade liberalization. These scenarios also are consistent with the magnitudes of expansion due to an FTA predicted by existing studies (INFORUM 1990, ITC 1990a, 1990b, 1989). We focus on the period projected from 1987 to 1995 by the INFORUM (1990) study, given our base employment figures are also for

Table 4.6
Other three-digit industries

	Plastics	Electrical industrial apparatus	
	Tobit	Probit	OLS
Log (wage)	−.913	−.794	−.689
	(2.71)	(1.30)	(1.34)
% medium education	−.430	−1.903	−1.429
	(.34)	(.80)	(.68)
% high education	1.690	−.096	−.796
	(1.64)	(.04)	(.34)
Distance to national business center	−.108	−.025	.222
	(2.15)	(.29)	(2.65)
Port dummy	−.120		
	(.96)		
Consolidated metrol area dummy	.193		
	(1.29)		
N.C. region dummy	.688	.311	.940
	(3.99)	(.97)	(3.46)
NE region dummy	.439	−.126	.047
	(2.93)	(.45)	(.20)
West region dummy	.149	−1.067	.259
	(.77)	(2.52)	(.69)
Log (metropolitan area population)	.226	.007	.259
	(2.08)	(.03)	(1.47)
Log (all other manu. employ)	.493	.659	.035
	(4.71)	(2.94)	(.151)
Diversity index	−3.532		
	(5.35)		
Log (chemical employ)	.115		
	(1.80)		
Log (other electrical machinery		.121	−.015
		(1.27)	(.19)
Log (instruments)		.263	.219
		(2.12)	(2.24)
Constant	−5.406	−5.189	−3.468
	(3.07)	(1.60)	(1.16)
R^2	.70		.36
% predicted correctly		82%	
N	313	313	105

Table 4.7
Scenarios of export expansion (Δ%)

150%	200%	300%	350%
Instruments	Textiles	Electrical industrial	Plastics
Machinery	Computers	apparatus	
	Electrical machinery		
	Telecommunications		
	Electronic components		

Table 4.8
Parameters utilized

η^D	
All industries	−1.5
ψ (1987)	
Textiles, plastics	.006
Machinery	.010
Electrical	.020
Instruments	.005
η^S	
Textiles	5
Plastics	2.5
Machinery	2.5
Electrical machinery	5
Instruments	5

1987. In table 4.7, we list the assumed impacts on exports, from 1987 to 1995, consistent with the INFORUM (1990) study. These incorporate both the impacts of existing trade liberalization and a future FTA that eliminates tariff and nontariff barriers. An FTA would also make permanent the existing trade liberalization measures. The impacts in Table 4.7 do not separate out estimates for the natural expansion of exports that would have occurred regardless of an FTA. The base from which these expansions occur is given in table 4.8 for two-digit industries.

The export expansion represents an increase in Mexican demand for U.S. production. The expansion stimulates a positive U.S. supply response, driving up domestic prices, which in turn creates a negative "domestic" (all other) feedback demand response. In particular, we assume a relationship

$$X_D^M(\cdot) + X_D^R(\cdot) = X_S^{US}(\cdot), \tag{7}$$

where $X_D^M(\cdot)$ is Mexican demand, $X_D^R(\cdot)$ is demand from everywhere else (principally the United States), and $X_S^{US}(\cdot)$ is U.S. supply. We differentiate

Table 4.9

Percentage change in overall domestic prices (β)			
Textiles	0.18%	Electrical machinery	0.62%
Plastics	0.18%	Instruments	0.12%
Machinery	0.38%		
Percentage change in overall domestic production at a national level			
Textiles	0.9%	Electrical machinery	3.1%
Plastics	0.9%	Instruments	0.6%
Machinery	1.0%		

this relationship and substitute guesstimates about the elasticity of domestic demand (η^D) and estimates of domestic supply η^S. Defining β as the percentage change in domestic prices due to an FTA, ψ as Mexico's share in U.S. production and Δ as the assumed elasticity of export expansion due to an FTA from table 4.7, we have

$$\beta = \frac{\Delta * \psi}{\eta^S - \eta^D(1 - \psi)}. \tag{8}$$

For the various industries the elasticities assumed for all variables except Δ are given in table 4.8. The ψ's are based on 1987 data (Mehl et al., 1991). The η^S figures are based on equation (6), where for machinery and plastics we assume $\hat{b} = -1$ and for the others $\hat{b} = -2$. We blow these numbers up by 2.5, reflecting a labor factor share between .2 and .3 and an elasticity of substitution less than 1.

Based on these elasticities, the predicted domestic price changes will be small, given the small size of the ψ's—Mexican imports relative to all U.S. domestic production. For each industry, the national price changes from equation (8) are listed in table 4.9. Based on these price changes, we can then calculate expansions for each product, for each metro area producing the product. The corresponding national changes in production are also given in the table 4.9 based on the price changes (β) and the assumed supply elasticities (η^s). They give us an aggregative picture. However, we do not use the numbers in table 4.9. Instead we redo the analysis to account for regional differences.

Regional Impacts of an FTA

We expect that these price effects, the initial shares, and output responses will vary by region within the United States. Indeed, some regions may experience much larger changes than the national averages. First, some localities may be more efficient producers of a product, selling at a lower price and attracting a larger market share. Second, localities' access to Mexico, or transport costs, will vary significantly with distance from Mexico. Unfortunately, we do not have direct information on how much of any product different localities export to Mexico. We do have state-level estimates of exports to Mexico by product, based on Shippers' Export Declarations as to "point (state) of origin" (Mehl et al., 1991). However, the point of origin may be a warehouse rather than a factory. The state data thus measure with error factory exports, and there may be some systematic biases. For example, inland states may have a greater tendency to have their exports attributed to coastal states, which are ports of export. Those professionals who construct these figures, however, believe any biases mostly are for export of nonmanufactured products. Although it could be misleading to use the data to predict for a specific state the impacts of an FTA, the data can be used for two purposes. First, it can be used to obtain reasonable estimates of the importance of access on exports to Mexico. Second, we can aggregate the data to the four regional levels to generate plausible specific numbers on regional exports of different products to Mexico.

At the state level, how do we model the importance of access and state scale of manufacturing on exports to Mexico? This problem must necessarily be cast in a varieties model, where as in Dixit-Stiglitz (1977), Mexican consumers value varieties. Otherwise, Mexico would simply buy each product from a single source—the cheapest and likely nearest supplier to it. While the location model in section 1 is not explicitly based on a varieties model, it is straightforward to reinterpret it as such. Consider a varieties model, where each two-digit industry comprises a commodity group within which consumers value variety. A Mexican demand equation for the two-digit industry then can be derived, in terms of Mexican expenditures on the product evaluated at factory prices. A very simple version of this equation is[6]

$$\ln(p_{ij}X_{ij}) = A + \frac{1 - \delta - \theta + 2\delta\theta}{(1 - \delta)(1 - \theta)}\ln s_{ij} - \frac{1}{1 - \theta}\ln(1 + T_i)$$

$$- \frac{1}{1 - \theta}\frac{\gamma_i}{(1 + T_i)} \cdot t_{j'} \tag{9}$$

where $p_{ij}X_{ij}$ are Mexican purchases of two-digit industry i product at location j at a factory price of p_{ij}. s_{ij} is the number of firms in industry i at location j, representing (a) the number of varieties and (b) the local scale of industry operation (and hence potential external economies of scale). θ is the varieties parameter for each commodity group where $0 < \theta < 1$. Within a commodity group variety becomes less valuable as $\theta \to 1$. The elasticity of demand in this model is $1/(\theta - 1)$. So an elasticity of demand of -1.5 implies a θ of .35.

δ is an economy of scale parameter. So for example, if $\theta = 0.7$ and $(1 - \delta - \theta + 2\delta\theta)/(1 - \delta - \theta + \delta\theta) = 1.3$, then $\delta = .11$, approximating the degree of localization economies of scale. These localization economies lower costs and local prices, increasing Mexican demand for the product. Quite apart from access considerations, one state may ship more to Mexico, because it sells at lower factory prices. And Mexicans may have stronger likings for some varieties than others, although the equation does not capture this feature per se.

In equation (9), T_i is the effective Mexican tariff rate imposed on all U.S. imports of commodity i. t_j is the distance from location j to Mexico; and γ_i is the cost (paid by Mexico) to ship a purchase of X_i (at price p_{ij}) a unit distance toward Mexico. Using state data for 1989 on exports to Mexico, I estimated equation (9) for relevant two-digit industries. s_{ij} is measured as the number of firms in 1987 in state j and industry i. t_j is the distance from the center of the state to the nearest point in Mexico. The OLS results from this simple equation are given in table 4.10.

From equation (9), we can assess the differential impact of a tariff reduction on states with different access to Mexico. In particular,

$$\frac{d\ln(p_{ij}X_{ij})}{d\ln(1 + T_i)} = -\left(\frac{1}{1 - \theta}\right)\left(1 - \frac{\gamma t_j}{1 + T_i}\right). \tag{10}$$

Table 4.10
Parameters of the demand model (t-statistics in pairs)

	$\frac{1-\delta-\theta+2\delta\theta}{(1-\delta)(1-\theta)}$	$-\frac{\gamma}{(1-\theta)(1+T)}$
Textiles	1.047	−.039
	(5.80)	(1.29)
Rubber and plastics	1.320	−.042
	(9.82)	(2.02)
Machinery	1.309	−.026
	(13.87)	(1.84)
Electrical machinery	1.519	−.011
	(10.19)	(.46)
Instruments	1.462	−.008

Suppose the effective rate of protection is $T_j = .35$. This doubles the typical official tariff rates of .17 of 1989, to incorporate further effective protection through quotas, licensing and other restrictions. If $\theta = .35$ and the estimated $-[\gamma/(1 - \theta)(1 + T)]$ is -0.03, then a 1% reduction in the tariff would increase sales by 1.5% for manufacturers at the border, but only .9% for manufacturers at $t_j = 20$ (approximately Chicago in the metric used), ceteris paribus. Ceteris paribus means that we have not factored in domestic demand and price responses.

Constructing Regional Scenarios Consistent with National Changes

Regional responses to an FTA will differ both because regional production concentrations and export concentrations to Mexico differ and because access differs. Together these imply that product price changes will vary by region relative to the national "average" price changes asserted in table 4.9. How do we calculate these differences so that they are consistent with national changes? I take as "given"—that is, as reasonable ballpark guesses—the overall export expansions listed in table 4.7. Next I work backward to get implied regional changes. For the envisioned export changes, I calculate an implied effective Mexican tariff reduction, regional differences in export responses, and regional differential price responses.

I define the access elasticity in table 4.10 as

$$m \equiv \frac{\gamma}{(1 - \theta)(1 + T)}, \tag{11}$$

and I define the national change in effective tariff protection as

$$\hat{T} \equiv -\frac{dT}{1 + T}.$$

Then I differentiate

$$X_T^e(\cdot) = \sum_{i=1}^{4} X_i^e(\cdot) \tag{12}$$

where X_i^e is exports to Mexico of a product group from region i and X_T^e is total U.S. exports to Mexico. Differentiating and utilizing equation (10), yields

$$\left[\sum_{i=1}^{4} \left(\frac{1}{1 - \theta} - mt_i \right) \frac{X_i^e}{X_T^e} \right] \hat{T} = \Delta$$

or

$$\hat{T} = \frac{\Delta}{\sum_{i=1}^{4}\left(\dfrac{1}{1 + \theta} - mt_i\right)\dfrac{X_i^e}{X_T^e}}. \tag{13}$$

Given this percentage change in the national effective tariff rate, the percentage change in regional exports can be calculated from equation (10), so that

$$\Delta_i = \hat{T}\left(\frac{1}{1 - \theta} - mt_i\right) \qquad i = 1, \dots 4. \tag{10'}$$

Next, I can reapply equation (8), to get regional percentage changes in product prices. That is

$$\beta_i = \frac{\Delta_i \psi_i}{\eta^S - \eta^D(1 - \psi_i)} \qquad i = 1, \dots 4. \tag{8'}$$

To calculate ballpark values of β_i I use the values of η^S in table 4.8, assuming those are the same across regions and varieties within a product group, and I set $\theta = 0.35$ and hence $\eta^D = -1.5$. Next I set $m = .04$ for textiles and plastics, $m = 0.025$ for machinery, and $m = 0.01$ for electrical machin-

Table 4.11

	% of regional output exported to Mexico (ψ_i)				% of U.S. exports produced in the region (X_i^e/X_i^T)			
	NE	NC	S	W	NE	NC	S	W
Textiles	.09	1.22	.53	36.80	3.01	1.54	79.50	16.4
Rubber and plastics	.22	.13	.96	1.48	7.35	8.04	54.42	30.62
Machinery	.47	.58	1.27	1.53				
Electric machinery	.30	.43	4.18	1.96	3.63	5.98	69.00	21.33
Instruments	.23	.88	.85	.32	19.37	26.59	34.27	18.56

	% Effective national tariff change ($\hat{T}$)	Regional percentage change in exports (Δ_i)				Regional percentage change in prices (β_i)			
		NE	NC	S	W	NE	NC	S	W
Textiles	177	60	131	209	209	.01	.25	.17	13.01
Rubber and plastics	321	109	238	379	379	.06	.08	.91	1.41
Machinery	128	100	132	166	166	.12	.19	.53	.62
Electric machinery	142	172	186	202	202	.08	.12	1.30	.61
Instruments	113	137	148	160	160	.05	.20	.21	.08

ery and instruments. Finally, in the assumed transport distance metric I set $t = 8$ for the South and West, $t = 19$ for the North Central region, and $t = 29$ for the Northeast. For example, $t = 29$ represents approximately the distance from Mexico to the regional heartland of the Northeast.

In table 4.11, I list the values of ψ_i and X_i^e / X_T^e calculated for 1987 from the data set. Given these and the Δ's in table 4.7 earlier, from (15) I calculate the assumed effective tariff reductions $\hat{T}$, which are very large. Based on these large tariff reductions I then calculate the Δ_i and $\beta_i's$ in equations (10) and (8) for each industry in each region.

Table 4.11 reveals the importance of access to Mexico in the analysis. Access affects both the initial position of regions and the incremental response to an FTA. Although price changes nationally remain very modest, there are significant regional differences. The percentage price rises in the South and West are generally multiples of those in the northern areas, signaling big differences in output and employment responses to be discussed next.

Impact on Urban Employment

The price rises and output increases in a region are realized at the local level, by expansions in outputs of cities producing the relevant products. We can calculate these for a "typical city" producing the product. The actual response in any one city in a region will vary according to both the idiosyncrasies of that city and its own initial export position to Mexico. If the product varieties produced in a particular city are more favored by Mexicans than the typical city case, the expansions in that city will probably exceed those of the typical city. However, we can't calibrate this, because we do not know exports of individual cities.

How do we proceed for the typical city in each region? Based on the elasticities of supply in table 4.8 and the $\beta_i's$ in table 4.11, for each industry and region we can calculate a typical output and, hence employment response (assuming homotheticity and approximately unchanged factor prices). The percentage employment response is simply the supply elasticity multiplied by the percentage change in regional price. These numbers are reported in table 4.12. Not surprisingly the responses in the South and West are generally much larger than in the North. The numbers in table 4.12 are the direct employment impacts of an FTA as they would affect a city in the center of the region with a typical export share to Mexico. The cities with the biggest impacts are those listed in table 4.1 in the South and West.

Table 4.12
Typical employment and output expansions due to direct effects of free trade (from 1987 to 1995)

	NE	NC	S	W
			(percentage)	
Textiles	.05	1.25	0.85	65.05
Rubber and plastics	.15	.20	2.28	3.50
Machinery	.16	.48	1.33	1.58
Electric machinery	.40	.60	6.50	3.50
Instruments	.25	1.00	1.05	.40

For Western textiles, which are heavily exported to Mexico, the impact of an FTA is enormous, in the order of magnitude of 65%. For the main city of Los Angeles, a 65% increase represents thousands of jobs. A caveat on such a calculation is that any employment expansion will affect wages. These wage effects will dampen employment effects, and this second-order effect is ignored. Also effected will be the textile industry, in the South Atlantic area of the South. Relevant cities include Dothan, Chattanooga, Greenville, Anderson, and other textile-belt cities nearer Mexico.

Rubber and plastics and machinery would both experience general output expansions. These would be heavier in the South and West. So a city such as Los Angeles with 30,000 workers in plastics could experience a direct employment expansion of over 1,000 workers in plastics. San Diego and Anaheim also currently employ over 10,000 workers in plastics. While the machinery percentages are smaller, the employment levels are enormous. Anaheim, Los Angeles, and San Jose respectively have 35,000, 65,000 and 56,000 machinery workers, and Houston has over 20,000. An FTA could result in direct employment increases of a 1,000 or so workers in each of these metro areas. This is simply the result of increased Mexican demand for capital goods.

The really large impacts of an FTA appear to lie in electric machinery, and the intersection of electric machinery with computers. Consider southern cities such as Dallas or Phoenix, each with around 30,000 workers in electrical machinery. A 6.5% direct increase in employment represents about 2,000 jobs. However, for these high-tech cities, a 6.5% increase in electrical machinery, a 1.3% increase in computer, and a 1% increase in instruments could each easily double with indirect, interactive effects. For Phoenix, with 52,000 jobs in computers, instruments, and electrical machinery (virtually all in communications and electronic components) combined, the total direct and indirect effects could involve 4,000 jobs.

While the percentage increases in high-tech industries are smaller in the West, the absolute number of jobs is much larger. For San Jose, there is a base of 175,000 workers in computers, instrument, and electrical machinery, and Anaheim has over 40,000. An FTA could translate into 10,000 manufacturing jobs. Our caveats remain, however. In particular, does San Jose export a typical amount to Mexico? Also, such an employment surge could be significantly retarded by local wage increases and deterioration in living conditions in San Jose.

Offsetting these caveats is the notion that manufacturing jobs generate jobs in the local service sector for services demanded by manufacturing workers. Typical multipliers lie in the range of 2 to 3. So before factoring in the retarding forces of wage increases and deterioration in living conditions resulting from employment and population increases, 10,000 manufacturing jobs could result in 25,000 or 30,000 jobs overall. Of course, these "jobs" come from somewhere. If San Jose's work force expands by 30,000, other cities' work forces will contract. What helps San Jose in the West may result in outmigration from declining cities in the Midwest and Northeast.

Conclusions

This chapter has examined the impacts of an FTA on industries likely to expand with an FTA. Losing sectors such as apparel or fresh and frozen vegetables and fruits, or domestic industries displaced by expanding industries, have not been examined. The focus has been to identify specific local areas that will benefit from an FTA because they contain high employment levels in favorably affected industries.

Because of expansion of high-tech industries, textiles, plastics, and machinery, we expect cities such as Austin, Houston, Anaheim, Los Angeles, San Jose, Phoenix, Boulder, and Dallas to gain thousands of jobs from the combined direct and indirect effects of an FTA.

In table 4.13, I list the cities where, based on the estimates in table 4.12, direct effects alone could exceed 2,000 and 4,000 jobs respectively. Indirect effects including derived demand and service sector effects could easily double these impacts, even accounting for adverse effects on local wages and other input costs.

Other cities such as Fort Smith, Melbourne, Oklahoma City, and Baltimore also could be significantly affected. Northern cities with their poor access to Mexico will have much smaller positive effects, as will Southern and Western cities whose employment patterns are geared to industries

Table 4.13
Expected direct employment effects of an FTA

MSA's with effects exceeding 2,000 jobs	MSA's with effects exceeding 4,000 jobs
Austin TX	Anaheim CA
Dallas TX	Los Angeles CA
Phoenix AZ	San Jose CA

not so favorably affected by an FTA. For example, whereas Los Angeles and San Jose stand to gain thousands of jobs, other California cities such as those engaged in food processing could suffer losses.

Notes

1. Instruments include the log (1982 wage rate in manufacturing), log (1982 total manufacturing employment), distance to a Rand-McNally national business center, percentage of adult population with high school or some college, percentage of adults with college or more, log (1984 resident population), median residential rent in 1980, 1982 manufacturing production workers, state fuel price for industrial users, number of persons over 65 years, number of 1980 housing units, number of 1980 housing units built before 1959, 1980 black population, and dummies for port, PMSA in a consolidated metro area, and regions.

2. We tried other price variables reflecting industrial electricity, fuel, and housing rental prices. These had no consistent impact on employment; and, with the exception of electricity price (weakly negative) in the Probit for textiles, they are omitted here.

3. Suppose we assume an elasticity of substitution of $1/(1 + \rho) = 0.6$ (or $\rho = 0.5$) in a CES function of the form $(\alpha L^{-\rho} + \beta K^{-\rho} + \gamma M^{-\rho})^{\delta/\rho}$, with inputs labor (L), capital (K), and materials (M). Assume $\alpha = 0.30$, $\beta = 0.15$, $\gamma = 0.55$, $\rho = 0.5$, where δ is a measure of diseconomies of scale. A 1% increase in output price produces a $1/(1 - \delta)$% increase in employment ignoring supply-side responses. A 1% decrease in wages produces a $A/(1 - \delta)$% increase in employment, where for $\delta - 0.5$, $A = .55$. Thus for all input prices normalized to 1, the response to an output price change is about 1.83 times the response to an input price change.

4. The t-statistics for communications and computers are based on regular OLS estimates because the relevant correlation coefficient to estimate correct standard errors lies outside the admissible range, for those industries. This is a standard small sample problem.

5. For the continuous equations, the coefficient for computers is little changed in electronic components, while the coefficient for instruments actually rises.

6. This is based on a utility function of the form (Krugman, 1981)

$$U = \alpha_1 \ln \left(\sum_{i=1}^{N_1} X_{1i}^{\theta_1} \right)^{1/\theta_1} + \alpha_2 \ln \left(\sum_{j=1}^{N_2} X_{1j}^{\theta_2} \right)^{1/\theta_2} + \cdots, \theta < 1,$$

where each term refers to a commodity group (e.g., two-digit manufacturing industry). N_1 is the number of firms nationally producing product group 1. For the specific form in equation (9) we assume $\theta_1 = \theta_2 = \cdots$, and normalize so $p_{ki} = p_{kj}$ for all i, j in a locality in commodity group k. We assume a production relationship where required inputs in a firm depend on scale (e.g., input $= \alpha + SX^{-\delta}x$, where x is firm output and X industry input) and all firms have the same technology. The scale economy parameter is δ. The transport-tariff parts of equation (9) represent a first-order expansion of $\ln(1 + \gamma t + T)$.

References

Carlton, D. 1985. "The Location and Employment of New Firms." *Review of Economics and Statistics* 65:440–449.

Dixit, A., and J. Stiglitz 1977. "Monopolistic Competition and Optimum Product Variety." *American Economic Review.* 67:297–308.

Henderson, J. V. 1988. *Urban Development: Theory, Fact and Illusion.* Oxford: Oxford University Press.

Henderson, J. V. 1993. "Where Does an Industry Locate?" *Journal of Urban Economics,* forthcoming.

INFORUM 1990. *Industrial Effects of a Free Trade Agreement Between Mexico and the USA.* Washington D.C.: Department of Labor.

International Trade Commission. 1990a. *Review of Trade and Investment Liberalization Measures by Mexico and Prospects for Future U.S.-Mexico Relations: Phase 1.* USITC Publication 2275.

International Trade Commission. 1990b. *Review of Trade and Investment Liberalization Measures by Mexico and Prospects for Future U.S.-Mexico Relations: Phase 2.* USITC Publication 2326.

International Trade Commission. 1989. *Production Sharing: U.S. Imports Under Harmonized Tariff Schedule Subheadings 9802.00.60 and 9802.00.80, 1985–1988.* USITC Publication 2243.

Krugman, P. 1981. "Intra-industry Specialization and Gains from Trade." *Journal of Political Economy* 89:959–973.

Lee, K. S. 1989. *The Location of Jobs in Development Metropolis: Patterns of Growth in Bogota and Cali.* Oxford: Oxford University Press.

Mehl, G. M. et al. 1991. *US Exports to Mexico: A State by State Overview, 1987–1989.* Washington, D.C.: U.S. Department of Commerce, ITC.

5 Mexico-U.S. Free Trade and the Location of Production

Paul Krugman and
Gordon Hanson

Economists normally approach issues of economic integration in general, and the move toward a North American Free Trade Area in particular, from the perspective of international trade theory. From that perspective, the effects of trade liberalization are most naturally thought of and described in terms of changes in national patterns of specialization, driven by comparative advantage and perhaps by the desire of firms to exploit economies of scale.

There is, however, another perspective from which to view the same issue: that of location theory. To the location theorist, the issue is not how countries will specialize, but where production will locate. In principle, of course, these are different ways of asking the same question, and should lead to the same answers; ideally, location theory and trade theory (as well as urban economics and regional science) would be seen as part of a unified theory of economic geography. Despite pleas for such a unified theory both traditional (Isard 1956) and modern (Krugman 1991c), however, the locational perspective tends to emphasize very different factors from those emphasized in conventional trade analysis. In location theory one tends to focus much more on the role of increasing returns and access to markets than is the case even in the "new" trade theory; the effects of factor mobility become central to the analysis; and the location of production *within* countries becomes as much a subject of interest as the division of production *between* countries.

Arguably the history of trade policy in North America—or at least of the intellectual rationales offered for trade policy—is better told in terms of location theory than in terms of trade theory. In the nineteenth century Canadians feared that the head start and sheer gravitational attraction of the huge U.S. manufacturing belt would, in the absence of protection, condemn Canada to a permanent status as part of the North American farm belt. In the twentieth century Mexico undertook import-substitution policies in an effort to free itself from what it saw as a colonial relationship to the U.S. economy. Whether these policies were right or wrong in their time, they are best described in spatial terms—as efforts by the neighbors of the United States to de-link themselves so as to avoid becoming peripheries to the U.S. core. The policies of protection in each case gave rise to a new, internal core-periphery pattern—centered on Ontario in the north, on Mexico City in the south—and a key issue in the political economy of NAFTA is the likely impact of regional integration on the location of production within each country.

In several recent papers one of us (Krugman 1991a, 1991b, 1991c) has attempted to build a bridge between the "new trade theory," which emphasizes the role of imperfect competition and economies of scale, and location theory. This chapter represents an effort to apply that style of thinking to the effects of U.S.-Mexican free trade on the location of production at two levels: the distribution of manufacturing between the two countries, and the location of production inside Mexico.

The chapter is divided into three main parts. The first section is primarily conceptual rather than empirical, arguing that when a small economy liberalizes trade with a much larger neighbor, issues of market access are likely to play as important a role as comparative advantage in determining the effect on production. The second section provides a partial and first-cut quantitative assessment of the effects of Mexico-U.S. free trade on the Mexican manufacturing sector. The third section then turns to some evidence on the effects of trade policy on the internal geography of Mexican manufacturing.

1 Market Access and Mexican Manufacturing: Theoretical Considerations

1.1 General Considerations

Mexico has traditionally been a net importer of manufactures from the United States. Large and indeed growing manufactures deficits in its bilateral trade continued until the onset of the debt crisis in 1982. That crisis forced Mexico to run large surpluses on its noninvestment account to secure the foreign exchange needed for debt service; the subsequent collapse of oil prices meant that large deficits in manufactures were no longer sustainable. Devaluation of the peso and harsh contraction of domestic demand were therefore used to achieve large surpluses in overall trade in

Table 5.1
Mexico-U.S. trade, 1988 ($1,000)

		Mexican exports	Mexican imports	Mexican tariff	U.S. tariff
20/21	Food, bev, tobac	2063214	1787937	14.1	10.5
22	Textiles	147620	335689	14.7	10.7
23	Apparel	460830	267042	20	18.7
24	Lumber and wood	153943	141554	13.5	2.6
25	Furniture	441789	235107	19.2	3.2
26	Paper/pulp	301612	696338	5.3	4.5
28	Chemicals	664892	1472489	13.4	6.8
30	Rubber, plastics	93430	261943	17	7.5
31	Leather	161554	160216	16.8	8.9
32	Stone, clay, glass	341890	100256	14.3	13
33	Primary metal prod	877263	731379	8.1	3.8
34	Fabric metal prod	323187	349507	15	4.4
35	Nonelectric machine	2266092	2943894	15.6	3.2
36	Electrical machine	5007714	3379570	17.4	4.7
37	Transport equip	1906567	1722666	14.3	2.7

Sources: OECD, *Foreign Trade by Commodities 1989*, Paris, OECD, 1990. United Nations, *International Trade Statistics Yearbook 1989*, New York: United Nations. Unpublished data from Secretaria de Comercio y Fomento Industrial (SECOFI).

spite of low oil exports. Nonetheless, even in the late 1980s Mexico ran only roughly balanced trade in manufactures.

Furthermore, this rough balance was achieved only through considerable protectionism. Table 5.1 summarizes U.S.-Mexican manufactures trade and tariff rates in 1988. By that time Mexico had already engaged in a historic liberalization of trade, scrapping most quantitative restrictions and taking a giant step toward free trade. Nonetheless, Mexican tariffs remained well above U.S. levels: whether the rates are weighted by Mexican or U.S. exports, the Mexican average was nearly three times as high as that of the United States.

To a conventional trade analyst, it would seem immediately clear that Mexico in general has a comparative disadvantage in manufactures, and should expect some deindustrialization as a result of NAFTA. Free trade with the United States would involve a much greater liberalization on Mexico's part than on the part of the United States, and thus on the whole one would expect a contraction of the Mexican manufacturing sector as a result—especially if the financial contraints that have forced Mexico to run trade surpluses were to be relaxed.

To a location theorist, however, the result is not nearly this obvious. The reason is that location theory emphasizes not only comparative costs, but also access to markets as determinants of location decisions. Trade liberalization between the United States and Mexico gives producers in each location better access to the other market. The value of such improved access is, however, far greater for a Mexican producer than a U.S. producer, because the U.S. market is so much larger. Indeed, in 1988 Mexican demand for manufactures was only 2.1% as large as that of the United States.

When the disparity in market size is this great, U.S. barriers to Mexican exports have much more impact than seemingly comparable Mexican barriers. Consider the following example. Imagine a product subject to sufficient economies of scale that it is normally worth concentrating production for the whole North American market in only one location. Suppose also that Mexico is the low-cost location—say, average production plus transportation costs for an optimum-size plant are $9 per unit if the plant is located in Mexico, versus $10 per unit if it is in the United States. Thus under free trade this would be a Mexican export.

Now suppose that Mexico and the United States both impose tariffs on this good. What happens if they impose the same tariff rate, say $1.50? The answer is that the location of production shifts to the United States. A Mexican plant would have to ship the bulk of its output to the United States, and would therefore incur the tariff on most units; a U.S. plant would have to ship relatively few units to Mexico, and would therefore incur little tariff. Thus an equal tariff rate would in effect bias the location of production toward the United States. Indeed, tariff barriers would still bias location toward the United States even if the Mexican rate were considerably higher—if demand were totally inelastic, with fifty-to-one disparity in market size Mexico would have to impose a $25 tariff in this example to make a Mexican location preferable to a U.S. site.

If tariffs are sufficiently high, of course, the assumption that this good is produced in only a single location needs to be reconsidered. At very high tariff rates, it will be worthwhile establishing a plant of inefficient scale to serve the Mexican market. As pointed out by Krugman and Venables (1990), this suggests that there should be a U-shaped relationship between the degree of integration and the output of manufacturing in peripheral regions. If barriers to trade are high, peripheral regions will be largely self-sufficient; if they are moderate, economies of scale will lead to concentration of production in the core; when barriers fall further, it finally becomes worthwhile to produce in the low-cost periphery to serve the core market.

We will return to the potential applicability of this discussion to the Mexican case later in this section. First, however, we turn to some simulation exercises. The concepts discussed above, though simple, are unfamiliar to most international economists, and often seem inconsistent with general equilibrium. They are not; but to show this it is useful to digress briefly into a formal model and produce some suggestive simulations.

1.2 Market Access and Manufacturing: Simulation Results from a Hypothetical Model

To think about the effects of North American trade liberalization on the location of production, we imagine a simplified model in which there are are only two countries and two sectors. One sector, primary production, is perfectly competitive and subject to diminishing returns. The other, manufacturing, is imperfectly competitive and subject to increasing returns. One of the countries has a much larger domestic market than the other. We suppose that both countries impose tariffs on manufactured imports; our question is how these tariffs affect the location of manufacturing production.

The equations of the model are given in the appendix; here we describe the structure briefly. There are two resources: land, which is used only in primary production, and labor, which is used in both primary and manufacturing production. The fixed supply of land gives rise to diminishing returns to labor in the primary sector.

Manufactures consists of a large number of differentiated products, not all of which will actually be produced. There are economies of scale in the production of each variety, leading to a monopolistically competitive market structure.

Each of the countries imposes ad valorem tariffs on imports of manufactures, while leaving trade in primary products free.[1] These tariffs cause consumers to shift expenditure from imported to domestic goods. They also generate revenue, which is assumed to be redistributed to consumers in each country.

Although the model is conceptually simple, it is a little too complicated to be analyzed completely with pencil and paper. Thus we must turn to simulations—which is a useful approach in any case, since we are interested in getting an idea about the likely importance of market size effects in practice.

Our base case involves two countries that have identical resource mixes —that is, where there is no comparative advantage in the usual sense, and all interindustry specialization arises from market access effects. This assumption obviously begs the question of why Mexico is so poor—it has one-third the U.S. population and probably one-quarter the U.S. potential labor force, yet has a far smaller domestic market than these numbers would suggest. We simply wave our hands and suppose that Mexican productivity is less, so that the effective labor force may be regarded as much smaller. For the purposes of the simulations, we consider a country that trades with a neighbor that has thirty times its endowment of both labor and land.

In addition to making an assumption about resources, it is necessary to make assumptions about a number of the model's parameters. These assumptions are given in the appendix. One key assumption that should be noted, however, is the assumed elasticity of substitution among products in the manufactured sector. This elasticity plays a crucial and double role: it serves both as the determinant of the monopoly power of firms and as the key determinant of how much tariffs affect trade flows. Typical empirical estimates of the elasticity of substitution between products from different countries are quite low (see the next section), and would imply extremely high degrees of monopoly power; much theory in international economics assumes conversely that firms have little monopoly power, implying unreasonably high substitution internationally. In our model, at least, there is no natural way to bridge this gap. We therefore carry out our simulations under the assumption that the elasticity of substitution is 5—too high to be consistent with most empirical work on trade, but implying a quite high degree of monopoly power.

Given the assumptions of the model, then, we can carry out a series of thought experiments. First, we examine the effect of tariffs imposed at equal rates by the two countries an the output of the small country's manufacturing sector. Then we examine the effect of moving from a situation where the small country is more highly protectionist than the large to free trade.

Our discussion above suggests that (i) protection at equal rates should tend to shift manufacturing to the larger country, and (ii) at sufficiently high rates of protection the small country's production should rise, as it turns toward production for its own domestic market. These expectations are borne out by the model. We consider the effects of a variety of ad valorem tariffs applied at equal rates by the two countries; figure 5.1 shows the results. Imposition of tariffs in both direction makes the larger country a more attractive location to produce, and production of manufactured goods in the small country is eventually reduced to about 55% of its free trade level. As the tariff rate continues to rise, however, production in the smaller country recovers. This is the same U-shaped relationship

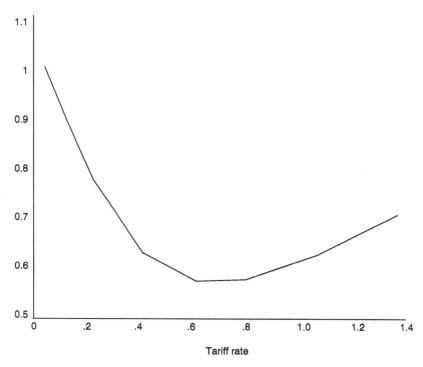

Figure 5.1
Small country manufacturing output

found in Krugman and Venables (1990); it suggests in general that closer integration has an ambiguous effect on the competitiveness of peripheral manufacturing.

Our second experiment asks a somewhat different question: given a tariff rate in the large country, how high a tariff rate in the small country is necessary to restore the free trade level of manufacturing output? Or, equivalently, what initial conditions of tariff rates are consistent with the expansion or contraction of manufacturing in the peripheral nation as a result of free trade?

Table 5.2 presents the results of a rough calculation. The first column presents a set of hypothetical tariff rates in the large country. The second column shows the approximate tariff rate needed by the small country to keep manufacturing output and employment at its free trade level. Thus suppose we observe an initial situation in which the large country's manufacturing is protected by a 10% tariff, while the small country's manufacturing is protected by an 80% tariff. One might suppose that in this case free

Table 5.2
Equal production tariffs

Large country	Small country
0	0
10	80
20	120
30	150
40	180

Source: Authors' calculations.

trade would have a devastating effect on the small country's manufacturing sector. Yet according to these estimates the small nation's manufactures output would not change. And if the small country initially had less protection—say 60%—free trade would actually cause its manufacturing to expand.

The potential implications of these results for Mexico are obvious. Mexico is more protectionist than the United States, but has a far smaller market. The model confirms the intuitive argument that in such a situation the gains from market access under free trade may outweigh the loss of protection, so that Mexico could actually expand its industrial output as a whole.

But are these potential implications likely to hold in practice?

1.3 Cautions Regarding the Market Access Argument

The stylized model described above and presented in full in the appendix suggests that market access should be extremely important as a determinant of specialization patterns between large and small countries, and that when the economic sizes are as different as they are is in the U.S.-Mexico case, the small country is likely to see its manufacturing expand after free trade even if it has much higher initial tariffs. Indeed, the numbers on U.S. and Mexican tariffs presented in table 5.1 would seem to place Mexico well within the range where free trade expands manufacturing.

This suggestion needs, however, to be treated with some caution, for three reasons. First, the stylized model neglects comparative advantage *within* the manufacturing sector. The representative manufactured good in the model is always cheaper to produce in the small country, and the only reason why more goods are not produced in the small country is the difference in market access. In reality, some Mexican protection is of goods in which Mexico has a straightforward, conventional comparative disadvantage; removing protection in such industries will lead to Mexican contraction regardless of any asymmetries in market access.

Second, the model neglects hindrances to market access other than tariffs —above all, natural barriers due to distance. This gives trade barriers huge locational significance, since in their absence every small-country plant would ship the great bulk of its output to the large country. In reality, transportation and transaction costs pose significant limitations to trade, and make the large-country/small-country distinction less relevant than it appears in the model.

Finally, whatever the effects of free trade on manufacturing in the aggregate, it is likely to have very uneven effects on different parts of the manufacturing sector. In part this is because there is comparative advantage within the manufacturing sector. It is also, however, because the same considerations of market access that apply across nations apply within Mexico—and free trade effectively turns the Mexican economy inside out, shifting it from a focus on an internal core to an outward orientation in a literal geographic sense. We will turn to some evidence on these shifts in the third section.

The immediate point, however, is that the simulation model, while suggestive, could be seriously misleading. We therefore turn next to an effort to put some empirical flesh on the theoretical skeleton by making some first-pass empirical estimates.

2 Free Trade and Mexican Manufacturing: Some Preliminary Results[2]

In principle it would be possible to devise a multisectoral version of the model described in the appendix, and to fit that model to Mexican and U.S. data. It would then be possible to derive general equilibrium estimates of the effects of free trade. We suspect that such estimates would be fairly unreliable, for reasons that will become clear shortly. In any case, however, we are not yet prepared for this exercise.

In this section we instead present a set of partial estimates. They are partial in two senses: they are partial equilibrium, and they do not allow for the free entry of firms that plays a significant role in the theoretical model in the appendix. We therefore regard the estimates as giving a sort of "impact" effect of free trade that may be a useful guide to the direction of final effects, without being complete.

2.1   The Model

We approach trade and output on an industry-by-industry basis. Within each industry we suppose that there are a large number of differentiated products, some produced in the United States, some in Mexico; we ignore third parties. Expenditure on the industry's goods is taken to be fixed within each country; this could almost be justified by assuming, as the appendix model does, that preferences are Cobb-Douglas at an upper level—although even under this assumption we are neglecting income effects. Given this maintained assumption, however, we then ask how these given expenditures are allocated between U.S. and Mexican products, to arrive at predicted trade flows and output in the industry.

We define the following variables for each industry (the industry subscript is suppressed to save notation):

p = f.o.b. price of a representative Mexican product

p^* = f.o.b. price of a representative U.S. product

n = the number of Mexican products

n^* = the number of U.S. products

τ = transportation/transaction cost (see below)

t = Mexican tariff rate

t^* = U.S. tariff rate

E = Mexican expenditures on the industry's products

E^* = U.S. expenditures on the industry's products

R = ratio of Mexican purchases of Mexican to U.S. goods

R^* = ratio of U.S. purchases of Mexican to U.S. goods

S = total Mexican sales

S^* = total U.S. sales

The f.o.b. prices p and p^* are the prices charged before transportation costs and tariffs. Their effects are, as will be apparent in a moment, confounded with those of the numbers of products n and n^*; for our purposes it is unnecessary to disentangle these variables. For simplicity we will therefore adopt the normalization $p = p^* = 1$.

Given this normalization, in the absence of any obstacles to trade, spending on each country's goods would simply be proportional to the number of goods it produces. We suppose, however, that there are two sorts of barriers to trade. First, there are the natural barriers caused by

transportation and transaction costs. Following the same problematic sim-
plification used in the appendix, these costs are assumed to be incurred in
the goods shipped: a total of $1 + \tau$ units of each industry's output must be
shipped for one unit to arrive. Second, there are the tariffs. These combine
to make imports more expensive than domestic goods. A Mexican, for
example, will pay a (normalized) price of 1 for a domestic good, a price of
$(1 + t)(1 + \tau)$ for a U.S. good.

We assume a constant elasticity of substitution a between any pair of
goods within an industry. Given this assumption, a Mexican resident will
consume $[(1 + \tau)(1 + t)]^{-\sigma}$ times as much of a representative Mexican
good as she will of a representative U.S. good. Taking into account valua-
tion effects, the ratio of Mexican spending on domestic to that on U.S.
goods is

$$R = \frac{n}{n^*}[(1 + \tau)(1 + t)]^{\sigma-1} \tag{1}$$

and the ratio of U.S. spending on Mexican goods to that on Mexican
goods is

$$R^* = \frac{n}{n^*}[(1 + \tau)(1 + t^*)]^{-(\sigma-1)}. \tag{2}$$

Equations (1) and (2) contain a mix of observable and unobservable variables. The spending ratios R and R^* can be calculated directly from imports
net of tariff and from apparent domestic consumption of domestic output
(sales less exports). The tariff rates are also directly observable. However,
neither the ratio n/n^* nor the transport cost τ are directly observable;
indeed, both should be viewed almost as metaphors rather than as concrete
variables.

It is possible, however, to extract considerable information from the
equations nonetheless. First, a measure of τ can be computed directly:

$$\frac{R}{R^*} = [(1 + \tau)^2(1 + t)(1 + t^*)]^{\sigma-1}, \tag{3}$$

from which τ can be calculated by

$$\tau = \left[\frac{R}{R^*}[(1 + t)(1 + t^*)]^{-(\sigma-1)} \right]^{1/(2(\sigma-1))} - 1. \tag{4}$$

The estimate of τ is of interest as a measure of the extent of natural (or at
any rate nontariff) segmentation of markets, which as we will see appears

to be considerable. It is also possible to bypass this measure and go directly to an estimate of the impact of free trade on industry output. To do this, we hold n/n^* constant. Then the R, R^* that result after free trade are simply

$$\hat{R} = R((1 + t)^{-(\sigma-1)} \tag{5}$$

$$\hat{R}^* = R^*(1 + t^*)^{\sigma-1}. \tag{6}$$

The total value of Mexican industry sales after free trade is the sum of the Mexican share of Mexican spending and the Mexican share of U.S. spending. This value may be calculated as

$$\hat{S} = E\frac{\hat{R}}{1 + \hat{R}} + E^*\frac{\hat{R}^*}{1 + \hat{R}^*}. \tag{7}$$

This predicted value of sales can be compared with the actual value of sales to derive the predicted change in output.

2.2 Quantitative Results

We used two-digit level data on Mexican and U.S. manufacturing. This involved some compromises and guesswork, because the trade and output numbers were classified under somewhat different schemes. Table 5.3 shows the basic data that we constructed. In the two cases of paper and pulp (industry 26/7) and electrical machinery (industry 36) our procedures led to estimates that the share of imports from the United States in Mexican domestic consumption exceeds one. This shows the roughness of our numbers. In each of these cases we simply assumed that all Mexican production is for export, ignoring the role of domestic demand. In a way, however, this makes a point: in several sectors U.S. production has a large, even dominant share of the Mexican market, while Mexican output is a minor share of all U.S. markets. Thus some of the increase in U.S. exports that results from free trade does not effectively compete with Mexican production.

To go from this data to estimates of the impact of free trade, it is necessary to have estimates of the industry-specific elasticity of substitution. There have been many surveys of estimates of such elasticities. As we discussed above, we regard such estimates, drawn from time series behavior, as problematically low. To deal with this, we made two different estimates: one using a set of elasticities given by Brown, Deardorff, and Stern (1991), and one assuming a uniform elasticity of substitution of 5.

Table 5.3
Domestic demand ($ million) and market shares

		Mexico domestic consump.	U.S. domestic consump.	U.S. share of Mexican market	Mexican share of U.S. market
20/21	Food, bev, tobac	11768	305412	0.152	0.007
22	Textiles	2487	54322	0.135	0.003
23	Apparel	1601	73154	0.167	0.007
24	Lumber and wood	694	60741	0.203	0.003
25	Furniture	953	36502	0.247	0.012
26	Paper/pulp	640	226749	1.087	0.001
28	Chemicals	5363	208037	0.275	0.003
30	Rubber, plastics	2048	80667	0.128	0.001
31	Leather	1005	13769	0.159	0.012
32	Stone, clay, glass	2845	137886	0.035	0.006
33	Primary metal product	2800	59147	0.261	0.006
34	Fabric metal product	1777	137886	0.196	0.002
35	Nonelectric machine	4101	207229	0.718	0.011
36	Electrical machine	3113	178664	1.086	0.028
37	Transport equip	2597	324950	0.663	0.006

Sources: OECD, *Foreign Trade by Commodities 1989*, Paris, OECD, 1990. United Nations, *International Trade Statistics Yearbook 1989*, New York: United Nations. United Nations, *Industrial Statistics Yearbook 1989, Vol. 1*, New York: United Nations, 1991. Nacional Financiea, *La Economia Mexicana en Cifras 1990*, Mexico City: Nacional Financiera, 1990.

Tables 5.4 and 5.5 report the results of free trade under these alternative assumptions. Two numbers are reported, for each industry and for all manufacturing: the percentage change in output and the absolute change in the trade balance, in thousands of dollars.

It turns out that qualitatively the two alternate sets of estimates are similar. In both cases the prediction is that free trade leads to a small decline in the Mexican trade balance in manufacturing—6.5% of the initial value of exports in the first case, 5% in the second—but a small *rise* in Mexican manufacturing output.

The rise in manufacturing output in spite of a negative movement in the trade balance is essentially a fiscal impact. That is, Mexican and U.S. tariffs act jointly as a tax on manufacturing in general; thus free trade has an expansionary effect that outweighs the small trade balance deterioration.

These results are not as striking as the numerical example might have suggested. We will turn to one reason why in a moment. But they do show that even on this first-pass estimate, the difference in market size is sufficient to wash out most of the adverse impact on Mexican manufacturing that a simple comparison of tariff rates might have led us to expect.

Table 5.4
Estimated impacts of free trade (survey elasticities)

		Percentage change in production	Change in trade balance ($1,000)
20/21	Food, bev, tobac	1.8	−35666
22	Textiles	0.6	−36477
23	Apparel	18.7	250617
24	Lumber and wood	−0.7	−25188
25	Furniture	−2.3	−85062
26	Paper/pulp	9.7	−12975
28	Chemicals	−2.1	−327966
30	Rubber, plastics	−9.1	−252968
31	Leather	0.9	−20654
32	Stone, clay, glass	3.7	94705
33	Primary metal prod	1.1	−30641
34	Fabric metal prod	−3.6	−132495
35	Nonelectric machine	1.9	−393313
36	Electric machine	11.4	−34812
37	Transport equip	0.1	−271371
	All manufactures	2.2	−1314271

Source: Authors' calculations.

Table 5.5
Estimated impacts of free trade (elasticity = 5)

		Percentage change in production	Change in trade balance ($1,000)
20/21	Food, bev, tobac	3.1	−14938
22	Textiles	−4.2	−173474
23	Apparel	23.2	321849
24	Lumber and wood	−6.3	−72454
25	Furniture	−6.1	−142521
26	Paper/pulp	34.6	48927
28	Chemicals	−7.3	−610579
30	Rubber, plastics	−7.4	−213990
31	Leather	−1.8	−61325
32	Stone, clay, glass	7.1	195154
33	Primary metal prod	−0.1	−75400
34	Fabric metal prod	−6.1	−185758
35	Nonelectric machine	−0.1	−559121
36	Electric machine	29.2	823826
37	Transport equip	−0.4	−295295
	All manufactures	3.7	−1015102

Source: Authors' calculations.

2.3 Segmentation of Markets

One important reason why the quantitative results do not look as striking as the theoretical model is that there appears to be substantial geographical segmentation of the North American manufacturing sector that goes beyond tariffs. This may be seen from the comparative market shares in table 5.3. In a fully integrated market, the Mexican share of the Mexican market would be the same as its share of the U.S. market—which is to say, a very small number. This is in fact the case for pulp/paper and electrical machinery. In other sectors, however, Mexican producers have a significant and indeed in most cases a majority share of the domestic market. Some disparity in market shares can be explained by the existing tariffs, some by quantitative restrictions that we have ignored. There is also, in practice, a significant overhang from past protection. Beyond these, however, are significant costs of transportation and large invisible transaction costs related to distance.

The important point about these transportation/transaction costs is that they reduce the importance of the relative size of markets. In the absence of transport/transaction costs, a Mexican firm that gains access to the U.S. market would in effect multiply its customer base by a factor of 50, while a U.S. firm gaining access to Mexico would gain only 2%. If distance effects imply that most U.S. consumers would continue to rely on domestic products, however, the advantage of greater legal access to the Mexican plant is much less, while the U.S.-based producer in effect has less to lose. This is captured crudely by the algebra of our calculations, and we would not argue that we have accurately represented what will happen. It is true, however, that free trade is worth less to Mexican production because distance remains as a significant barrier to trade.

3 Location inside Mexico

As noted above, from a locational point of view trade liberalization effectively turns the Mexican economy inside out. Under the import substitution regime, Mexico developed a strong core-periphery pattern centered around Mexico City. This was a natural development as long as industry was largely aimed at the domestic market. Once trade is liberalized, however, and industry is aimed at the North American market, the forward and backward linkages that have created and sustained the Mexico City core become relatively unimportant; and the new industrial areas in the north of Mexico become advantageous not only because they avoid some of the capital's congestion, but because they are closer to the now dominant U.S. market. A process of dissolution of Mexico's internal core-periphery pattern began during the 1980s, and will almost surely accelerate following free trade.

3.1 Import Substitution and the Mexican Core-Periphery Pattern

The logic of the formation of core-periphery patterns is circular; it is a natural extension of the logic of market access described in section 1, with the additional point that when factors are geographically mobile, the location of markets depends on the location of production as well as vice versa.

Imagine that there are two possible locations of production, each of which is also a center of demand, and that economies of scale for some manufactured good are sufficiently important that even given transportation costs it is cheaper to produce that good in only one of the two locations. Suppose also, however, that costs of transportation are significant, and that if a plant is placed in one location it must incur these costs in order to serve the market at the other. Then, other things equal, it will be preferable to place the plant at the location with larger local demand, so as to minimize the required transportation—just as in our tariff example, tariff barriers make a U.S. location, with its better access to the bulk of the North American market, preferred to a Mexican site.

But within a country the location of factors of production including labor, and hence of demand, is endogenous—and depends on the location choices of firms. Firms will tend to locate where local demand is large; but local demand will be large precisely where large numbers of firms choose to locate. Thus there is a basic circularity, in which a site that gets a head start for whatever reason tends to attract footloose industry in a snowballing process of growth.

This circularity via "backward linkages" is reinforced by "forward linkages" via the supply of intermediate goods, which add to the pull of an established economic core.

The process of core-periphery formation depends on three factors (see Krugman 1991b for a formal general-equilibrium treatment). First, non-agricultural tradeable production—traditionally manufacturing, although some services also fit the bill—must be sufficiently large as a share of the economy to get the process going. Second, transportation costs must be low enough to permit production to serve a national market. Third, economies of scale must be large enough relative to the size of the market to

Table 5.6
Mexico City share of manufacturing employment (percent)

1930	19
1940	24.6
1950	25
1960	46
1970	41.9

Source: Gustavo Ganza, *El Proceso de Industrializacion en la Ciudad de Mexico*. Mexico City: El Colegio de Mexico, 1985.

make it worthwhile to serve the national market from centralized production facilities.

In the case of the United States, a strong core-periphery process, the differentiation of the country into a "manufacturing belt" and a "farm belt", occurred in the nineteenth century, as industrialization, railroads, and the rise of mass production provided the three necessary conditions. In the second half of the twentieth century that pattern has eroded, perhaps in part because the continuing growth of the economy has made economies of scale less important relative to market size.

Mexico showed little sign of a core-periphery pattern before the beginning of import-substitution policies. Most manufacturing was resource-based, and as late as 1930 the Mexico City area accounted for only 19% of manufacturing employment. As table 5.6 shows, however, over the next thirty years the great bulk of manufacturing employment growth was concentrated in Mexico City.

The maquila program provided some incentive for export-oriented manufacturing in the border area during the 1970s. Growing congestion also provided some incentive for decentralization of industries aimed at the domestic market, such as the apparel sector. Nonetheless, as late as 1980 the core-periphery pattern of Mexican manufacturing remained overwhelming, with Mexico City and environs accounting for 42% of employment and a higher share of value-added.

Since 1980, however, there has been a dramatic relocation of industry. Manufacturing employment in Mexico City and environs, battered both by economic slump and by competition from imports under increasingly liberal trade, fell almost 14% between 1980 and 1988. Meanwhile, employment in the five border states rose 149%. The extent of the unravelling of Mexico City's dominance is documented in table 5.7.

This relocation can be viewed as a natural consequence of an outward-looking trade policy. Mexico City is a crowded and expensive location

Table 5.7
Spectoral employment and regional shares: Mexico City and the five border states, 1980 and 1988

	National	1980 Mex. City	Border	National	1988 Mex. City	Border
Manufact.	2,247,620	950,595	205,378	2,484,377	820,318	511,199
		0.4299	0.0914		0.3302	0.2058
Consumer	1,099,968	392,515	122,615	1,179,662	366,202	164,621
goods		0.3568	0.1115		0.3104	0.1395
Capital	664,362	343,173	40,343	744,524	245,151	271,370
durable goods		0.5165	0.0607		0.3293	0.3645
(Maquiladora production is subsumed within the three sectors above)						
Maquiladora	119,546	N/A	106,290	369,489	N/A	298,863
			0.8891			0.8089

	1980	1988	Change
Share of border employment in maquila	0.5175	0.5309	
Border employment 1988/border employment 1980			2.489
Share of border employment increase due to maquila employment growth			0.6297

Sources: Instituto Nacional de Estadistica, Geografia e Informacion (INEGI), *XI Censo Industrial*. Mexico City: INEGI, 1981. INEGI, *Resultados Oportunos*, Aguascalientes: Ags: INEGI, 1989. INEGI, *Industria Maquiladora de Exportacion 1981–1988*. Aguascalientes, Ags: INEGI, 1989.

for production, able to hold marginal producers only through its central market position. With increased reliance on external rather than domestic markets, this centrality is greatly reduced. Furthermore, in the geography of an integrated North American market, plants in the border area actually have better access to the relevant market.

As table 5.7 shows, in 1988 maquila employment still accounted for more than half of the manufacturing jobs in the border area, and this share actually increased slightly during the period 1980–88. The growth of manufacturing in the north is almost surely not, however, essentially driven by the special maquila incentives. For one thing, these incentives have become increasingly less valuable as Mexican trade is liberalized. Further-more, anecdotal evidence suggests that the most recent growth, especially of foreign direct investment, is not in maquilas or in the narrow border area but in cities located some distance behind the border. We would argue that the shift of manufacturing to the north, while it has taken advantage of special privileges offered by the government, would have taken place in any case as a result of the opening of the Mexican economy.

The crucial point is that it is a process that will continue. The opening of the Mexican economy has reduced the gravitational attraction of Mexico City, and already led to a major shift of economic activity outward. Free trade will reinforce this shift. As industry locates away from Mexico City, however, this will further reduce the core's economic pull, leading to a further outward shift. That is, the decline of the Mexican core-periphery pattern is likely to be a cumulative process that will gather strength over time.

Ideally we would like to model this process quantitatively. We are not yet in a position to do so; but this will be a priority for future research.

4 Summary and Conclusions

This paper has offered a prelimary look at Mexico-U.S. free trade from a locational perspective. It presents three different pieces of the puzzle, linked by a common focus on the issue of market access given an enormous disparity in the sizes of the two countries' domestic markets for manufactured goods.

The first section offered a theoretical justification, backed by suggestive simulations, for supposing that free trade might actually lead to an expansion of Mexican manufacturing. This is true even though Mexico has traditionally been a net importer of manufactured goods from the United States, and is much more protectionist. The reason is that access to the U.S. market is much more valuable than access to the Mexican market, and free trade may therefore increase the relative attractiveness of Mexican production locations.

The second section made a preliminary effort to quantify the effects of free trade. The results do suggest that relative market size matters. Mexico's trade deficit in manufactures does, according to these calculations, widen slightly as a result of free trade; but the output of Mexican manufacturing expands nonetheless. This effort helps to suggest some quantitative dimensions of the real problem.

Finally, the third section draws attention to perhaps the most interesting locational issue, that of the geography of production within Mexico itself. It offers a theoretical argument and suggestive evidence that trade liberalization is leading to a dissolution of the core-periphery pattern that emerged under Mexico's import-substitution regime.

This work obviously needs to be extended. We hope, however, that it is suggestive and helps make the case that a locational approach is useful in thinking about the impacts of North American free trade.

Appendix: A Model of Trade and Protection

This chapter emphasizes the effects of tariffs on the pattern of industrial location via market access considerations. This is an unfamiliar concept to most international economists, and often seems inconsistent with general equilibrium. To show that such effects can be important, and that they are consistent with general equilibrium, this appendix lays out a simple, suggestive computable model.

We consider a world of two countries, Mexico and the United States. Both countries have the same tastes and technologies, but they differ in their resource endowments: Mexico is smaller, and may have a higher land-labor ratio. In the equations that follow, an asterisk indicates that a variable refers to the United States; where equations are identical or symmetric for the two countries, only the Mexican equation is presented.

In both countries, consumers derive utility from consumption of a manufactures aggregate and from agricultural goods. We assume a Cobb-Douglas form for demand:

$$U = C_M^\mu C_A^{1-\mu}, \tag{1}$$

where μ is the share of manufactured goods in expenditure. Following Dixit and Stiglitz (1977), the manufactures aggregate C_M is in turn a CES function of consumption of a large number of individual manufactured goods, not all of which will actually be produced

$$C_M = [\textstyle\sum_i C_i^{\sigma-1/(\sigma)}]^{\sigma/(\sigma-1)}. \tag{2}$$

Output of agricultural goods is a Cobb-Douglas function of labor and land input:

$$Q_A = L_A^\gamma T^{1-\gamma}. \tag{3}$$

Manufactured goods are produced with labor only. For any good that is actually produced, there is a fixed cost, with additional labor proportional to output:

$$L_{Mi} = \alpha + \beta q_{Mi}. \tag{4}$$

Finally, there is full employment, with labor mobile between agriculture and manufacturing:

$$\textstyle\sum_i L_{Mi} + L_A = L_M + L_A = L. \tag{5}$$

The properties of the Dixit-Stiglitz model are by now well known. Provided that a large number of goods are produced, each will be produced by a single firm facing a perceived elasticity of demand σ. This implies a profit-maximizing price that is a markup on the wage rate w:

$$P_M = \frac{\sigma}{\sigma - 1} \beta w. \tag{6}$$

This pricing rule, together with free entry, imply a determinate size of the output of a representative firm:

$$q_M = \frac{\alpha(\sigma - 1)}{\beta}. \tag{7}$$

And the number of manufactured products is therefore proportional to employment in the manufacturing sector:

We also note that in the agricultural sector, there is a

$$n = \frac{L_M}{\alpha + \beta q_M} \tag{8}$$

downward-sloping demand curve for labor. Let us measure w in terms of the agricultural good; then the demand curve takes the form

$$L_A = \kappa T w^{-1/(1-\gamma)}, \tag{9}$$

where κ is a constant term, and output of agricultural goods—which is equal to income earned in the agricultural sector—takes the form

$$Y_A = \kappa' T w^{-\gamma/(1-\gamma)}. \tag{10}$$

We now suppose that Mexico trades with a second country, the United States. The United States is described by a similar set of equations; indeed, it differs only in its resource endowments T^* and L^*. We assume, however, that the United States and Mexico are divided by tariff barriers. Specifically, each of them imposes an ad valorem tariff against the other's manufactured goods at the rates τ and τ^* respectively. We assume that trade in agricultural products is free.

The basic procedure for analyzing this type of model was laid out in Krugman (1980). We first compare the expenditure of residents of each country on representative manufactured goods from each country. Consider, for example, a Mexican resident. For her, the price of a U.S. manufactured good relative to a local product depends both on the ratio of f.o.b. prices—which is the same as the ratio of wage rates—and on the tariff rate. She also faces an elasticity of substitution a between any pair of manufactured goods. So her consumption of a representative imported good will be $[(w^*/w)(1 + \tau)]^{-\sigma}$ times her consumption of a representative

Mexican good. To calculate relative expenditure, we multiply relative consumption by relative prices, and find that Mexican expenditure per U.S. good will be ρ times Mexican expenditure per Mexican product, where

$$\rho = \left[\frac{w}{w^*(1 + \tau)} \right]^{\sigma-1}. \tag{11}$$

The corresponding ratio for U.S. residents is

$$\rho^* = \left[\frac{w^*}{w(1 + \tau^*)} \right]^{\sigma-1}. \tag{12}$$

The total income earned in Mexican manufacturing is the sum of expenditure by Mexican residents on Mexican goods, plus expenditure by U.S. residents on Mexican goods, less that part of the U.S. expenditure that represents tariff revenues to U.S. customs. After some rearrangement, we find that

$$Y_M = \mu \frac{n}{n + \rho n^*} Y + \mu \frac{1}{1 + \tau^*} \frac{n\rho^*}{n\rho^* + n^*} Y^*, \tag{13}$$

where Y, Y^* are Mexican and U.S. national income, respectively.

Mexcian national income is the sum of three components: income earned in the agricultural sector, income earned in manufacturing, and tariff revenue. Tariff revenue may be calculated as

$$Y_R = \frac{\tau}{1 + \tau} \frac{\rho n^*}{n + \rho n^*} Y, \tag{14}$$

and national income is simply

$$Y = Y_A + Y_M + Y_R. \tag{15}$$

We may note finally that the demand for labor in the manufacturing sector is

$$L_M = \frac{Y_M}{w}. \tag{16}$$

This model, although conceptually simple, is too complex in detail to yield easily to analytical methods. It is, however, easy to solve numerically; and numerical examples are sufficient to make the point that a move from protection to free trade may well cause trade to move in the opposite direction from that suggested by revealed comparative advantage.

To solve the model, we start with a guess at the wage rates w and w^*, measured in terms of agricultural output. We then use the demand for labor in agriculture (10) together with the full-employment condition (5) to derive the sectoral allocation of labor; (8) to derive the number of manufactured goods produced in each country; and (13), (14), and (15) iteratively to derive national income and income in manufacturing. When this process converges, we can use (16) and (10) to get an estimate of the demand for labor in both manufacturing and agriculture in each country, and hence of the excess demand for labor in each. We can therefore use these excess demands to make a new guess at equilibrium wage rates, either by Newton's method or (the approach used here) simply by gradually adjusting each wage in proportion to that country's excess labor demand. When both labor markets clear, we have found the model's general equilibrium.

In the calculations described in the text, certain assumptions were maintained:

(i) The ratio of U.S. to Mexican land, T^*/T, was assumed to be 30; the ratio of U.S. to Mexican labor was also assumed to be 30. Units were chosen so that the free trade equilibrium wage was 1.

(ii) The labor share in agriculture was set at 0.5.

(iii) The share of manufactures in expenditure was set at 0.5.

Under these common assumptions, figure 5.1 was constructed by setting $\tau = \tau^*$ and varying τ; table 5.2 was constructed by choosing values of τ^* and searching for the value of τ that restored the free trade level of manufacturing output.

Notes

1. This is, of course, not a very realistic way to model protection. In particular, qantitative restrictions play a key role in practice. It is very difficult, however, to consider anything other than ad valorem tariffs, for technical reasons.

2. There have been a number of carefuL efforts to model the effects of free trade in North America; Brown (1992) offers an excellent survey of these efforts. We use our own approach in order to focus more directly on the market access issue. It is reassuring, however, to note that in a rough way our results seem to accord with those of other models. In particular, the distribution of size changes across Mexican industries is not too different from that in Brown et al. (1991).

References

Brown, D. 1992. "The Impact of North American Free Trade Area: Applied General Equilibrium Models." Presented at Brookings Conference on NAFTA, April, 1992.

Brown, D., Deardorff, A., and Stern, R. 1991. "Some Estimates of a North American Trade Agreement." University of Michigan Discussion Paper No. 288.

Dixit, A., and Stiglitz, J. 1977. "Monopolistic Competition and Optimum Product Diversity." *American Economic Review* 67 : 297−308.

Isard, W. 1956. *Location and Space-Economy*. Cambridge, MA: MIT Press.

Krugman, P.1980. "Scale Economies, Product Differentiation, and the Pattern of Trade." *American Economic Review* 70 : 950−959.

Krugman, P. 1991a. "History and Industry Location: the Case of the US Manufacturing Belt." *American Economic Review*, May.

Krugman, P. 1991b. "Increasing Returns and Economic Geography." *Journal of Political Economy*. June.

Krugman, P. 1991c. *Geography and Trade*. Cambridge, MA: MIT Press.

Krugman, P., and Venables, A. 1990. "Integration and the Competitiveness of Peripheral Industry," in C. Bliss and J. de Macedo, eds., *Unity with Diversity in the European Community*. Cambridge: Cambridge University Press.

III

Effects on Specific Industries

6

Trade with Mexico and Water Use in California Agriculture

Robert C. Feenstra and Andrew K. Rose

1 Introduction

Agriculture is an important part of global trade, constituting a tenth of all international trade flows. This is true despite the fact that historically, agriculture has been the most heavily distorted industry in the industrial countries. Pervasive and significant barriers to trade have been, and continue to be, exceedingly difficult to remove in agriculture, which remains the industry least susceptible to freer trade. The current Uruguay Round of GATT negotiations almost foundered in December 1990 on the issue of agricultural subsidies. To quote an even more relevant example for the case of the North American Free Trade Area (FTA), the U.S.-Canadian free trade agreement did not fully liberalize agricultural trade, instead leaving many barriers to agricultural trade unresolved.

In this chapter, we examine the effect of the proposed Mexico-U.S. FTA on agricultural trade with California, which, together with Florida, faces potentially significant competition from Mexico. Mexican imports compete with different crops in California and Florida, due to differences in growing seasons, and so separate analyses of the FTA in the two states would be required.[1] By focusing on California, we are able to combine our discussion of the U.S.-Mexico FTA with another important policy issue: water use in agriculture.

California is now at the end of its fifth consecutive year of drought; this crisis provides the impetus for a general rethinking of the system of water allocation. Water in the Western United States is inefficiently allocated for historical reasons. Freer trade in agriculture commodities may lead to large indirect costs as a result of these inefficiencies in the water market. Specifically, freer trade in agriculture encourages American producers to switch from horticultural crops where the United States has a comparative disadvantage to commodities such as rice, beef, and dairy goods, in which the United States has a comparative advantage. But without water reform, this switch could entail a substantial increase in agricultural water consumption; the indirect costs (to California industry and municipalities) of this switch are potentially large. Unless the system of water allocation is changed along with the system of trade barriers, the indirect costs of more inefficiently allocated water could outweigh the gains of more efficiently allocated agricultural resources. Freer markets in water can also be justified either as compensation to farmers facing adjustment costs while crops are changed during the transition to a FTA, or because subsidized agricultural water represents an unfair American producer subsidy.

Liberalizing trade with Mexico, but keeping current regulations in water use intact, should therefore be viewed as a "second-best" policy. We also consider the "first-best" policy of creating a market for water sales within California, while also liberalizing trade. Since the price for water now paid by some urban users (often over $200 per acre-foot) is much higher than that paid by agricultural users (usually less than $40 per acre-foot), it is sometimes feared that opening up a market for water would result in a large increase in the price paid (or received) by farmers. However, we argue that under a free market, the equilibrium price for water would probably be only a *modest* amount higher than current agricultural prices.[2] The reason is that the excess demand from urban users is very small compared to the current water use in crops such as pasture, alfalfa, rice, and cotton, and some of this land would be switched out of production after a small increase in the price of water. The welfare gains available from opening up a Western water market are potentially quite large. If the FTA negotiations provide any opportunity for water reform, we urge the American representatives to seize the opportunity.

In the next section we provide an overview of U.S. agricultural trade with Mexico. In section 3 we discuss the California crops that face potential import competition under the FTA, and in section 4 describe our methodology for estimating the impact of the FTA on California production. The resulting social efficiency gains, and implications for water use, are presented in section 5. Section 6 provides background material on water markets, while section 7 analyzes the effect of creating a free market for water sales in California. They are followed by a brief summary and conclusions.

2 Agricultural Trade

The total value of Mexican-American agricultural trade was approximately $5 billion in 1989 and has been growing steadily recently.[3] Much in line with global patterns, agricultural trade now constitutes around a tenth of all bilateral trade between two countries. In terms of bilateral trade volume, agriculture is comparable with energy and only superseded in importance by automotive products, machinery and equipment, and electronic equipment. The United States ran a bilateral agricultural trade surplus with Mexico of approximately $400 million; the United States has run a cumulative, though irregular, bilateral trade surplus in agriculture over the 1980s.

Mexico accounts for about a tenth of all American agricultural trade; Mexico is the second-largest exporter of agricultural goods to the United States (after Canada), and the third-largest market for American exports (after Japan and the former Soviet Union). The United States is overwhelmingly the most important export market for Mexican agriculture. About two-thirds of American agricultural exports to Mexico consist of grains and oilseeds. This sector is highly protected in Mexico; consequently, an FTA could lead to increases in American exports of grains and oilseeds (though these will likely be small relative to total American production). Mexico is also a major recipient of American livestock and fish products.[4]

Many Mexican agricultural exports to the United States do not compete with American production; examples include coffee, cocoa, and tropical fruit. The most important markets where Mexican imports compete directly with American production are horticultural.[5] Mexico is the largest exporter to the United States of horticultural products such as fresh and processed fruits and vegetables (Mexico is also the seventh-largest importer of American horticultural products). Over a third of American agricultural imports from Mexico are horticultural products, and the United States is a large net importer of horticultural goods from Mexico.[6] The USITC (1991, pp. xi–xii) states that "The elimination of tariffs and NTBs under an FTA would generate a significant increase in U.S. imports from Mexico and a moderate increase in U.S. exports to Mexico [of horticultural products] ... U.S. growers of these products are expected to experience losses in production, particularly growers in Florida. California and other warm-climate States who compete directly with products during the same growing seasons in Mexico." The USITC believes that of *all* American industries likely to be affected by the FTA (including manufacturing goods), horticulture is the industry likely to be most affected. Hufbauer et al. (1991) also argue that Mexican exports of fruits and vegetables should expand significantly.

Protectionism

A variety of American trade barriers affect potential Mexican agricultural imports, including 1) tariffs; 2) quotas; 3) marketing orders; and 4) health and sanitary requirements.[7] Border processing and other "administrative" barriers to trade are of uncertain importance in both the United States and Mexico (although each country complains of such problems). An FTA can in principle affect all, or most of these barriers to trade. In all likelihood, especially given historical precedent, an FTA will result in somewhat freer, but not free trade in agriculture.

In agriculture, as in other sectors, average *tariffs* are low with a few important exceptions, and a large fraction of total trade enters the United States without any duties at all (40% in the case of agricultural imports from Mexico). The average American trade-weighted tariff rate in agriculture is 7%. Some of the tariffs are seasonal (especially in horticultural products) and are directed toward limiting imports during the main summer marketing period. Mexico is included in the GSP (Generalized System of Preferences) program, although many agricultural products are not covered by GSP rates.

In addition to tariffs, the United States maintains a number of nontariff barriers that also affect bilateral trade in agriculture. *Quotas* are for the most part relatively unimportant in bilateral agricultural trade. Although a number of quotas exist, many are not currently binding. Quotas are currently in place for imports of meat and dairy products, sugar, peanuts, and cotton.

"Marketing orders" act as an important impediment to agricultural competition, from both domestic and international sources. Marketing orders consist of regulations potentially governing a variety of different aspects of agriculture, including: advertising; research; shipping procedures; quality; shipment volumes; and the operation of buffer stocks for price-smoothing. Regulations issued under a domestic marketing order must also be issued on imports. In California, federal marketing orders affect a number of fresh and dried fruits (oranges, lemons, grapes, olives, raisins, etc.); nuts; and potatoes.[8]

Phytosanitary regulations and animal health requirements protect domestic industry against potential pests and diseases. These may be viewed as a final set of potentially important barriers to trade. This is especially true if such regulations are enforced through border checks rather than on-site checks, as it typically the case for Mexico, since border checks lead to costly administrative delays. Phytosanitary regulations are the reason for the prohibition (since 1914) of imports of fresh Mexican avocados (which are potentially affected by the seed weevil), but are also important in a number of other agricultural products.[9]

3 California Crops

To determine which crops in California would most likely be affected by the Mexico-U.S. FTA, and particularly those that might be negatively affected, telephone interviews were conducted with representatives from various farm and commodity groups in California.[10] Combined with the published material from these groups and government sources, we obtained the breakdown of crops presented in table 6.1, depending on whether the FTA will likely result in losses, gains, or little impact on each crop.

Import-Competing Crops

We expect that the crops shown in the first column of table 6.1 will face increased Mexican competition from the removal of U.S. import barriers. Generally, these crops have fairly high tariffs now, as shown in table 6.2, and their growing seasons overlap between California and Mexico. The most important of these crops (in terms of Mexican sales) is tomatoes, which totaled $222 million in import sales in 1989, and was the third-largest agricultural import from Mexico (after coffee and live cattle).[11] The

Table 6.1
Effect of Mexico-U.S. FTA on California production

Lose from FTA	Small effect of FTA	Gain from FTA
Asparagus ⎫	Citrus (fresh)	Apples
Broccoli ⎬ (fresh and frozen)	Cucumbers	Peaches
Cauliflower ⎭	Peppers	Pears
Lettuce	Strawberries (fresh)	Kiwi fruit
Melons (cantaloupe)		Prunes
Onions		Raisins
Table grapes*	—	Table grapes
Tomatoes		Wine
Olives	Alfalfa	Beef
Strawberries (frozen)	Cotton	Dairy
Freezer vegetables	Sugar beets	Dried beans
Citrus (frozen)	Wheat	Nuts
Cut flowers		Rice

*From the Coachella Valley.
Sources: "North American Free Trade Agreement: Concerns of California's Agricultural Industry," Report prepared for the Coordinating Council for International Programs, Department of Food and Agriculture, State of California (undated); "U.S.-Mexico Trade: Extent to Which Mexican Horticultural Exports Complement U.S. Production, United States General Accounting Office, March 1991; and interviews with industry representatives in California.

Table 6.2
Tariffs and value of Mexican imports (1988)

Product	Product type and time of year	Tariff (percent)[1]	Import value ($1,000): to CA	to U.S.
Asparagus	fresh	25%	n.a.[2]	n.a.[2]
	frozen	17.5%	339	458
Broccoli	fresh	25%	332	4,220
	frozen	17.5%	14	39,849
Cauliflower	fresh, 6/5–8/15	5.5%	0	1
	fresh, other times	12.5%	11	1,014
	frozen	17.5%	6	13,368
Cantaloupe	8/1–9/15	20%	0	1
	1/1–5/15[3]	0%	14	14,126
	other times[4]	35%	776	15,984
Lettuce	6/1–10/31	0.4¢/lb. (1.7%)	2	39
	other times	2¢/lb. (7.2%)	3,719	9,275
Onions	sets	0.6¢/lb. (1.4%)	17	61
	pearl	1.2¢/lb. (8.4%)	5	16
	all other	1.75¢/lb. (8.6%)	33,621	74,750
Olives	fresh	5¢/lb. (15.0%)	265	265
	in brine	20¢/gal. (10.4%)	1,038	1,038
Strawberries	fresh, 6/15–9/15	0.2¢/lb. (1.0%)	542	542
	fresh, other times	0.75¢/lb. (1.7%)	9,278	14,276
	frozen	14%	32	14,136
Tomatoes	fresh, 3/1–7/14 and 9/1–11/14	2.1¢/lb. (11.8%)	32,195	74,750
	fresh, 7/15–8/31	1.5¢/lb. (8.4%)	15,076	15,089
	fresh, other times	1.5¢/lb. (7.1%)	3,652	62,517
	sauce or paste	13.6%	1,663	11,666

Notes:
1. For products with specific tariffs, the *ad valorem* equivalents are calculated using the unit-value of Mexican imports to the U.S. in 1988.
2. Import values for fresh asparagus were not available after 1984.
3. The import values are for 12/1–3/31.
4. The import values are for 4/1–8/31 and 9/16–11/30, but for the period 4/1–5/15 the imports were duty free.
Sources: *Tariff Schedules of the United States*, U.S. International Trade Commission (annual); *U.S. Imports for Consumption and General Imports, Commodity by Consumption*. FT 246, Bureau of the Census (1988).

Mexican growing season in *fresh market* tomatoes overlaps to some extent with California's summer and fall crop. However, industry sources felt that import competition with Mexico will be especially important in tomatoes intended for processing, and those products.[12]

California citrus fruit and strawberries are primarily subject to import competition from Mexico in their processed forms. For oranges, the California Valencia and navel varieties are marketed as fresh, and have an established reputation for quality; they would not compete with current Mexican varieties. Only the oranges that are too small for consumer sales are used for orange juice, and in this limited sense would compete with Mexican sales. For fresh strawberries, the tariff is already very low (0.2–0.75¢/lb., depending on the season), and not surprisingly, Mexican sales to the United States have increased from $3.4 million in 1980 to $13.5 million in 1989. In contrast, the tariff on frozen strawberries is 14%, while sales from Mexico have dropped by half from $25 million to $12.5 million during 1980–89. Thus the FTA will probably result in import competition in only the frozen strawberry market.

Other crops in the first column of table 6.1 will face import competition from Mexico in both their fresh and processed forms, including asparagus, broccoli, and cauliflower. Generally, all frozen vegetables will face potential displacement if the processors decide to move their plants to Mexico. This has occurred with the movement of Green Giant, Simplot, and United Foods plants to Mexico, and the trend could likely accelerate under the FTA.[13] In addition to the fruit and vegetable crops, both cut and dried flowers would face significant import competition, according to industry representatives. Due to data limitations, however, this crop is not analyzed in this study.

In the second column of table 6.1, we show a number of crops for which significant import competition, or export opportunities due to the FTA, are not anticipated. The crops above the dashed line have different growing seasons in California and Mexico, or low tariffs (as in fresh strawberries). It should be noted that most of these crops *would* face stiff import competition in Florida, because of the overlap between the winter growing season there and in Mexico. The crops shown below the dashed line are grown in substantial amounts in California, but industry representatives in these cases did not anticipate increases in export sales to Mexico.

Exports

In the third column of table 6.1 we show crops for which a rise in export sales to Mexico may occur. This list is taken directly from a report by the

California Department of Food and Agriculture (undated). These products are listed to highlight the diverse effects the proposed FTA will have on California agriculture, though in our empirical work we focus on products facing import competition.

In a few cases, the crops with potential export opportunities according to the CDFA study differed from the results of our industry interviews. For example, the CDFA study listed rice, but industry sources noted that Mexican millers have been quite successful in keeping out this crop, even when the U.S. loaned Mexico funds to purchase the rice. (In addition, during the current drought in California, rice growers have had difficulty in obtaining sufficient water.) The CDFA study also listed table grapes as a beneficiary of the FTA, but this would not apply to grapes grown in the Coachella valley of California. These producers have an overlap in growing season with Mexico, and feel that removal of the tariff would result in substantial import competition. Due to the difficulty with modeling the effects of the FTA on grapes grown in different areas of California, this product was not analyzed. Also, given the absence of past data on which to predict the effects of removing the restriction, we do not include avocados in our study. Our methodology for estimating the effects of eliminating tariffs on the demand for crops grown in California is discussed in the next section.

4 CES Demand System and Data

We shall treat each California crop that faces potential import competition from Mexico as a differentiated product, with six sources of supply: grown in California; grown in the rest of the United States; Mexican imports to California; Mexican imports to the rest of the United States; imports from other countries to California; and imports from other countries to the rest of the United States. As in the Armington approach, each of these six sources of supply is treated as a distinct product, which will be estimated as a CES demand system.[14] Our methodology for estimating the elasticity of substitution across the six sources is taken from Feenstra (1991, 1993).

To provide some motivation for the estimator we shall use, we can start with the results of Leamer (1981), which considers a simultaneous demand and supply system in the absence of any instruments or identifying restrictions. Under the assumption that the errors in the demand and supply equations are uncorrelated, he shows that the maximum likelihood estimates of the demand and supply elasticities lie on a *hyperbola* defined by the second-moments of the data: the nonuniqueness of the estimates illustrates the identification problem. Now consider a panel data set, such as we have, where the elasticity of demand for a given crop is equal across the sources of supply (due to the CES demand structure), and the elasticity of supply from each source of supply is also equal (by assumption). Then, by using the time series data for *each* source of supply, we obtain a hyperbola of elasticity estimates as in Leamer. Combining these over all six sources, we obtain multiple hyperbolas, whose intersection defines a unique estimate for the demand and supply parameters.[15] Our estimate of the elasticity of substitution across the six sources of supply will be obtained in essentially this manner, though our presentation will differ from that of Leamer.

CES Framework

We suppose that consumption of each crop from the six sources of supply enters a CES subutility function, summarizing the aggregate preferences of U.S. consumers. The expenditure needed to obtain one unit of utility for the CES function is given by

$$e(p_t) = \left[\sum_{i=1}^{6} (p_{it}/b_{it})^{1-\sigma} \right]^{1/(1-\sigma)} \tag{1}$$

where p_{it} is the price of a particular commodity from source $i = 1, \ldots, 6$ in year $t = 1, \ldots, T$; p_t is the price vector: σ is the elasticity of substitution between this commodity obtained from the various sources; and b_{it} is a taste parameter for the commodity from source i in each year. Notice that an *increase* in b_{it} *lowers* expenditure when $\sigma > 1$, meaning that the commodity from this source is providing a greater contribution to utility. We can think of the b_{it} as acting as *shift parameters* on the demand curves for the commodity from each source, and we will allow b_{it} to vary randomly over time.

Let $\varepsilon_{it} \equiv \ln b_{it} - \ln b_{it-1}$ denote the change in the taste parameter for source i, where we assume that $E(\varepsilon_{it}) = 0$ and that $E(\varepsilon_{it}^2) = \sigma_{\varepsilon i}^2$.[16] By differentiating (1), we can compute the change in the share of expenditures devoted to purchasing the commodity from each source as

$$\Delta \ln s_{it} = \alpha_t - (\sigma - 1)\Delta \ln p_{it} + (\sigma - 1)\varepsilon_{it}, \tag{2}$$

where $\alpha_t \equiv (\sigma - 1)\ln[e(p_t)/e(p_{t-1})]$ is a random effect in (2), since the taste parameters b_{it} are random.

Equation (2) summarizes the demand size of our model, and in principle could be estimated over a panel data set (six sources of supply over multiple years) for a single commodity. A difficulty arises, however, if the random errors in demand ε_{it} are correlated with prices p_{it}, as we would expect whenever the supply curves are upward sloping. We will address this difficulty by incorporating supply curves for the commodity from each source, and simultaneously estimating the demand and supply elasticities.

Let us write the supply curve for good i in first-differences as

$$\Delta \ln p_{it} = \gamma \Delta \ln x_{it} + \xi_{it}, \tag{3}$$

where $\gamma \geq 0$ is the inverse supply elasticity, x_{it} is the quantity supplied, and ξ_{it} is a random error. For the purpose of estimation we treat γ as equal over all sources of supply. It will be useful to express (3) in terms of market shares s_{it} rather than quantities x_{it}. From (1) we can write the change in the cost-minimizing quantities $x_{it} = y_t \partial e(p_t)/\partial p_{it}$ as

$$\Delta \ln x_{it} = \Delta \ln(y_t e_t^\sigma) - \sigma \Delta \ln p_{it} + (\sigma - 1)\varepsilon_{it}, \tag{4}$$

where y_t is the total utility obtained from the commodity.

Using (3) and (4), we can solve for the equilibrium change in price of the good from each source as

$$\Delta \ln p_{it} = \pi_t + \rho \varepsilon_{it} + \delta_{it}, \qquad 0 \leq \rho < 1, \tag{5}$$

where $\delta_{it} \equiv \xi_{it}/(1 + \gamma\sigma)$, $\pi_t \equiv [\gamma/(1 + \gamma\sigma)]\Delta\ln(y_t e_t^\sigma)$, and $\rho \equiv \gamma(\sigma - 1)/(1 + \gamma\sigma)$. The parameter ρ satisfies $0 \leq \rho < (\sigma - 1)/\sigma < 1$ with $\sigma > 1$, and $\rho = 0$ if and only if $\gamma = 0$, meaning that the supply curve is horizontal. To interpret (5), a positive value of ε_{it} indicates an increase in the taste parameter b_{it}, and an outward shift in the demand curve for good i when $\sigma > 1$. If this good has an upward-sloping supply curve, we obtain a corresponding increase in its price. We shall refer to (5) as a "reduced form" supply curve, and use it instead of (3).

The key assumption we shall make is that the error δ_{it} in the supply curve (5) is independent of ε_{it} in the demand curve (2).[17] As is well known, independence of the errors across equations can sometimes be used as an identification condition, and we shall argue that this is the case in our system. Our estimation method is described next.

Estimation

To write (2) and (5) in a form more suitable for estimation, eliminate the (random) terms α_t and π_t in each of them by subtracting the same equation for source k. Denoting $\tilde{\varepsilon}_{it} \equiv \varepsilon_{it} - \varepsilon_{kt}$ and $\tilde{\delta}_{it} \equiv \delta_{it} - \delta_{kt}$, the resulting equations are

$$\tilde{\varepsilon}_{it} = (\Delta \ln p_{it} - \Delta \ln p_{kt}) + (\Delta \ln s_{it} - \Delta \ln s_{kt})/(\sigma - 1)$$

$$\tilde{\delta}_{it} = (\Delta \ln p_{it} - \Delta \ln p_{kt}) - \rho \tilde{\varepsilon}_{it}$$

$$= (1 - \rho)(\Delta \ln p_{it} - \Delta \ln p_{kt}) - \rho(\Delta \ln s_{it} - \Delta \ln s_{kt})/(\sigma - 1).$$

In order to take advantage of the independence of $\tilde{\varepsilon}_{it}$ and $\tilde{\delta}_{it}$, we can multiply these two equations, and divide by $(1 - \rho) > 0$, to obtain

$$Y_{it} = \theta_1 X_{1it} + \theta_2 X_{2it} + u_{it}, \tag{6}$$

where

$$u_{it} \equiv \tilde{\varepsilon}_{it}\tilde{\delta}_{it}/(1 - \rho), \tag{7a}$$

$$Y_{it} \equiv (\Delta \ln p_{it} - \Delta \ln p_{kt})^2, \tag{7b}$$

$$X_{1it} \equiv (\Delta \ln s_{it} - \Delta \ln s_{kt})^2, \tag{7c}$$

$$X_{2it} \equiv (\Delta \ln s_{it} - \Delta \ln s_{kt})(\Delta \ln p_{it} - \Delta \ln p_{kt}), \tag{7d}$$

$$\theta_1 \equiv \frac{\rho}{(1 - \rho)(\sigma - 1)^2}, \qquad \theta_2 \equiv \frac{(2\rho - 1)}{(\sigma - 1)(1 - \rho)}. \tag{7e}$$

Since the prices and market shares are correlated with the errors ε_{it} and δ_{it}, u_{it} is correlated with X_{1it} and X_{2it} in equation (6). Feenstra (1991) formally shows how consistent estimates of θ_1 and θ_2 can still be obtained, by exploiting the panel nature of the data set. Given these values, consistent estimates of σ and ρ can then be obtained from (7e). An intuitive exposition of this estimator is as follows.

Consider averaging (6) over all t, and let $\bar{Y}_i$, $\bar{X}_{1i}$, $\bar{X}_{2i}$, and $\bar{u}_i$ denote the sample means of the variables. Then (6) can be rewritten as

$$\bar{Y}_i = \theta_1 \bar{X}_{1i} + \theta_2 \bar{X}_{2i} + \bar{u}_i, \tag{6'}$$

where this equation has $i = 1, 2, \ldots, 5$ observations (since differences have been taken with one source k). Note that the data in (6') are the second-moments of the changes in price and market share, while $\bar{u}_i$ is the cross-moment of the errors in the demand and supply equations. From our assumption that these errors are independent, we have $E(\bar{u}_i) = 0$. Moreover, as the number of time periods T approaches infinity, we can presume that $\text{plim}(\bar{u}_i) = 0$. This means that as $T \to \infty$, the error in (6') vanishes, and so it is uncorrelated with $\bar{X}_{1i}$ and $\bar{X}_{2i}$.

Let $\hat{\theta}_1$ and $\hat{\theta}_2$ denote estimates of θ_1 and θ_2 obtained by running OLS on (6'). Since for large T there is no correlation with the error, we can treat $\hat{\theta}_1$ and $\hat{\theta}_2$ as consistent estimates provided that one additional condition is satisfied: the vectors $\bar{X}_1 = (\bar{X}_{11}, \ldots, \bar{X}_{15})$ and $\bar{X}_2 = (\bar{X}_{21}, \ldots, \bar{X}_{25})$, which are the regressors in (6), cannot be proportional as $T \to \infty$. If the probability limits of these vectors were proportional, so the regressors were colinear, then it is immediate that we could not separately identify θ_1 and θ_2 from (6'). It turns out that the probability limits of $\bar{X}_1$ and $\bar{X}_2$ are *not* proportional provided that there exist sources of supply $i \neq k$ and $j \neq k$ such that,

$$\left(\frac{\sigma_{\varepsilon i}^2 + \sigma_{\varepsilon k}^2}{\sigma_{\varepsilon j}^2 + \sigma_{\varepsilon k}^2}\right) \neq \left(\frac{\sigma_{\delta i}^2 + \sigma_{\delta k}^2}{\sigma_{\delta j}^2 + \sigma_{\delta k}^2}\right). \tag{8}$$

Condition (8) requires that there must be some differences in the relative variances of the demand and supply curves across the goods. Provided that this condition is satisfied, the estimates of θ_1 and θ_2 obtained from running OLS on (6') are consistent, and then consistent estimates of σ and ρ can be obtained by solving the quadratic equations (7e).[18] Feenstra (1991, 1993) discusses how the standard errors of the estimates are constructed.[19] When the identification (8) is satisfied, then the errors u_{it} in (6) are heteroskedastic, and Feenstra also discusses the construction of efficient estimates of θ_1, θ_2, σ, and ρ, which will be reported in section 5.

Data

The import values summarized in table 6.2 were obtained from Bureau of the Census, *U.S. Imports for Consumption and General Imports, Commodity by Country*, FT146 (annual). These data were obtained from magnetic tapes for the years 1976–88. Included in the tapes was the port of entry for each import, which allowed us to separate imports into those coming to California, and those going to the rest of the United States. Imports of the agricultural products listed in table 6.1 were collected for both Mexico and all other countries selling to the United States.

For each crop, the annual price and quantity of California production were obtained from California Department of Food and Agriculture, *California Agriculture*, for the years 1976–88. Values for total U.S. production were obtained from U.S. Department of Agriculture, *Agricultural Statistics* (annual), so that production in the U.S. *other than* California could be computed. The corresponding export values for both California and the rest of the United States were obtained from California Department of Food and Agriculture, *California Agricultural Exports* (annual), and these exports were subtracted from the California and other U.S. production data.[20] Thus for each crop the data consists of the various sources of supply for apparent U.S. consumption over 1976–88.[21]

Table 6.3
Expenditure shares for each source of supply, 1988

| | Imports | | | | Domestic | |
Product	Mexico to CA	Mexico to U.S.	Other to CA	Other to U.S.	CA	U.S.
Broccoli (fresh)	0.002	0.018	0	0.001	0.89	0.09
Cauliflower (frozen)	0.002	0.38	0	0.024	0.40	0.19
Lettuce	0.004	0.006	0	0.0004	0.68	0.31
Onions	0.071	0.081	0.004	0.020	0.18	0.64
Strawberries (frozen)	0.0004	0.16	0.001	0.048	0.50	0.29
Tomatoes	0.045	0.090	0.0002	0.009	0.58	0.28

Notes:
"CA" refers to California, while "U.S." means the rest of the United States.
"Other" means all importing countries other than Mexico.

The 1988 expenditure shares for each of the six sources of supply are reported in table 6.3 for each crop. In comparison with table 6.2, we have aggregated and omitted a few of the products.[22] Several crops—fresh broccoli and lettuce—have very small shares of Mexican imports to either California or the rest of the United States. We might expect removal of the tariffs on these items to have a correspondingly small impact on California agriculture. The frozen products—cauliflower and strawberries—have negligible shares of Mexican imports to California, but large shares of Mexican sales to the rest of the United States. For these items, California has a dominant share of domestic production, and so removal of the tariffs will lead to substantial competition with Mexico for the U.S. market. In the two remaining crops—onions and tomatoes—Mexico has a significant share of sales in both California and the rest of the United States. For these two crops we can expect the greatest impact of removing tariffs with Mexico, as will be estimated in the next section.

5 Estimation Results

In table 6.4 we present our estimation results for the eight crops considered, using annual data for 1976–88. For each crop, either Mexico or other importing countries had zero sales in some years; these observations are omitted from (6) and when forming the second-moments in (6'). The actual number of observations used (after differencing over time and sources of supply) is shown as N in column one.[23] Production from the rest of the United States (other than California) was used as the supply source k in (6) and (6').

Table 6.4
Parameter estimates

Product	N	θ_1	θ_2	σ	ρ	$1/\gamma$
Asparagus	25	0.061	−0.606	2.44	0.112	10.42
		(0.029)	(0.491)	(0.87)	(0.149)	(10.67)
Broccoli (fresh)	31	0.013	−0.043	8.18	0.409	9.35
		(0.009)	(0.149)	(5.70)	(0.294)	(6.12)
Cauliflower (frozen)	33	0.143	0.119	4.10	0.578	1.26
		(0.036)	(0.113)	(0.91)	(0.082)	(0.09)
Lettuce	54	0.163	−0.994	1.88	0.112	6.00
		(0.065)	(0.571	(0.38)	(0.102)	(4.50)
Onions	56	0.407	0.276	2.94	0.606	0.26
		(0.065)	(0.147)	(0.27)	(0.054)	(0.17)
Strawberries	34	0.067	0.415	9.06	0.813	0.85
		(0.043)	(0.240)	(2.77)	(0.075)	(0.85)
Tomatoes	55	0.137	0.726	7.45	0.850	0.13
		(0.075)	(0.176)	(2.42)	(0.038)	(0.26)

Note: Standard errors are in parentheses.

In the second and third columns of table 6.4 we report the estimates of θ_1 and θ_2 that appear in (6) and (6'). Using these, the estimates of σ and ρ are obtained by solving the quadratic equations (7e). Our estimates of the elasticities of substitution range between 1.9 and 9.1, and in most cases have low standard errors.[24] Although the variation of the elasticities across products is hard to explain, quite strong degrees of substitution between the various sources of supply seems plausible when there is some overlap in growing seasons.

The parameter p is related to the inverse supply of elasticity γ by $\rho = \gamma(\sigma - 1)/(1 + \gamma\sigma)$. Using the estimates of σ and ρ, we report the supply elasticity for each product in the final column. These elasticities differ considerably across products, with high standard errors in some cases. Although the elasticities apply to our annual data, over several years it would be quite easy to shift production in and out of the crops we are considering. Accordingly, we will treat the long-run supply curves for each source of supply as horizontal. This means that to evaluate the effects of the FTA with Mexico, we can focus on the direct reduction in import prices due to removing the tariffs.

Consumption Gains

For the CES utility function, the elasticity of demand from each supply source is given by

Table 6.5
Welfare effects of removing tariffs

Product	Social gain ($ million)	Total consumer gain ($ million)	Displaced California production (percent)	Water savings ($ million)
Asparagus	1.44	6.94	8.6	3.72
Broccoli (fresh)	0.64	1.78	3.6	1.51
Broccoli (frozen)[a]	1.76	8.74	21.2	2.67
Cauliflower (frozen)	0.60	2.94	20.7	0.43
Lettuce	0.06	1.00	0.06	0.03
Onions	1.06	10.38	2.5	0.48
Strawberries (frozen)	1.08	3.06	18.1	0.24
Tomatoes	4.52	18.97	8.3	11.28
Total	11.16	53.81	5.2[b]	20.36

Note:
a. Using the estimate of σ from cauliflower (frozen).
b. Computed as a weighted average of the percentage displacement of each crop, using the 1988 acreage for each crop as weights.

$$\frac{\partial \ln x_i}{\partial \ln p_i} = -\sigma + (\sigma - 1)s_i < 0, \tag{9}$$

where s_i is the share of expenditure on the product from source $i = 1, \ldots,$ 6. The cross-elasticities of demand are

$$\frac{\partial \ln x_i}{\partial \ln p_j} = (\sigma - 1)s_j > 0 \qquad \text{if} \qquad \sigma > 1. \tag{10}$$

With the expenditure shares in table 6.3 (for 1988), and the elasticities of substitution in table 6.4, we can use (9) and (10) to calculate the welfare effects of eliminating the tariffs on each crop.[25]

Let τ denote the ad valorem tariff, p_{mex} the price of the import from Mexico (net of the tariff), and x_{mex} the import quantity. Then the triangle of social gains due to increased purchases of the import is

$$\frac{1}{2}\tau p_{mex}\Delta x_{mex} = [\sigma - (\sigma - 1)s_{mex}]\frac{\tau^2 p_{mex}x_{mex}}{2}, \tag{11}$$

where we have calculated the increase in imports Δx_{mex} using (9). These social gains are shown in the first column of table 6.5. The largest triangle of gains is obtained for tomatoes, where we include the increased consumption of both fresh tomatoes and those for processing.[26] Following this, each of asparagus, frozen strawberries and broccoli have social gains exceeding $1 million. Several other crops have gains exceeding $0.5 million, and the total social gain due to elimination of the tariffs is about $11 million.

Of course, *total* consumer gains are much larger than the social gains, and are obtained by adding to (11) the reduction in price on the Mexican imports already purchased. The result of this calculation is shown in the second column of table 6.5. The largest consumer gains, of nearly $20 million and $10 million, respectively, are obtained for tomatoes and onions. The total gains for frozen broccoli and cauliflower exceed $10 million, while smaller consumer gains are obtained for the other products. In sum, consumers benefit by $54 million for the eight crops we have analyzed, which account for about 40% of all horticultural imports from Mexico. Thus, if the other horticultural products had the same tariffs on average as those we have analyzed, the total consumer gains from eliminating their tariffs could exceed $100 million.

California Production and Water Use

Using (10), we can calculate the percentage reduction in the quantity of California production due to tariff elimination as $\tau(\sigma - 1)s_{mex}$. Note that this includes the direct effect of consumers in California shifting toward Mexican imports, and also the indirect effect of consumers in the rest of the United States purchasing from Mexico rather than California. The result of this calculation is shown in the third column of table 6.5.

For three crops—frozen cauliflower, broccoli, and strawberries—the displacement of California production is estimated as about 20%. This high degree of competition could plausibly apply to other frozen fruits and vegetables that we have not analyzed. For California production of tomatoes, the displacement is estimated as 8%, which corresponds to over 20,000 acres of production.[27] A similar estimate is obtained for asparagus. For other crops, the estimated displacement is smaller, though we would still expect some impact on the pattern of production in California.

Because we are treating the supply curve from each source as horizontal, we cannot calculate a triangle of efficiency gains due to replacing California production with (lower-cost) Mexican imports. However, it is possible to calculate a social gain due to the reduced consumption of water, provided that the water is evaluated at a proper shadow price. The price for water deliveries from the Metropolitan Water District, which distributes water to much of Southern California, is $233 per acre-foot.[28] In contrast, federal water is often sold to agriculture at $3.50 per acre-foot, while state water for agriculture costs between $20 and $50 per acre-foot. If we take $33 as an average price within agriculture, then each acre-foot of water which is freed for sale to urban users generates a social gain of $200.

To apply this idea to California production displaced due to the FTA, we need to assume that the water used for this production is not switched to some other crop, but instead is transferred to urban users. This scenario is unlikely under current water regulations, which limits the extent to which farmers can sell water and retain the right to future deliveries. On the other hand, there are currently bills at both the state (AB 2090) and Federal (S.484) levels that would allow greater marketing of water.[29] If these policies are enacted, they could lead some farmers faced with import competition to sell water to urban users, where the proceeds from such sales could be viewed as a form of adjustment compensation. The social gains we calculate due to these water transfers should be viewed as illustrative, and not an actual prediction of the effects of the FTA.

For each of the crops in table 6.5 we obtained information on the actual water deliveries in various areas of California during 1973–83, from Department of Water Resources (1986). The annual deliveries to each of the crops was between 1.5 and 3 acre-feet per acre, with the exception of asparagus, which used 6.5 acre-feet/acre. Combining this information with the acres devoted to each crop in California in 1988, and the percentage displacement in column three of table 6.5, we can estimate the amount of water freed by the import competition. Evaluating this water at $200 per acre-foot, we obtain the estimate of social gains due to water savings shown in the last column of table 6.5.

The largest amount of water savings is from displaced production of tomatoes in California evaluated at over $11 million. Asparagus and broccoli each give social gains of about $4 million, while several other crops have water savings evaluated at close to $0.5 million. In total, the social gains due to water freed from displaced California production of the eight crops is $20.4 million. which exceeds our estimate of the social gains due to increased consumption. Summing the social consumption gains and those due to water savings, we obtain a total social gain of about $31 million.

As discussed above, the potential gains due to water savings should be viewed with caution, since the markets to transfer such water from rural to urban users are currently limited. Moreover, we have not considered the possibility that the FTA may lead to *increased* agricultural water consumption. This would be the result of California production shifting out of horticultural products and into more water-intensive products such as rice and dairy (the latter uses alfalfa and pasture as intermediate inputs). Both rice and dairy are included in table 6.1 as products whose exports from California to Mexico may increase under the FTA, which would have a negative effect on social welfare through the increased use of water for agriculture.

Whether or not this perverse "second-best" result would actually occur under the FTA depends on whether farmers faced with import competition decide to leave their land fallow or switch crops, and in the latter case, whether the crops are water-intensive. Although we have not modeled these decisions, an understanding of the current regulations on water use in California suggests that the import competition would *not* result in fallow ground. The reason is that farmers must continue using water allocations for agricultural purposes or lose the right to future deliveries. The institutional details of this and other regulations affecting water use are discussed in the next section. In section 7 we then consider the "first-best" policy of creating a market for water sales in California, while also liberalizing trade with Mexico. In this case the possibility of "second-best" losses due to increased use of low-priced water is avoided.

6 Water Regulations in California

There are four important causes for the inefficient agricultural use of water: 1) subsidies to water deliveries, made by both the federal and state government; 2) federal crop subsidies; 3) the (state) doctrine of "prior appropriative rights" and associated other legal technicalities; and 4) other constraints (legal and otherwise) on "water marketing" (also known as "water transfers"). The last two are the most important impediments to the efficient operation of a free market for water.

Subsidies

Federal reclamation policy (which is administered on, for example, Central Valley Project water in California) states that irrigation water charges should not include repayment of interest on construction costs (California Department of Water Resources (1983)), and that prices are based on amortized *historical* construction costs, not replacement costs. For this reason, federal water is considerably cheaper than state water, since the policy of the State Water Project is to require full repayment by the users of all (historic) costs associated with water delivery (CDWR (1983)). While this effect is of questionable importance, by not charging marginal *opportunity* cost for water deliveries, government policy encourages farmers to pro-duce low-value crops profitably.[30,31]

It is unnecessary to review the effects of federal crop subsidies on agri-cultural water consumption. As is well known, crop subsidies are large and pervasive, currently averaging almost $15 billion annually: government-promoted agricultural production clearly encouraged use of all intermedi-ate inputs, including water. It is interesting to note that rice and cotton, crops that use water intensively, are also in chronic surplus. Thus rice and cotton farmers are allowed to engage in "double-dipping," that is, receiving federal water subsidies to produce crops that are then bought and stored (and often eventually destroyed) by the federal government.

Legal Issues

While excessive agricultural consumption of water is encouraged by gov-ernment policy, more basic institutional arrangements also discourage the efficient operation of the water market. The most important of these im-pediments are fundamental legal principles.

The doctrine of "prior appropriative rights" is the primary rule govern-ing water allocation in the American West.[32] The rule is essentially a formalization of the phrase "first in time, first in right." The precept recog-nizes superior rights for the first party to withdraw water and put it to "beneficial" use, such as irrigation; the water need not be used next to the original water source, (As such, the Western law is intrinsically based on water use, not landownership, and stands in contrast to the Eastern water doctrine of "riparian rights" in which water rights reside with the owner of the property located on the banks of a watercourse.[33])

This tenet of the prior appropriative rights doctrine is clearly important in affecting the distribution of surpluses that arise from water use. As water becomes increasingly scarce, rents accrue to historical water users. Never-theless, the critical cause of allocative inefficiency in the water market is a different principle. For another tenet of prior appropriation law is the rule that once an appropriative right has been established, it continues to exist *so long as the water is beneficially used*. This right is relinquished if the appropriator does not use the water for several years (whether intention-ally or not). The rule can be summarized as "use it or lose it."[34] This principle essentially denies water users the right to use their water in whatever way they see fit, and as such is the most important legal impedi-ment to the efficient operation of the market for water. In particular, sales of water (e.g., from agricultural interests in one water district to municipal and industrial (M & I) interests elsewhere in the state) are of unclear legal status, and may lead to loss of the initial appropriative right to water use.[35]

Water Marketing

Water marketing is the sale (either temporary or permanent) of water rights. Water transfers can involve option clauses for drought years and are sometimes seasonal. Most existing California water transfers have involved the sale or lease of agricultural water inside water districts (public agencies governed by boards organized under state legislation to manage water deliveries to agricultural lands) rather than from agricultural water districts to urban areas.

Transfers of federal water are of unclear legal validity; water transfers are neither expressly authorized nor prohibited by law. The fact that Congress does not seem willing to express its views on water transfers explicitly is an important deterrent to potential large-scale water transfers. In any case, even without legal ambiguities, the federal bureaucracy does not seem to encourage water transfers actively.

The state of development of water marketing in California noticeably lags behind that of other Western states (such as Colorado), despite its rapid population growth and the lack of new reservoirs. In part this is due to the large amount of federal water (12 million acre-feet annually, primarily in the Central Valley Project (CVP), but also in the Coachella and Imperial Irrigation Districts (IID)). Also, the state water project, which accounts for 2.5 million acre-feet annually, has issued many contracts that restrict or prohibit water transfers. These two sources alone effectively preclude water transfers for half of California's developed surface water. Reisner and Bates (1990, p. 104) state that no permanent rights to CVP or IID water have ever been sold.[36]

7 Reform of the Water Market

Three facts are extremely salient in understanding the potential impact of opening the market for water. First, in California (as elsewhere in the West and indeed the United States), the vast majority of all water used is consumed in irrigation. In California, a typical Western state, around 85% of all developed water is used for irrigation (CDWR (1983, 1987)).

Second, while the demand for M&I water is inelastic, it is also small relative to total supplies.[37] Thus population and economic growth per se need not necessitate a water crisis. In California, a modest (10%) reduction in agricultural water consumption would double the amount of water available for M&I purposes.

Third, much of the water used to irrigate the West is used for low-value agricultural production. For example, in 1986, irrigated pasture in California used over 4 million acre-feet of water (of the approximately 32 million acre-feet annually available). This pasture yielded a crop whose *total* value was only some $90 million (much of which was not value-added). By way of contrast, Los Angeles used approximately 700,000 acre-feet of water, and total California M&I water use totaled less than 6 million acre-feet. Alfalfa worth $570 million also used 4 million acre-feet. Rice and cotton are also low-value heavy consumers of water. These four crops account for 40% of irrigated California cropland, but only 15% of total agricultural income. Moreover, California's Mediterranean climate supports many alternative, high-value crops. From this, we conclude that the demand for agricultural water is currently extremely elastic. Indeed, the inefficient use of agricultural water is key in understanding why agricultural interests are reluctant to move to a less regulated and more transparent market for water. *Alternatively, California's water shortages for municipal and industrial usages can be eliminated at almost no economic cost.*

The last extensive survey of California water prices was conducted by the Department of Water Resources (CDWR) in 1985. At that time, the average California price for irrigation water was $22 per acre-foot; prices for other agricultural uses are slightly lower.[38] On the other hand, the price for M&I users was above $230 per acre-foot, although no good estimate appears to be available in the literature.[39] (Some of the difference between agricultural and M&I water prices is due to treatment and distribution costs.) There are few reasons to believe that the character of the market has changed noticeably since 1985.

Figure 6.1 portrays the current supply and demand curves for water. The demand curve for agricultural water has been reflected through the ordinate so that its origin is the right-hand lower corner. The supply of water can be approximated by an L-shaped curve. An exact L-shaped curve would be the result of fixed water storage and conveyance facilities that can be run below capacity at a fixed marginal cost, and cannot provide water deliveries above capacity. Although this picture is not exactly right, it works well for our simplified analysis.[40] The current allocation of water is given by α, with different prices prevailing for agricultural and M&I water. However, because of the inelasticity of M&I water demand, the price in the latter sector is currently extremely high.

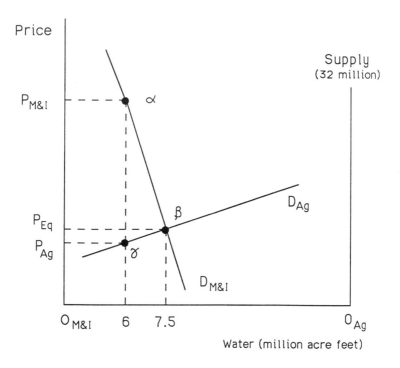

Ag   = Agricultural users
M&I = Municipal and industrial users
Eq   = Market equilibrium

Figure 6.1

A Free Water Market

If all legal impediments to water marketing were removed, and a free water market was created, the equilibrium occurs at β. Farmers would reduce agricultural production slightly, selling water to M&I. The latter interests would experience a large decrease in the price of water, but because of the inelastic nature of their water demand, the quantity of water used for M&I purposes would increase only slightly. Hence the current (inefficient) status quo water allocation is altered only slightly. The equilibrium price of water that would prevail under a competitive system is shown to be low, only marginally above the current price for agricultural water.

The social gains from a unified water market can be easily calculated; they correspond to triangle $\alpha\beta\gamma$ in figure 6.1. If we assume that M&I interests would increase their water consumption by 25%, this would still only amount to a water reallocation of 1.5 million acre-feet (i.e., less than half what is currently used for irrigated pasture). Treating the difference between the current M&I and agricultural price as about $200 per acre-foot, the welfare gains are $150 million annually. While this calculation has been made on the basis of a hypothetical increase in M&I water consumption of 25%, the same social gains of $150 million are obtained in the detailed regional analysis of Vaux and Howitt (1984).[41] They analyze regional trade between rural and urban areas in California, taking into account the costs of transporting water. Allowing trade between the regions leads to increases in the price of agricultural water of about 5% for many users (though a larger price increase in the Imperial Valley), and very substantial reductions in prices to M&I users. Thus a market-based system of water allocation could have large social gains that exceed the direct effect of the FTA on California agriculture, while entailing only a small change in the current status quo, and a small increase in the price currently paid for most agricultural water.

8 Summary and Conclusions

In this chapter, we have analyzed the potential effects of the Mexico-U.S. FTA on American agriculture, focusing on the horticulture sector in California. The crops most likely to be affected by the FTA are tomatoes and frozen fruit and vegetables. Although California production will be somewhat adversely affected, the effects in other crops should not be that large. The direct social gains are estimated at about $11 million annually, or closer to $31 million if we incorporate the social value of potential water savings. The gains to consumers exceed this amount, of course, and if we extend our results to all horticultural products, the consumer gains could exceed $100 million.

The FTA may also have large *indirect* effects on agricultural water consumption. First, virtually all agricultural producers, even potential exporters with greater access to Mexican markets, are likely to have transitional adjustment costs as a result of the FTA. It is possible to imagine a trade whereby agricultural interests permit freer international agricultural trade in exchange for compensation in the form of a better water deal for agriculture. Alternatively, the current system of water distribution may have to be renegotiated as a result of Mexican complaints that water subsidies represent an unfair producer subsidy.[42] Finally, freer trade in agricultural goods combined with the status quo in water markets may lend to net welfare losses for the United States. This could easily occur as American agricultural production shifts out of horticultural crops and into rice and dairy products.

Agricultural interests need only be given more well-defined water rights and the ability to sell water in order for a more efficient water market to develop. The welfare effects that may arise from reform of the system of water distribution are potentially larger than the social gains in agriculture due to the FTA, and are on the order of $150 million annually. Both agricultural interests and municipal and industrial users would gain from a more efficient water market. Perhaps the political momentum of the North American Free Trade Agreement can provide the opportunity for reform of the water distribution system in the American West, thereby generating social gains from both these actions.

Notes

For comments we thank Rudiger Dornbusch, Andrew Feltenstein, Peter Garber, Edward Leavee, Santiago Levy, Clinton Shiells, and Sweder van Wijnbergen. For discussions we thank: Linda Calvin, Economic Research Service, U.S. Department of Agriculture; Frank Dimick of the Bureau of Reclamation, U.S. Department of Interior; Lloyd Dixon, Rand Corporation; Colin Carter and Alex McCalla, University of California, Davis; and David Runsten, University of California, Berkeley. For research assistance we thank Wen Hai, Yongxin Cai, Joann Lu, and David Bunn. This research was initiated when Rose was a visiting scholar in the International Finance Division of the Federal Reserve Board.

1. A more general treatment of agriculture in the U.S.-Mexico FTA is provided by Levy and van Wijnbergen (1991a,b).

2. This point is recognized in, e.g., Bay Area Economic Forum (1991), which draws on the analysis of Vaux and Howitt (1984).

3. Many of the numbers we quote are drawn from Council of Economic Advisors (1991), or U.S. Department of Agriculture (1991).

4. Hufbauer et al. (1991) argue that U.S. exports of field crops and processed food should expand dramatically as a result of an FTA.

5. Horticultural products, including fruits, vegetables, nuts, and flowers, account for an eighth of all American farm receipts.

6. Coffee and live animals are other important Mexican agricultural exports to the United States, though processed foods are rapidly rising in importance.

7. U.S. General Accounting Office (1990, 1991c) provides further details.

8. Powers (1990) provides further detail on the federal marketing orders. Sales of fruits and vegetables are covered in some states by minimum quality standards (which are identical for all producers, domestic and foreign). Crops covered by a state marketing order within California include tomatoes and strawberries.

9. For example, imports of Mexican limes have effectively been banned in the United States since 1983.

10. These interviews were conducted by David Bunn, agricultural consultant, Davis, CA. The results from the interviews are available on request.

11 . See U.S. General Accounting Office (1991b).

12. Note that tomatoes intended for processing are a different crop from those grown for fresh sale. Tomatoes grown in the Baja peninsula of Mexico have a summer growing season, and compete directly with California fresh market tomatoes; see Cook (1990).

13. Movement of processing plants could also occur for olives. These plants generate a substantial amount of polluted water from processing the olives, and so environmental regulation in Mexico would be particularly important.

14. Alson, Carter, Green, and Pick (1990) have strongly criticized the Armington assumption in the context of agricultural goods, by showing that tests of separability (and sometimes homotheticity) are rejected on the data. As described below, our approach allows a more flexible error structure than is usually considered, so their negative results do not necessarily apply when these errors are incorporated.

15. In small samples, the hyperbola will not generally intersect at a point, so the estimates are chosen to minimize the sum of distance to the hyperbola. Asymptotically, an intersection will occur, and it will be unique provided that the identification condition in (8) is satisfied; if this condition does not hold, it means that the hyperbola all coincide asymptotically.

16. Other assumptions on the errors ε_{it} are detailed in Feenstra (1991, Assumption 1). In brief, we assume that ε_{it} is stationary, and that for each i the sample variance computed over all t approaches $\sigma_{\varepsilon i}^2$ almost surely as $T \to \infty$.

17. Other assumptions on δ_{it} are detailed in Feenstra (1991, Assumption 2), and they are analogous to the conditions assumed on ε_{it}.

18. Provided that $\hat{\theta}_1 > 0$, then (7e) yields two real solutions for $\hat{\sigma}$, one of which exceeds unity while the other is less (possibly negative). We choose the former solution as our estimate.

19. Note that the standard errors of $\hat{\theta}_1$ and $\hat{\theta}_2$ are not obtained by running OLS on (6'), but rather, are obtained by using fixed-effects for each source of supply as instrumental variables in (6). The standard errors of σ and ρ are then obtained by linearizing (7e) in first-order Taylor series expansions around the estimated parameters. See Feenstra (1991, section 6 and Appendix).

20. In a number of cases the *value* of exports showed erratic behavior, though the *quantity* did not. We therefore used the latter to subtract from the quantity of California or other U.S. production. Note that export data for frozen broccoli or cauliflower were not available.

21 . An independent estimate of total U.S. consumption of each crop was obtained from U.S. Department of Agriculture, Economic Research Service, "Vegetables and

Specialties: Situation and Outlook Yearbook," November 1990. We cross-checked that estimate of U.S. consumption with our own and found a very close correspondence. We thank Linda Calvin for providing this information.

22. Cantaloupe and olives are omitted, since the domestic production data were either not available or in different units than imports. Frozen broccoli was omitted due to unreliable import data in some years, though it will be included in table 6.5 using only the 1988 data. Asparagus combines both fresh and frozen, but is omitted from table 6.3 since the former values are not available after 1984. An estimated 1988 import share from Mexico of 0.24 is used to calculate the results for asparagus in table 6.5.

23. U.S. production of asparagus was missing for several years, leading to the small number of observations. The maximum value of N is 12 years $\times$ 5 sources = 60, though every crop had some omitted observations due to zero sales.

24. When domestic production of tomatoes for processing and fresh sales are aggregated, and estimated with imports at various times of the year, the estimated elasticity ranges between 10 and 20 with a standard error of equal magnitude. The estimate reported in table 6.4 is obtained when California and U.S. annual production of *fresh market* tomatoes is used, together with imports during the $3/1-7/14$ and $9/1-11/14$ period, during which the tariff is highest.

25. An estimated 1988 import share from Mexico of 0.24 is used to calculate the results for asparagus (U.S. Department of Agriculture, 1992, p. 98).

26. The tariff for tomatoes is calculated as 9.5%, which is a weighted average of the tomato tariffs in table 6.2.

27. Industry specialists suggested that displacement would occur primarily in tomatoes intended for processing. If we consider only this crop, the estimated displacement is 5%, which corresponds to over 10,000 acres of production.

28. The acre-foot is the standard measure of water volume; it is the quantity of water necessary to submerge a field of one square acre under a foot of water, and represents approximately 326,000 gallons.

29. Bill Bradley, chairman of the Senate subcommittee on water and power, is the chief architect of S.484, the "Central Valley Project Improvement Act," which is considered likely to pass Congress. Section 5 (a & b) of S.484 make it possible for individuals and agencies to buy and sell water. As well as ensuring adequate water for California fish and wildlife, Bradley's bill makes California law (not federal regulations) determine distribution of the 8 million acre-feet distributed annually by the Central Valley Project. At the state level, California Assemblyman Richard Katz has introduced pertinent legislation in the form of AB 2090 (which passed the House 46-25 in the Spring of 1991, but has since been defeated). This bill permits individual farmers to sell water rights. Currently, there are no specific statutory provisions allowing water transfers by individuals, and only water districts transfer water.

30. In the United States about 60 million acres are currently irrigated (Reisner and Bates (1990, p. 27)), almost all in the West. Almost a fifth of this is directly

irrigated by the Federal Bureau of Reclamation (excluding important federal programs such as flood-control protection or river flow regulation). Bureau water deliveries are highly skewed toward irrigation; Reisner and Bates (1990, p. 27) state that in 1987, 3.2 million acre-feet of water were used for M&I use of the total of 29.9 million acre-feet delivered. The gross value of all livestock and crops on lands irrigated by bureau water was $8 billion in 1987; this represents just over 5% of gross national farm product (Reisner and Bates (1990, p. 30)). In California, 40% of water deliveries to irrigated land are managed by the Bureau of Reclamation.

31. Parenthetically, subsidized water in principle is only supposed to be delivered to farms of 960 acres or less. But Reisner and Bakes (1990) state that the J. G. Boswell company farms about 150,000 acres (in "paper farms") in the San Joaquin Valley and uses more water than San Diego. "Paper farms," which are used to circumvent the 960-acre rule, are common in California. More efficient legal enforcement of the 960-acre rule could help to reduce the effects of the current drought on M&I, although the consequences of these violations are more distributional than allocative.

32. The rationale for prior appropriative rights is to protect parties who invest in water diversion projects from later diversions. The prior appropriative rights rule has its origins in the California Gold Rush, since much gold was extracted using mining processes in which water plays an integral role (such as the hydraulic and placer techniques).

33. California has adopted a complicated set of five types of water rights, essentially including the doctrine of prior appropriation with some riparian rights.

34. A by-product of this rule is that, until recently, costly water salvage that could be attained through individual acts of conservation often did not benefit the individual bearing the conservation costs because the rights to conserve water revert to either the state or the individual who next used the conserved water. This discourages water conservation (although wasteful water use may not be judged "beneficial," as was the case in the Imperial Valley case). Some cities have proposed paying water districts to salvage water through lining ditches and other conservation techniques, in exchange for the water thereby salvaged. California has recently passed legislation allowing appropriators to retain rights of water gained through salvage efforts, and the Metropolitan Water District has worked out a relatively important arrangement to this effect with the Imperial Irrigation District.

35. The 1935 Warren Act is another legal impediment to more efficient water allocations. This act excludes the use of federal water facilities to carry nonproject water for nonagricultural uses.

36. The Metropolitan Water District (MWD), which controls water for much of Southern California, has recently negotiated a sale of water-conservation technology to IID. Under the terms of the contract, the MWD provides the means for conservation of IID water; the MWD has first call on the 100,000 acre-feet of water annually salvaged. The IID fiercely resisted the arrangement.

37. An urban price elasticity of demand for water of -0.40 is reported in CDWR (1982).

38. This estimate is quoted in private correspondence with the CDWR. There is substantial variation in the price of water across regions; the price of irrigation water varied in 1985 from $1.2 to $300 per acre-foot.

39. Numerous examples are available, however. The CDWR has informed us in private correspondence that in 1990, the city of Oceanside charged retail costs of $490 per acre-foot of residential water, $412/AF for small industrial water, and $348/AF for agricultural water (all water is treated). Oceanside buys its water from San Diego for $237/AF for M&I water and $193/AF for agricultural water. San Diego in turn buys its water from the Metropolitan Water District of Southern California for $197/AF for M&I water and $153/AF for agricultural water. Finally, the MWD received slightly over half of its water from the Colorado river (at a cost of $20/AF), and the rest from the State Water Project at a cost of $240/AF.

40. Marginal costs of water delivery below capacity are not constant, because different water storage and conveyance facilities have varying degrees of efficiency (depending on, for example, distance and climate). However, California's extensive system of aqueducts and canals makes the physical conveyance of marginal quantities of water relatively easy. Further, the existence of groundwater, water tankers, desalination plants, and a variety of other devices imply that the supply curve probably does not become vertical in any interesting range. Nevertheless, a rough characterization of the supply for water can probably omit both sources of curvature without serious loss.

41. For 1995 they project social gains of $156 million, whereas for the earlier period of 1980 the gains are one-half of this amount.

42. Twenty % of arable Mexican land is irrigated, at negligible subsidies, compared with ten % for the United States. The USITC states that greater American water resources constitute one of the competitive advantages that the United States enjoys over Mexico (USITC (1991, pp. 4–6)); also see Becker (1991).

References

Alston, Julian M., Colin A. Carter, Richard Green, and Daniel Pick. 1990. "Whither Armington Trade Models?" *American Journal of Agricultural Economics* (May): 455–467.

Bay Area Economic Forum. 1991. "Using Water Better."

Becker, Geoffrey S. 1991. "Fruits and Vegetables in a U.S.-Mexico-Canada Free Trade Agreement." Congressional Research Service 91-362-ENR.

California Department of Food and Agriculture. Undated. "North America Free Trade Agreement: Concerns of California's Agriculture Industry." report prepared for the Coordinating Council for International Programs.

California Department of Water Resources. 1982. "The Price Elasticity of Demand for Water in the SWP Service Area." Staff memorandum report, Sacramento.

California Department of Water Resources. 1983. *The California Water Plan: Projected Use and Available Water Supplies to 2010.* Department of Water Resources Bulletin 160-83 (Sacramento, Resources Agency).

California Department of Water Resource. 1986. *Crop Water Use in California.* State of California, Resources Agency.

California Department of Water Resources. 1987. *California Water: Looking to the Future.* Department of Water Resources Bulletin 160-87 (Sacramento, Resources Agency).

California Department of Water Resources. 1990. *Drought Conditions in California.* Department of Water Resources Bulletin (Sacramento, Resources Agency).

California Department of Water Resources. 1991a. *California's Continuing Drought.* Department of Water Resources Bulletin (Sacramento, Resources Agency).

California Department of Water Resources. 1991b. *Water Conditions in California.* Department of Water Resources Bulletin 120-91 (Sacramento, Resources Agency).

Cook, Roberta. 1990. "Evolving Vegetable Trading Relationships: The Case of Mexico and California." Journal of Food Distribution Research (February): 33–44.

Council of Economic Advisers. 1991. *Economic Report of the President.* Washington, D.C.: GPO.

Feenstra, Robert C. 1991. "New Goods and Index Numbers: U.S. Import Prices," NBER Working Paper No. 3610.

Feenstra, Robert C. 1993. "New Product Varieties and the Measurement of International Prices," *American Economic Review*, Forthcoming.

Hufbauer, Gary C., Jeffrey J. Schott, and Lee J. Remick. 1991. "Trade Effects of NAFTA: A Survey," taken from draft of "Prospects for North American Free Trade," Institute for International Economics, mimeo.

Leamer, Edward E. 1981. "Is it a Demand Curve or is it a Supply Curve? Partial Identification through Inequality Constraints." *Review of Economic Studies* 63(3): 319–327.

Levy, Santiago, and Sweder van Wijnbergen. 1991a. "Labor Markets, Migration and Welfare: Agriculture in the Mexico-US Free Trade Agreement." IBRD, mimeo.

Levy, Santiago, and Sweder van Wijnbergen. 1991b. "Maize and the Mexico-United States Free Trade Agreement." IBRD, mimeo.

Powers, Nicholas J. 1990. "Federal Marketing Orders for Horticultural Crops." USDA Agricultural Information Bulletin Number 590.

Reisner, Marc, and Sarah Bates. 1990. *Overtapped Oasis* (Washington, D.C.: Island Press).

United States Department of Agriculture. 1991. "Agriculture in a North American Free Trade Agreement." USDA, mimeo.

United States Department of Agriculture. 1992. *Agriculture in a North American Free Trade Agreement.* Economic Research Service, Foreign Agricultural Economic Report No. 246.

United States General Accounting Office. 1990. *US-Mexico Trade: Trends and Impediments in Agricultural Trade.* GAO/NSIAD-90-85BR.

United States General Accounting Office. 1991a. *US-Mexico Trade. Extent to Which Mexican Horticultural Exports Complement U.S. Production.* GAO/NSIAD-91-94BR .

United States General Accounting Office. 1991b. *US-Mexico Trade: Impact of Liberalization in the Agricultural Sector.* GAO/NSIAD-91-155.

United States General Accounting Office. 1991c. *US-Mexico Trade: Trends and Impediments in Agricultural Trade.* GAO/NSIAD-91-155.

United States International Trade Commission. 1990a. *Review of Trade and Investment Liberalization Measures for Future United States-Mexican Relations.* USITC Publication 2275.

United States International Trade Commission. 1990b. *Summary of Views on Prospects for Future United States-Mexico Relations.* USITC Publication 2326.

United States International Trade Commission. 1991. *The Likely Impact on the United States of a Free Trade Agreement with Mexico.* USITC Publication 2353.

Vaux, H. J., Jr., and Richard E. Howitt. 1984. "Managing Water Scarcity: An Evaluation of Interregional Transfers." *Water Resources Research* 20(7), (July): 785–792.

7 The Automobile Industry and the Mexico-U.S. Free Trade Agreement

Steven Berry,
Vittorio Grilli, and
Florencio Lopez de Silanes

The recent growth of automotive imports from Mexico and the prospect of a new North American free trade agreement have raised fears of a massive movement of North American automobile production to low-wage Mexican plants. In common with many other industry observers, we argue that such a movement is unlikely.[1] In brief, the primary current impediments to North American trade in autos consist of restrictions on imports into Mexico. Thus the primary long-term effect of a free trade agreement will be the opening of the (potentially large) Mexican market to North American producers, rather than a movement of production to Mexico.

We begin with a discussion of the world automobile industry and of prior experience with free trade in automobiles. We note that the automotive sector is now a world industry that escapes the narrow limits of national boundaries. In analyzing the international position of U.S., European, and Japanese firms, we show that U.S. firms have the greatest involvement abroad. However, despite the relocation of production across the world, the ratio between the output of foreign affiliates of U.S. firms and the domestic output of U.S. firms changed little during the 1980s. During this same period, the overseas competitors of U.S. firms followed very different strategies. While Japanese manufacturers demonstrated an unprecedented willingness and ability to move production abroad, European companies have retrenched inside the European Community.

To identify the consequences of a possible free trade agreement, we analyze the effects of the Auto Pact of 1965 on both the Canadian and the U.S. auto industry. We show that the Canadian industry enjoyed spectacular growth after the Auto Pact, mostly fueled by exports to the United States. However, the most relevant aspect of this episode for the Mexican case is that the Auto Pact opened a new, large market to U.S. manufacturers.

Mexico, however, with its very low wages, is clearly a different case from Canada. We therefore turn to a discussion of the history and current structure of the Mexican auto industry. We note that this industry is increasing its integration into the world market and is particularly integrated into the operations of U.S. manufacturers. Current policies, however, prohibit most imports of finished automobiles and give indirect subsidies to exports. Both Mexican exports and imports have been increasing, with many exports coming from maquiladora plants near the border. We provide new data on maquiladoras that is consistent with claims that these plants specialize in labor-intensive production unlikely to take place in the United States. We conclude that the export-oriented sector of the Mexican auto industry will continue to prosper, relying heavily on production from United States-owned plants and on inputs imported from the United States and Canada. However, much of the existing domestically oriented industry is likely to be replaced by other North American producers.

Finally, via an econometric demand analysis, we consider the potential size of the Mexican market that could be opened up to U.S. producers. This demand analysis treats recent changes in Mexican national income and government policy as experiments that help to reveal underlying demand elasticities. Although the Mexican market is currently small, we find that declines in prices to world levels and, even more important, economic growth, could rapidly expand its size.

I The World Auto Market: Some Stylized Facts

Worldwide Trends

It would be beyond the scope of this chapter to analyze in depth the worldwide evolution of the automobile industry. However, to put the issue of the free trade agreement in its proper perspective, it is important to recall some essential features of the automotive sector. After the 1980–82 recession, worldwide motor vehicle production experienced several years of sustained growth. Between 1982 and 1988, motor vehicle production grew by 33%, and by 1988 production was 13% higher than the previous peak of 1978.

More important, the recent history of the industry is characterized by increased globalization of both production and markets. The increasing multinational nature of most car producers makes it difficult to draw clear national boundaries for the industry. With few exceptions, auto companies continued to diversify the location of their production in the 1980s. As

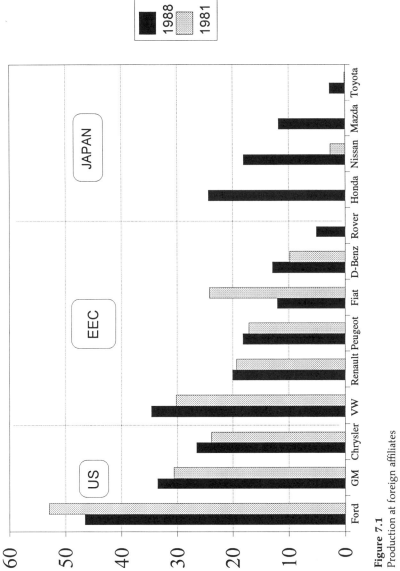

Figure 7.1
Production at foreign affiliates

shown in figure 7.1, the major auto companies typically produce between 10% and 50% of their total output abroad. American companies still exhibit the largest share of production manufactured at foreign affiliates, but European and Japanese companies have increased their foreign activity in the last decade. The changes in the location of production of Japanese companies have been especially remarkable. For example, while Honda's production in 1981 took place completely inside Japan, by 1988 almost a quarter of it took place abroad, mainly in the United States. Typically, changes in the international location of production are guided by a desire to move manufacturing closer to end markets, thus saving on transport costs and, more important, avoiding local protectionist measures. With few noticeable exceptions, mentioned below, the bulk of production at foreign affiliates is not reimported for sale in the home market.

It is important, therefore, to keep in mind that the relevent definition of, say, the American auto industry depends on the issue to be addressed. For example, if we are concerned with the profitability of U.S. companies, the relevant criterion is the nationality of the manufacturer, independent of where it operates. On the other hand, if we are concerned with the effects of the industry on domestic employment and output, what is important is the production location and not nationality. As shown in figure 7.2(a)–7.2(d), the two criteria do not always suggest similar conclusions. In 1988, American car manufacturers had the largest share of world production (34.1%), followed by Japanese (28.8%) and European (24%) manufacturers. Perhaps surprisingly, Japanese and European Community shares decreased from 1981, while the American share actually increased.[2]

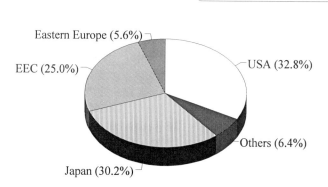

Figure 7.2.a
World auto production, 1981

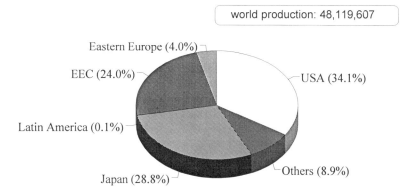

Figure 7.2.b
World auto production, 1988

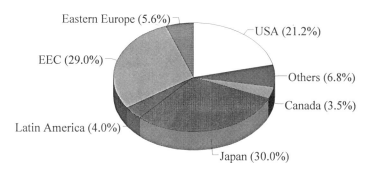

Figure 7.2.c
Location of auto production, 1981

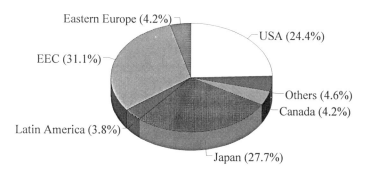

Figure 7.2.d
Location of auto production, 1988

If we consider the location of production, the situation is reversed. The European Community has the largest world share (31.1%), followed by Japan (27.7%) and the United States (24.4%). Both the European and American shares increased from 1981, while the Japanese share fell slightly. A major cause of this pattern is the relocation of Japanese production from Japan to the United States and Europe.

The U.S. Industry

Data on worldwide employment and foreign direct investment of U.S. firms are not available at the auto industry level, so we first analyze data referring to the whole transportation equipment sector. Between 1983 and 1988, worldwide employment of U.S. multinationals in transportation equipment increased by 20% (from 2.7 million to 3.2 million employees). The increase in employment, however, occurred only at U.S. parent, where it rose by 32%. In contrast, the aggregate employment of foreign affiliates decreased by almost 10% in the same period, although this employment displayed substantial cross-country variation. As shown in figure 7.3(a)– 7.3(b), employment in European affiliates dropped from 63% to 45% of total foreign employment. Conversely, considerable growth took place in Canada, where employment increased from 111,000 to 137,000 and in Japan, although by a smaller extent. Similarly, the share of employment in Latin America almost doubled, with Mexico enjoying the largest growth. Because of this increase, U.S. multinationals in transportation equipment

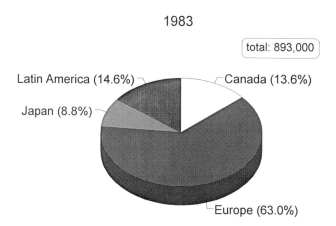

Figure 7.3.a
U.S. multinationals: Foreign affiliates employment in transportation equipment

now employ almost 83,000 in Mexico, comparable to their Brazilian employment of 89,000.

Similar trends are present in the pattern of the U.S. direct investment position. After a decline between 1980 and 1983, the U.S. foreign investment position in transportation equipment increased sharply and more than doubled between 1984 and 1989 (figure 7.4). This period was characterized by a marked shift away from Europe toward Canada and Japan (figure 7.5(a)–7.5(b)). While the direct investment position in Latin America increased by almost 70% between 1980 and 1989, its world share decreased, although this decrease largely stems from divestment in Argentina (figure 7.6(a)–7.6(b)). Both Brazil and Mexico, in fact, experienced a rapid growth, higher than the world average. In Mexico, as we will see, this growth is largely due to the expansion of the "maquiladora" sector.

We will now turn from the transportation equipment sector to data on the automobile industry alone. Between 1981 and 1988, production in the U.S. automotive industry increased by 42%, a rate of growth greater than in the European Community (32%) and Japan (13.6%).[3] As shown in figure 7.7(a), foreign manufacturers' production has increased from 2.6% to 8% of total output. The upward trend in foreign producers' output is entirely due to the commencement of Japanese production.[4] Since 1984, output of Japanese transplants has been growing at an annual average rate of 55%. Although far from Japanese performance, the U.S. production of American manufacturers displayed a considerable growth, increasing by 34% between 1981 and 1988. This contrasts with the behavior of European pro-

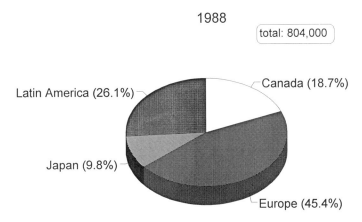

Figure 7.3.b
U.S. multinationals: Foreign affiliates employment in transportation equipment

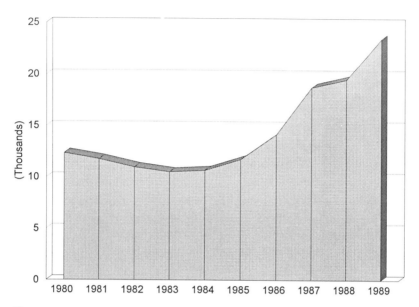

Figure 7.4
U.S. direct investment position, 1980–89: Transportation equipment

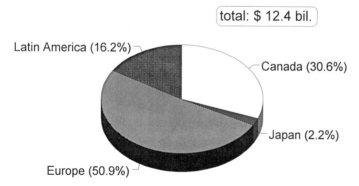

Figure 7.5.a
U.S. direct investment position, 1980: Transportation equipment

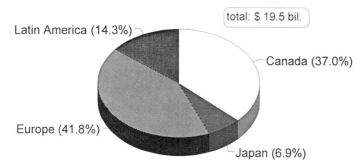

Figure 7.5.b
U.S. direct investment position, 1988: Transportation equipment

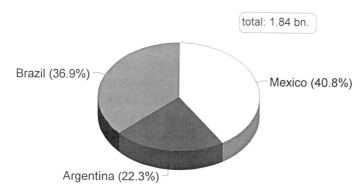

Figure 7.6.a
U.S. direct investment position, 1980: Transportation equipment

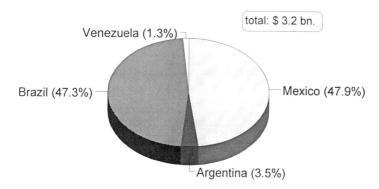

Figure 7.6.b
U.S. direct investment position, 1989: Transportation equipment

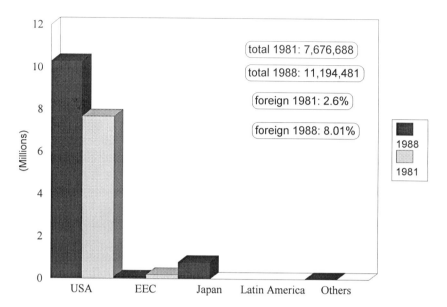

Figure 7.7.a
Auto production in the United States

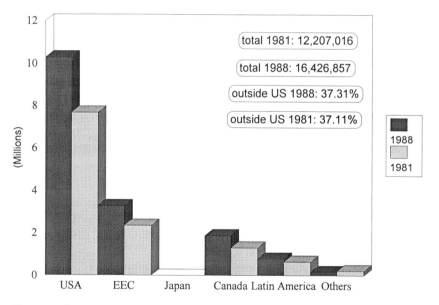

Figure 7.7.b
Location of U.S. auto production

ducers, whose output more than halved in the same period, due to the closure of Volkswagen's plant in 1988.

We now turn to the nationality of producing firms. As shown in figure 7.7(b), worldwide production of American manufacturers increased by 34.5% between 1981 and 1988. The figure also shows that the increase in production was a global phenomenon.[5] The largest increases took place in Canada (43.5%) and in the European Community (39%). To a lesser extent, production also increased in Latin America (21.7%).

In summary, it is important to stress that American foreign investment and production in transportation equipment is quite considerable. In 1988, more than 37% of the American production of motor vehicles took place abroad. This ratio remained almost constant during the 1980s, despite the considerable changes in the degree of involvement of American manufacturers across different world regions. In comparison, the production of foreign companies in the United States is small, but increased sharply in the 1980s, mainly because of the operations of Japanese transplants.

The European Community, Japan, and Latin America

The situation in the European Community is almost opposite from the United States. The production of foreign manufacturers in the Community is large, a quarter of total production in 1988, up from 22.5% in 1981 (figure 7.8(a)). European production in the United States decreased by almost 60%, between 1981 and 1988. In contrast, U.S. production in the European Community increased by 39%, well above the 28% growth rate of the European manufacturers. Japanese companies have also begun production in the Community, a process started with Nissan's factories in Spain (1983) and the United Kingdom (1988). Japanese production in Europe, however, is less than one sixth of their production in the United States. In contrast to their American counterparts, European manufacturers produce relatively little outside the Community, and such production decreased in the 1980s from 10.2% in 1981 to 7.4% in 1988 (figure 7.8(b)). The only sizable foreign production takes place in Latin America, mainly because of the VW and FIAT plants in Brazil and VW's operation in Mexico. It should be kept in mind, however, that a substantial part of the production of European manufacturers occurs within the Community, but in countries other than the country of residence of the parent company. Also, this production diversification within the Community showed an upward trend in the 1980s, increasing from 9.2% in 1981 to 12% in 1988.

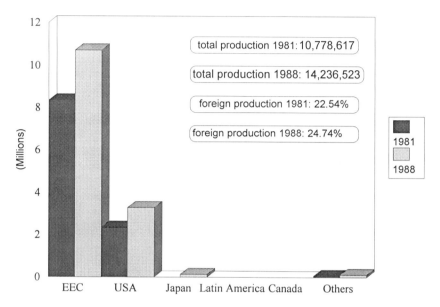

Figure 7.8.a
Auto production in the EEC

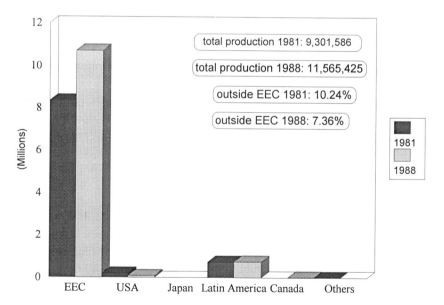

Figure 7.8.b
Location of EEC auto production

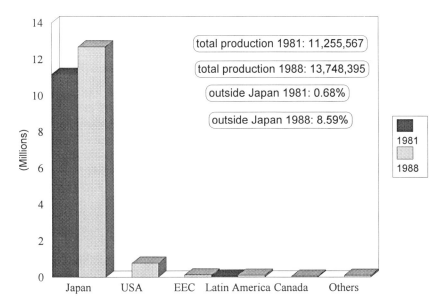

Figure 7.9
Location of Japanese auto production

Until the early 1980s, Japanese automobile production was isolated from the rest of the world. No foreign production of motor vehicles took place in Japan, and virtually all of Japanese manufacturers' output was produced in Japan. While foreign producers have not established a noticeable presence in Japan, Japanese manufacturers have shifted their production abroad at an increasing rate. Between 1981 and 1989 they opened new fronts in the United States, Canada, the European Community, and Australia, while increasing their production in Latin America by almost 40%. In 1988 production of foreign affiliates represented 8.6% of total production, higher than that of the European Community (figure 7.9).

In section 3, we analyze in detail the recent evolution of the automobile sector in Mexico. It is worthwhile, however, to put the Mexican case in the wider context of the Latin American market. While some assembly plants operate in Columbia, Chile, Peru, and Venezuela, the bulk of Latin American production takes place in Argentina, Brazil, and Mexico. As shown in figure 7.10(a)–7.10(b), Brazil is the largest producer, manufacturing in 1988 over 60% of Latin American motor vehicles. The Brazilian share of Latin American production has increased considerably in the 1980s, while the opposite was true for both Mexico and Argentina. In fact, between 1981 and 1988, production in Brazil increased by 37%, while in Argentina it

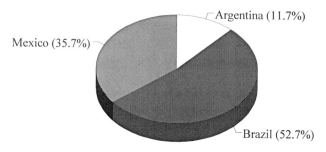

Figure 7.10.a
Auto production in Latin America, 1981

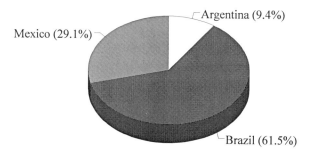

Figure 7.10.b
Auto production in Latin America, 1988

decreased by 6%, and in Mexico it decreased by 4.5%. However, while production in Argentina never recovered from the contraction of the early 1980s, Mexican production has displayed a positive trend since 1983, with particularly significant gains in the most recent years. By 1988, U.S. manufacturers were the largest producers in Latin America, with 45.8% of total output. European Community producers, which had the largest share up to 1987, decreased to 43.8% from 50.49% in 1981. Looking across countries in Latin America, in 1988 U.S. companies produced the majority of motor vehicles in Mexico (68%,), while Japanese companies produced 20% and European companies 12%. In Argentina and Brazil, however, European manufacturers still had the lead in 1988, with 59% and 41.8% of total production respectively. That year, U.S. companies produced only 39% of Brazil's output and 19.8% of Argentina's output.

One crucial issue in view of a possible trade liberalization is the current degree of openness of the sector in Latin America, especially in Mexico. All three countries under consideration have a high degree of protection against foreign-produced autos, and consequently imports have remained negligible. As shown in figure 7.11(a)–7.11(b), Argentina's production is almost completely absorbed by the domestic market, and exports have been very small. However, both Mexican and Brazilian export patterns have changed dramatically in recent years. While in 1970 exports represented less than 1% of Brazilian production, they increased to 13% in 1980 and 30% in 1988 (figure 7.12(a)). While most exports are directed to other Latin American countries and Europe, about 20% of exports were shipped to the United States in 1988 (figure 7.12(b)). We will analyze the Mexican case in more detail in the next section. At this point, however, it is worth mentioning that Mexican exports increased by a factor of 10 in the 1980s. Moreover, 86% of exports were directed to the United States in 1990 (figure 7.13(a)–7.13(b)).

These developments in Latin America raise the central issue of whether a free trade agreement with Mexico will induce American firms to relocate across the southern border, in an attempt to reduce their production costs. Some useful information in debating this issue can be derived by analyzing the recent history of the trade relationship between Canada and the United States. We turn to this issue next.

The Canadian-U.S. Auto Pact

Looking at the recent history of the U.S.-Canada market is instructive for several reasons. First, the type of free trade agreement now negotiated between Mexico and the United States has many points in common with the Free Trade Agreement (FTA) signed in 1989 between Canada and the United States. Moreover, it is most likely that a Mexico-U.S. agreement would not even be an issue now without the successful conclusion of the previous Canada-U.S. negotiations. Second, the common geographical proximity to the United States makes several aspects of the Canadian experience relevant to understand the likely consequences of a free trade area with Mexico. Finally, there are unavoidable interactions and spillovers between trade relationships north and south of the U.S. border. The Canadian experience, however, should be interpreted with caution because there are obvious differences between the Canadian and Mexican cases. Probably the most important difference is the dissimilar stage of economic development in which the two countries are entering the free trade area. Later we will argue that the particular growth position of Mexico is an essential element in evaluating the medium- to long- run consequences of a free trade agreement.

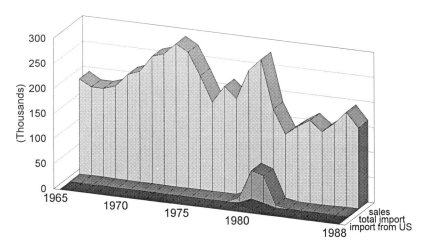

Figure 7.11.a
Argentina auto sales and imports, 1965–1988

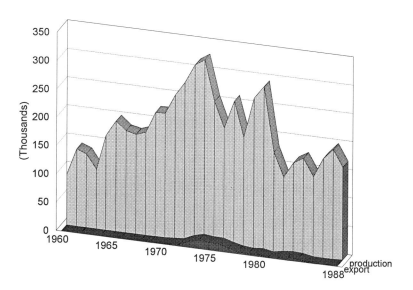

Figure 7.11.b
Argentina auto production and exports, 1960–1988

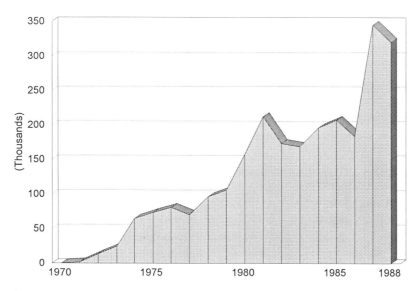

Figure 7.12.a
Brazil auto exports, 1970–1988

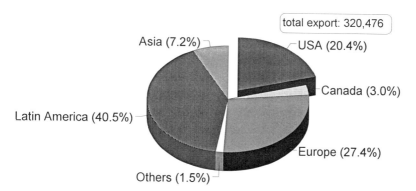

Figure 7.12.b
Brazil auto exports, 1988

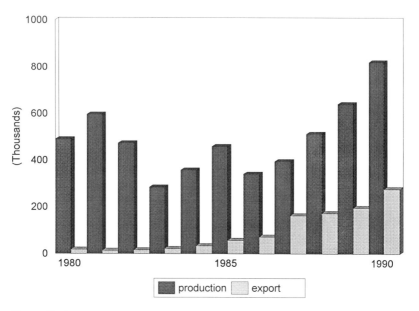

Figure 7.13.a
Mexico auto production and exports, 1980–1990

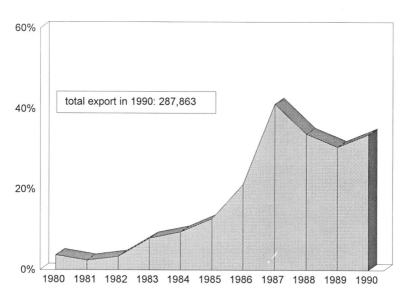

Figure 7.13.b
Mexican auto exports, 1980–1990 (% of production)

The relevant episode for our purposes is not, however, the Canada-U.S. FTA of 1989, but the Canada-U.S. Auto Pact of 1965. The FTA, in fact, has not changed the basic car industry environment created by the 1965 Pact. Compared with the scope of the 1965 Auto Pact, the FTA introduces only minor modifications. It calls for the phasing out (to be completed by 1998) of the remaining duties on Canada-U.S. automotive trade, and it changes the procedure for computing the North American content requirement (now 50% of direct manufacturing costs instead of 60% of invoice value). More important is the provision that prevents new manufacturers from enjoying the privilege of free trade import into Canada from third countries.

The 1965 Auto Pact eliminated most of the tariffs between the United States and Canada. The Auto Pact also introduced the 50% minimum North American requirement for products flowing from Canada to the Unites States, as mentioned above. Canada took a more global approach to trade liberalization than the Unites States, granting free entry to all imports (not just from the Unites States) as long as they satisfied a number of production safeguards. These safeguards were designed to guarantee a minimum ratio of Canadian production to total Canadian sales and value added.

The effects of the pact on the Canadian auto industry were enormous. Production more than doubled between 1965 and 1970, and almost tripled by 1979 (figure 7.14(a)). Most of the increase in production has been exported, mainly to the Unites States. As shown in figure 7.15(a), before the Auto Pact, Canadian exports were negligible and were mostly directed to countries other than the Unites States. The Pact changed the situation dramatically. By 1970, over 70% of Canadian production was exported to the Unites States (figure 7.15(b)). Trade, however, has not been one-sided. As shown in figure 7.14(b), before 1965 Canadian imports of motor vehicles were small and came primarily from outside North America. After the Auto Pact, imports increased sharply, mainly because of the acceleration of imports from the Unites States. While prior to 1965 U.S. imports represented around 5% of Canadian sales, by 1971 this ratio surpassed 40% and it is now over 50% (figure 7.16(a)). Exports to Canada represented less than 1% of U.S. production before 1965 and are now over 7% (figure 7.16(b)).

The Auto Pact thus profoundly changed the Canadian auto industry. Production rose spectacularly and a major component of this surge in production was exported to the Unites States. But the most important lesson for the U.S.-Mexican trade agreement is that the Auto Pact created a new, large market for U.S. manufacturers. In the next section we will

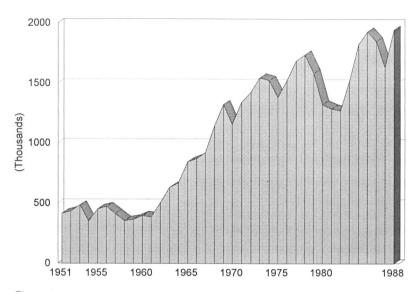

Figure 7.14.a
Canada auto production, 1951–1988

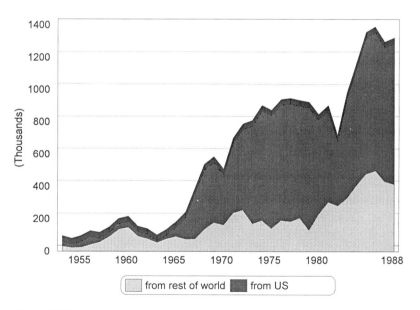

Figure 7.14.b
Canada auto imports, 1953–1988

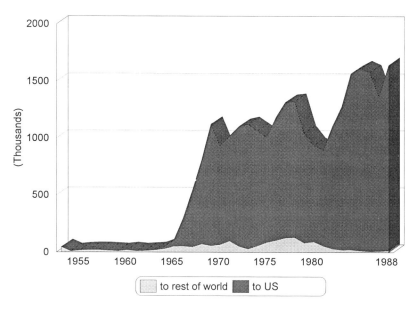

Figure 7.15.a
Canadian automobile exports, 1953–1988

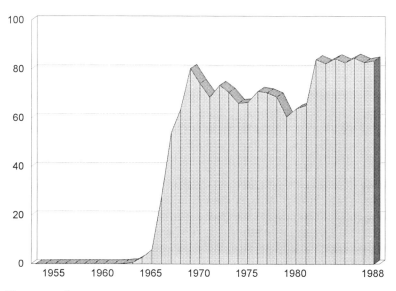

Figure 7.15.b
Canada auto exports to the United States, 1953–1988 (% of Canadian production)

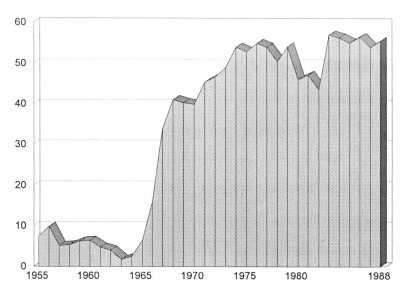

Figure 7.16.a
Canada auto imports from the United States, 1955–88 (% of Canadian sales)

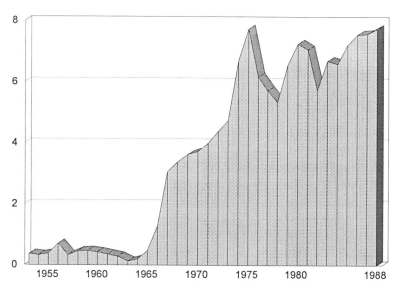

Figure 7.16.b
Canada auto imports from the United States, 1953–88 (% of total U.S. production)

consider the Mexican auto market in greater detail. We will then turn, in section, to the potential size of this market under a free trade agreement.

II The Mexican Auto Industry in Relation to the United States

In this section, we will analyze in some detail the history and current structure of the Mexican automobile industry. We will emphasize that, despite years of avowedly protectionist policies, the Mexican industry is dominated by foreign producers and has remained a large importer from the Unites States. In considering the current structure of the industry based in Mexico, we will show that Mexican auto exports to the Unites States are concentrated in products typically imported by the Unites States from low-wage countries. But in contrast to similar products imported from overseas, the Mexican products are frequently manufactured by U.S. based firms and contain a high percentage of U.S.-made parts.

The Initial Relationship

The automobile industry represents one of the most important examples of industrial integration between the Unites States and Mexico. The multiple backward and forward linkages of automobile manufacturing have captured the attention of both governments in the last three decades, and the relationship has been influenced by world trends and country-specific regulations on both sides of the border. In this section, we will look at the series of Mexican "Automobile Decrees" as a mechanism to promote sectoral growth and, more important, as a response to the overwhelming automobile trade deficits since the 1950s.

The growing Mexican market led Ford to open the first Mexican assembly plant in 1925. In the following years, all the other U.S. producers as well as some foreign and domestic firms started assembling vehicles. Nevertheless, by 1960, 53% of domestic demand for passenger cars was still supplied by imports, while close to 80% of the value of parts used in domestic assembly was also imported. Exports amounted to a little over $200,000, producing a sectoral deficit of more than $119 million, almost 85% with the Unites States alone (table 7.1).

These facts motivated the Mexican government's 1962 Automotive Decree, establishing a new regulatory framework intended to foster domestic production and reduce the trade deficit. Other countries (such as Brazil and Argentina) employed protectionist policies, but because of its links with the U.S. industry, Mexico's rules were far less restrictive. The decree included

Table 7.1
Mexican automotive trade balance, 1960–1990 (millions of U.S. dollars)

Year	Automotive exports				Automotive imports			Automotive Trade balance	U.S./Total		Automotive/National		
	Total	Vehicles	Engines	Auto parts	Total	Vehicles	Auto parts		Exports to	Imports from	Exports	Imports	Balance
1960	0.2	0.0		0.2	119.3	86.5	32.7	−119.1	65.4%	86.4%	0.0%	10.1%	26.6%
1965	0.8	0.1		0.8	182.6	131.7	50.9	−181.7	63.8%	87.1%	0.1%	11.7%	39.7%
1970	26.6	0.2		26.4	219.7	166.4	53.3	−193.1	67.7%	88.8%	2.1%	9.4%	18.6%
1975	184.0	9.6	35.4	139.0	807.3	189.6	617.6	−623.3	73.9%	65.4%	6.0%	12.0%	17.1%
1980	366.2	128.7	32.7	204.8	1,896.7	657.7	1,239.0	−1530.4	66.9%	66.3%	2.4%	10.1%	41.4%
1981	339.5	113.8	61.5	164.2	2,219.4	681.6	1,537.8	−1879.9	69.1%	73.5%	1.7%	9.3%	41.7%
1982	420.2	79.2	191.3	149.6	1,192.8	213.4	979.4	−772.6	62.8%	77.9%	1.9%	6.1%	NS
1983	940.6	124.2	602.8	213.6	397.9	33.5	364.5	542.7	72.4%	68.1%	4.4%	5.4%	3.9%
1984	1,303.6	145.9	840.2	317.5	684.6	97.5	587.1	619.0	74.2%	68.5%	5.8%	7.1%	4.8%
1985	1,426.8	140.7	1,039.2	246.9	993.2	135.0	858.2	433.5	85.5%	72.0%	6.6%	7.1%	5.8%
1986	2,083.1	545.8	1,152.7	384.6	728.9	91.3	637.2	1,354.2	86.4%	75.0%	12.8%	5.0%	32.0%
1987	2,839.1	1,207.0	1,179.6	452.5	1,135.8	108.6	1,027.2	1,703.4	87.7%	75.1%	14.7%	8.9%	23.0%
1988	3,335.3	1,452.0	1,371.9	511.4	1,909.7	225.8	1,683.9	1,425.6	81.8%	81.1%	15.5%	9.9%	78.6%
1989	3,477.7	1,674.4	1,335.9	467.4	3,951.1	161.3	3,789.9	−473.4	84.1%	75.9%	15.3%	15.6%	18.2%
1990	4,635.0	2,691.0	1,478.4	465.7	4,936.8	345.3	4,591.5	−301.8	89.8%	77.5%	17.2%	15.9%	7.3%

Note: NS = Nonsignificant.
Source: Calculated with data from INEGI, Banco de Mexico and SECOFI.

a 60% domestic content regulation, price controls, and production quotas. Foreign investors faced no restrictions in vehicle production, but were limited to 40% ownership of component plants.

The government envisioned an industry consisting of only four domestically owned companies. However, in 1964 the final outcome allowed seven producers: General Motors, Ford, American Motors, Fabricas Automex (with Chrysler participation), Nissan, Volkswagen, and DINA, a government-owned firm.

U.S.-Mexican sectoral relations continued to deepen. To meet the domestic content requirement, U.S. subsidiaries, led by Ford, linked U.S. component producers with Mexican capital to create auto part companies. Tremec and Spicer are the result of these efforts, supplying most of the domestic market for transmissions (and several other components) since then. Other U.S.-based parts companies like Eaton made substantial direct investments in the components industry.

Nonetheless, the sector's significant trade imbalance persisted; in 1970 the deficit with the Unites States alone represented $170 million or close to 17% of the nation's 1970 trade deficit. After numerous disputes between domestic and foreign producers, the government opted for an export promotion policy formalized in the 1972 Automotive Decree. Imports were to be balanced by growing exports containing at least 40% of auto parts not made by the car manufacturer. This policy strongly favored foreign auto makers. Automex faced Chrysler's opposition to its U.S. exports, leading to financial difficulties and acquisition by its U.S. partner.[6]

Private domestic (i.e., Mexican) capital in vehicle production disappeared. Exports of auto parts increased as the Big Three implemented globalization strategies, but the deficit persisted. In 1975, imports from the Unites States were almost three times larger than exports from Mexico (figure 7.17.)

The 1977 Auto motive Decree created a new balance-of-payments mechanism, requiring each auto maker to increase exports in order to balance its imports and payments abroad by 1982. This provided an additional incentive for multinationals, especially the Big Three, to focus on Mexican export strategies instead of investing in other developing countries like Brazil. By 1981, General Motors increased its maquiladora operations (discussed further below), and opened two new plants for the production of engines and vehicles. Chrysler also started engine production operations, joined by Ford's Chihuahua plant two years later (table 7.2).

The growth of auto parts companies, supplying the rapidly growing domestic market with high-quality components, was the outcome of a

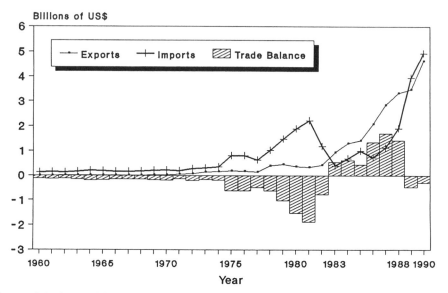

Source:Calculated with data from
INEGI, Banco de Mexico and SECOFI.

Figure 7.17
Mexican automotive trade

second wave of joint ventures between U.S. auto makers and large Mexican industrial groups. In 1981, Ford joined with Grupo Alfa to open Nemak, still one of the largest suppliers of aluminum engine heads. A few months later, General Motors and Grupo Condumex together created Condumex Autoparts, supplying wire harnesses. Two other Ford ventures with Grupo Vitro and Grupo Visa created Vitroflex, the largest auto glass producer, and Carplastic, producing plastic boards. The multinational auto makers benefited in several ways from such associations. They could produce and supply the domestic market with higher-quality products, profit from the comparative advantage of their Mexican partners, meet export requirements, and even source their U.S.-based plants, reducing production costs.

The 1977 decree also increased maquiladora incentives allowing up to 20% of the compensating exports of car producers to accrue through the value added of maquila plants. U.S. auto makers, and in particular General Motors, increased their involvement in this sector with electrical components assembly.

The significant growth of the domestic market, peaking at 600,000 units in 1981, also entailed the worsening of the sector's trade balance and made

Table 7.2
Plants and installed capacity of the automobile assembly industry in Mexico (1983–1991)

Auto maker	Plant location (year)	Region	Product	Installed capacity (units/yr.)			Announced investment plans: 1990–1991		
				1983	1988	1990	Amount	Purpose	Resulting planned exports to U.S.
Chrysler	1) Mexico City	Center	Light trucks	73,440	73,440	73,440			
	2) Toluca	Center	Passenger cars	120,960	120,960	150,000			
			Engines (6, 8 cil.)	137,088	169,646	90,000			
			Condensers	806,400	806,400	806,400*			
			Automatic transmission	—	60,480	60,480*			
	3) Saltillo (1981)	North	Engines (4 cil.)	270,000	270,000	270,000			
Ford	1) Cuautitlan	Center	Passenger cars	59,280	61,900	61,900	1) $840 million	1) Expand Hermosillo from 130,000 to 170,000 units.	1) All units from its Hermosillo plant.
			Light trucks	44,640	49,700	49,700			
			Engines (4, 6 cil.)	60,000	n.a.	90,000			
			Engines VB	120,000	n.a.	n.a.			
			Forge	33,225	n.a.	n.a.	2) $700 million	2) Double Chihuahua's engine capacity.	2) 500,000 engines/yr.
	2) Chihuahua (1983)	North	Engines (4 cil.)	400,000	400,000	400,000			
	3) Hermosillo (1986)	North	Passenger cars	—	130,000	Expanding			
G. M.	1) Mexico City	Center	Light trucks	71,300	60,480	60,480	$ 50 million	Increase in wire harnesses. in the maquiladora segment.	
			Spark plugs	5,520,000	5,520,000	5,520,000*			
	2) Toluca	Center	Engines (4, 6, 8 cil.)	118,750	142,538	142,538			
			Forge	33,500	33,500	33,500*			
	3) Saltillo (1981)	North	Passenger cars	87,500	103,156	120,000			
	4) Saltillo (1981)	North	Engines (6 cil.)	451,200	451,200	451,200			

Table 7.2 (continued)

Auto maker	Plant location (year)	Region	Product	Installed capacity (units/yr.)			Announced investment plans: 1990–1991		
				1983	1988	1990	Amount	Purpose	Resulting planned exports to U.S.
Nissan	1) Cuernavaca	Center	Passenger cars	78,000	78,000	100,000	$1 billion (1990–1994)	1) Shift component from Japan to Mexico.	1) 1992: $120 million in components
			Light trucks	48,000	48,000	48,000			
	2) Lerma	C-N	Engines (4 cil.)	84,000	144,000	144,000		2) By 1994: 200,000 vehicles	2) 1993: 32,000 Sentras 1995: 64,000 Sentras
			Gray iron forge	30,000	40,000	40,000*			
	3) Aguascalientes (1982).	C-N	Engines (4 cil.)	—	192,000	192,000			
			Aluminium forge	n.a.	n.a.	n.a.			
			Transaxes	n.a.	150,000	150,000*			
	4) Aguascal. II (1990)	C-N	Passenger cars	—	—	Construction			
VW	1) Puebla	Center	Passenger cars	168,000	129,800	200,000	$ 1.5 billion (1991–1994)	Expand vehicle production to 300,000 units by 1991, and 450,000 units by 1993.	By 1993 up to 310,000 vehicles.
			Light trucks	24,000	22,000	22,000			
			Eengines (4 cil.)	540,000	440,000	440,000			
			Gray iron forge	64,800	64,800	64,800*			
			Aluminium forge	21,600	21,600	21,600*			
			Magnesium forge	14,400	14,400	14,400*			
Renault/ Jeep	1) Mexico City	Center	Light trucks	17,500	Closed	—			
	2) Cd. Sahagun	Center	Passenger cars	40,000	Closed	—			
			Engines (4 cil.)	40,000	Closed	—			
	3) Torreon	C-N	Engines (6 cil.)	40,000	200,000	300,000			

*Represents own estimate drawn from previous production or capacity data.
n.a. Information not available.
C-N Stands for Center-North.
Source: AMIA, several issues.

it impossible for producers to meet the "balanced-growth" goal of 1977. In 1981, the auto deficit with the Unites States alone was close to 27% of Mexico's total trade deficit (table 7.1).

The 1983 Auto motive Decree followed shortly, undertaking stronger measures aimed at a zero trade balance for each company. Three main policies were outlined: stringent domestic content rules for vehicles and parts, required balance-of-payments (allowing no deficits), and limits to one line and a maximum of five models per car maker by 1987. The more restrictive rules and a decline in the domestic market convinced Renault and American Motors to stop vehicle production.[7] The Big Three, Volkswagen, and Nissan, all 100% foreign owned, are the sole remainders of twenty years of "protectionist" policies in the passenger car segment.

The 1989 Automotive Decree

We will now turn to the recent evolution of the Mexican auto industry and its integration with the Unites States. We will begin by explaining the present regulatory framework in Mexico, which has not only altered the tone and thrust of the previous two decades of industrial policies, but also led to an enormous increase in imports ending the period of sectoral trade surplus.

By 1989, Mexico was already embarked on a path of stabilization, trade liberalization, and structural change, but the automotive industry remained isolated from these movements, ranking third in protection after oil and tobacco. To find a solution to this imbalance, all industry players were involved in consultations, resulting in three 1989 decrees designed to promote the industry's development in both domestic and foreign markets.

The Mexican automobile market is almost 1/25th of the U.S. size, and the ratio of cars per consumer is eleven times lower in Mexico. These issues were addressed in the 1989 "Auto Popular" Decree. Tax exemptions were granted to popular cars subscribing to the program, which required the auto maker to reduce its profit margin as well. The general idea was to provide consumers with a small car at more reasonable prices. Only the Volkswagen Sedan model (the "Beetle") embraced the scheme. By the end of that year, VW had become the leader in domestic sales with a 70% increase in the Sedan's production and sales. In 1990, monthly sales of this car had quadrupled, capturing 24% of total passenger car sales in the country.

In December, two other decrees followed. One pertaining to buses, truck, and other similar vehicles established, for the first time since 1962, a clear path for the elimination of trade and entry barriers (to be achieved by 1994.) Finally, new rules pertaining to the manufacturing of passenger vehicles and light trucks were outlined in a third decree that significantly relaxed the restrictions on foreign-owned producers and broke with a closed market for imports. The third decree became effective in November 1990 with the 1991 year models.

Auto makers established by 1989 now have some freedom to choose the lines they wish to produce in Mexico and those to import from the same manufacturer abroad. However, imports of vehicles are restricted to 15% of total domestic production (this increases to 20% in 1993). To gain permission to import, manufacturers must still maintain a positive trade balance, with diminishing proportions of exports to imports. Auto parts imports continue to be open to trade with an average tariff rate close to 10 percent.

Individual automobile, truck, and auto parts domestic content requirements have been eliminated. A more flexible 36% of the National Value Added for all the auto makers' production must still come from the National Value Added of the domestic auto parts industry, or from other domestic suppliers.[8] The general deregulation of the sector includes the elimination of limits in lines and models, the compulsory list of domestic auto parts to be included in each vehicle, the mandatory gasoline engines on medium-sized trucks, and the restrictions on the proportion of base vehicles marketed.

The previous balance-of-payments requirement was replaced by a less restrictive trade-balance mechanism eliminating the need to compensate for payments abroad. Trade surpluses can accumulate beginning with the 1992 car model year. Even the transferability of trade-surplus rights among manufacturers is allowed.

The pricing of imported vehicles is said to be closely watched by the authorities. A manufacturer could lose its temporary "import exclusivity rights" if its listed price exceeds international public prices for equivalent vehicles.

Resulting Industry Structure

Today's Mexican automotive industry is the result of regulations in the series of decrees just outlined, the macroeconomic conditions of the country in the 1980s and intense international market competition. These three factors have created a two-tiered industry and, until recently, defined separate trends for domestic sales and exports.

An important reason for the failure of the 1969–1982 measures in promoting exports was the stream of incentives favoring the opposite: production for the domestic market. This has created a relatively inefficient domestic assembly industry, which frequently relies on outdated production techniques and short production runs. This industry is unlikely to survive a free-trade agreement in its present form.

Trade liberalization measures starting in 1983 have eliminated some of the anti-export bias; indeed the strict balance-of-payments rules can be seen as an implicit export subsidy. The U.S. auto manufacturers, as well as some large component companies, are among the most favored by the implementation of special export programs. The new, globally oriented sector of the Mexican auto industry is likely to flourish under a free-trade pact. This industry, typically located in Northern Mexico to take advantage of its close links with the United States, can be roughly divided into three parts: engine plants, maquila auto parts plants, and a high-tech auto assembly sector. We will examine these sectors in some detail, arguing that exports to the United States from this sector largely compete with imports from other (often low-wage) countries, rather than with U.S. production. The North American industry is aided by the relatively low cost and high quality of the Mexican products and (perhaps more important to U.S. and Canadian producers) the fact that the Mexican exporters are large demanders of inputs from the rest of North America.

Of the three sectors, production in the engine and high-tech assembly plants most resembles similar U.S.-based production. However, production in the famed maquiladora sector is concentrated in highly labor-intensive stages of production. This sector takes U.S. inputs and creates products that otherwise might be produced in other areas of the world.

A detailed analysis of the manufacturers' installed capacity per plant is provided in table 7.2. We show the data for 1983 and 1988, covering the period of one of the most important investment waves in the industry. Installed capacity and announced investment plans with their possible consequences for exports are also shown. After reviewing the various export-oriented sectors, we will turn to a discussion of the prospects for the domestically oriented industry.

The Engine Plants

The engine export take-off in 1982–1984 marks a first stage in the export movement. Triggered by the intense competition from Japanese imports, U.S. producers searched for low-cost production bases in Third World countries. The new market for smaller engines and front-wheel drives was reoriented to these countries, among which Mexico presented appropriate cost-saving conditions for engine production. In 1981, General Motors and Chrysler opened new high-technology engine plants in Saltillo, significantly increasing their installed capacity to 570,000 and 395,000 units respectively. Ford's 1983 Chihuahua plant uses advanced technology and a skilled labor force. The engines produced in this plant have quality comparable to U.S.-manufactured engines and require similar labor input. Another example of the quality and high productivity of this segment is Renault's engine plant in Center-North Mexico. Renault's Mexican operations, after withdrawing from the passenger car market in 1986, consist solely of an engine plant in Torreon producing nearly 150,000 units per year; this plant produces some of the best-quality engines of the French manufacturer.

Total engine exports quadrupled in value in two years and reached over 1.4 million units by 1988. Practically all of the Big Three exports are directed to the United States. Nevertheless, they still constitute less than 14% of the total amount of engines used every year in the U.S.-based production. The satisfactory results of these plants in world markets has led Ford to announce increased investments to double its capacity in its Chihuahua engine operations (table 7.2).

High-Tech Vehicle Plants

The second stage in export growth began in 1987 with the high-tech vehicle plants. Ford's Hermosillo plant, one of the most advanced in the world, became operational that year and was to annually assemble, largely from Japanese parts, 130,000 units of Mercury Tracers for export to the United States. However, due to the appreciation of the yen the units became more expensive than expected, halving actual production to 65,000 per year. Originally, about 65% of components were Japanese, 3% from the United States, and 32% Mexican, but with time the input composition has dramatically changed. The 1990 model contained nearly 75% U.S. parts, 15% from Japan, and only 5% from Mexico. In this new phase, after a partial shutdown of the plant in 1989 that nearly halved exports, the new Ford-Mazda Escort model is being produced with exports reaching over 40,000 units in 1990.

Exports from General Motors since 1986 have been erratic, with total units fluctuating between 20,000 and 40,000. Chrysler's vehicle exports include an almost constant 22,000 units of the D-150 light truck and, until

1989, mostly compact K-models. More recently, Volkswagen's shutdown in the United States (due to reduced demand) resulted in its operational shift to Mexico, thus creating a flow of small car exports to the United States. Finally, Nissan's exports, steadily growing since 1987, are almost completely directed to other Latin American countries.

In summary, total vehicle units exported jumped from 20,000 in 1983 to 278,000 seven years later. In 1983, Volkswagen was responsible for 90% of exports and only 1% of vehicles were directed to North America, while in 1990 86% were sent to the United States alone. Of these, 87% represented exports of the Big Three back home (table 7.3).

Maquiladoras and Auto Parts

The maquiladoras ("in-bond" plants) are another recent component of North American automobile integration, exemplifying a cost-efficient combination of inputs between the two countries. The basic operation of a maquila plant consists of the import of components and assembly in Mexico for later export. These plants are exempt from Mexican majority ownership rules governing the auto parts industry, and are able to import components free from duties as long as they export at least 80% of their output.

These plants have experienced dynamic growth in the past decade, especially since 1984. From about 12,000 workers in 1982, transportation equipment maquiladoras employed about 100,000 workers in 1990. That year, their total value added represented an average of 23% of exported value and had multiplied sevenfold since 1982. Automotive maquiladoras are the second most important maquila group following electronic materials and accessories. They contribute one out of five workers in the total maquiladora operations located in Mexico (table 7.4).

In order to clarify the sometimes misrepresented nature of this industry, we will study a sample of 178 maquiladora plants out of the total of 187 transportation plants in May 1991 (table 7.5). Because of the paucity of available data on the maquiladoras, we provide fairly detailed information about these plants. Our results show that one out of four of these plants is engaged in the production of wire harnesses, an extremely labor-intensive activity. In 1990, Mexico was the most important exporter to the United States of this product, followed by Taiwan and the Philippines. Japanese data also show large imports of these products into Japan from other Asian countries like Taiwan. From our data, almost all components used in Mexican wire harness plants are imported from the United States, representing

Table 7.3
Mexican-based passenger car production for domestic sales and exports (before and after the 1989 Auto Decree)

Auto maker	Models	(Type)	1988				1990				
			Production	For: Domestic sales	Exports U.S.	(%)	Production	imports	For: Domestic sales	Exports U.S.	(%)
Chrysler	Dart/Aries	(C)	21,385	14,406	6,960		0		0	0	
	Volare/Reliant	(C)	21,930	13,159	8,725		0		0	0	
	Shadow	(C)	19,029	15,005	3,980		29,344		23,703	4,714	
	Sundace	(C)	3953		4,220		0		0	0	
	Spirit	(C)					32,494		23,941	8,640	
	Acclaim	(C)					8,618			8,612	
	Phantom	(L)	8,021	3,191	4,587		35,053		2,009	33,389	
	New Yorker	(L)	2,161	2,152	2		2,862		2,850		
	Magnum	(S)	819	819			0		0		
	Imperial	(L)						77	77		
	Total		77,299	48,732	28,474	92.6%	108,371	77	52,580	55,355	99.2%
Ford	Topaz	(C)	19,512	19,116			28,664		35,355		
	Tracer	(C)	66,361		66,361		47,702			47,702	
	Escort	(C)					40,902			40,902	
	Guia	(C)					3,670		3,470		
	Taurus	(L)	6,974	6,855			3,502		4,073		
	Cougar	(L)	2,919	2,961			5,647		6,553		
	Thunderbird	(S)	3,049	3,069			4,504		5,431		
	Lincoln Town	(L)						940	940		
	Total		98,815	32,001	66,361	97.8%	134,591	940	55,822	88,604	100.0%

Maker	Model	Type									
G. M.	Celebrity	(C)	40,449	4,080	36,385		0		267	0	
	Cavalier	(C)	9,012	9,152	3		15,024		13,212		
	Cutlass	(C)	2,016	2,050			13,676		13,686		
	Century	(L)					45,075		4,084	40,993	
	Cadillac	(L)						789	789		
	Corvette	(L)						313	313		
	Total		51,477	15,282	36,388	99.7%	73,775	1,102	32,351	40,993	100.0%
Nissan	Tsuru	(P)	71,201	60,247	12,319		98,450		79,945	18,737	
	Maxima	(L)						438	438		
	300 ZX	(L)						119	119		
	Total		71,201	60,247	12,319	0.0%	98,450	557	80,502	18,737	0.0%
VW	Sedan	(P)	19,008	19,348	51		84,930		84,245	83	
	Golf	(P)	17,380	16,988	286		58,482		27,948	29,075	
	Jetta	(C)	12,879	12,293	24		39,494		21,390	17,074	
	Corsar	(C)	3,095	3,996	75		0		49		
	Passat	(C)						1,129	1,129		
	Total		52,362	52,625	436	9.3%	182,906	1,129	134,761	46,232	77.4%
Totals	Populars	(P)	107,589	96,583	12,656		241,862	0	192,138	47,895	
	Compacts	(C)	217,605	91,207	126,733		259,588	1,129	136,202	127,644	
	Luxury	(L)	22,092	17,209	4,589		92,139	2,676	22,245	74,382	
	Sports	(S)	3,868	3,888	0		4,504	0	5,431	0	
	Total		351,154	208,887	143,978	85.7%	598,093	3,805	356,016	249,921	86.8%

Note: The letters in parenthesis represent the type of car as classified in Mexico:
Populars: (P)
Compacts: (C)
Luxury: (L)
Sports: (S)
Source: AMIA, several issues.

Table 7.4
Automotive maquiladora industry, 1979–1988

| | | | Transportation equipment | | | | | Transp. equip./National total | | |
| | | | Imported inputs | Value added (millions of U.S.$) | Exported value | V.A./ imp. inputs (percent) | V.A./ exp. value (percent) | Workers | Value added (percent) | Exported value |
Year	Plants	Workers								
1980	53	7,500	—	62.2	—	—	—	6.3%	8.1%	—
1981	44	10,999	—	125.5	—	—	—	8.4%	13.0%	—
1982	44	12,288	—	130.7	—	—	—	9.7%	17.0%	—
1983	47	19,048	—	171.8	—	—	—	12.8%	21.1%	—
1984	51	29,079	—	222.8	—	—	—	14.6%	19.4%	—
1985	62	39,848	—	329.5	1,438.8	—	22.9%	18.8%	26.0%	28.2%
1986	76	48,140	1,313.9	307.9	1,621.8	23.4%	19.0%	19.6%	23.8%	28.7%
1987	107	59,278	1,704.5	381.6	2,082.2	22.4%	18.3%	19.4%	23.9%	29.3%
1988	131	83,290	2,253.5	596.3	2,849.8	26.5%	20.9%	21.4%	25.5%	28.1%
1989	149	87,813	2,664.2	725.1	3,389.3	27.2%	21.4%	20.1%	23.8%	27.1%
1990	187	100,461	2,989.2	908.3	3,897.5	30.4%	23.3%	22.5%	25.2%	27.7%

Source: INEGI and Banco de Mexico, several issues.

Table 7.5
Survey of the Mexican automotive maquiladora industry (May 1991)*

Product	Number of plants	Capital ownership				Location	
		U.S. (above 90%)	U.S.-Mexico joint ventures²	Mexico (above 50%)	Other nations	Northern states	Other
Wire harnesses	43	34	2	5	2 (Japan)	43	
Other electrical components	9	4		4	1 (Jan-Mex)	8	1
Radio receivers	3	2			1 (Panama)	3	
Seat covers, interior trim and parts	14	12	1		1 (Canada)	13	1
Seat belts	5	5				5	
Plastic parts and boards	9	8³		1		9	
Windshields or safety glass	5	2		3		3	2
Air conditioners and air compressors	7			3		7	
Bumpers and body parts	7	4	1	1	1 (US-Jap)	6	1
Metallic structures for trailers	8	2	1	4	1 (Canada)	7	1
Body repairs and modifications	6	3	1	2		5	1
Golf cars	2			2		2	
Reconstruction of parts	7	2	1	4		6	1
Chromizing and shining of rims	11	6	1	4		11	
Rims	2	2				2	
Wheel components	2	1		1		2	

Table 7.5 (continued)

Product	Number of plants	Capital ownership				Location	
		U.S. (above 90%)	U.S.-Mexico joint ventures[2]	Mexico (above 50%)	Other nations	Northern states	Other
Radiators	3	2	1			2	1
Hydraulic mechanisms	3	3				3	
Assembly of gear boxes	3			3		3	
Assembly of aluminium parts	2			2		2	
Brake components	6	4	1	1		4	2
Mufflers	2	2				2	
Other small components[1]	13	9		3	1 (Panama)	12	1
Total	172	111	10	43	8	160	12
		64.5%	5.8%	25.0%	4.7%	93.0%	7.0%

Notes:

*This reflects a survey of 180 Transportation Equipment Maquiladoras. Here we only include those engaged in automotive related activities.

1. It includes (1) Speedometers; (1) Ceramic Magnets; (1) Catalytic Converters; (2) Metallic components; (1) Transmission components; (1) Windshield Wipers.

2. With US percentage ownership below 90% but above 50%.

3. It includes 1 US-German Joint Venture with 96% US capital ownership.

Source: Direction of the Maquiladora Industry, SECOFI Mexico.

close to 70% of Total Production Value. Presumably, the proportion of U.S.-made components is much less in East Asian production.

Seat covers and interior trim constitute another 8% of maquiladora plants. Chromizing and shining of rims takes 5%, followed by various other components. Mexico is the main supplier to the United States of seats, safety belts, and windshield wipers. All of these operations are labor intensive; lower Mexican wages are obviously of great benefit to U.S. producers. Japan similarly uses neighboring Taiwan and Singapore, and more recently Thailand, for producing such components.[9] If U.S. producers were denied access to the Mexican labor market for these production stages, they would be at a disadvantage relative to Japanese access to neighboring low-wage countries. (Presently, European producers may gain similar access to labor markets in Eastern Europe.)

To explore this issue further, we looked at the U.S. Import Tariff by item from 1982 until 1990, covering the period of the Mexican automotive export surge. We chose a sample of seventeen of the highest U.S. imports from Mexico, which are almost completely supplied by maquiladoras.[10] Table 7.6 presents the participation of Mexican imports in total U.S. imports as well as Mexico's ranking among exporters to the United States in each product analyzed. Similarly we also show the percentage of U.S. imports coming from the first, second, or third countries in the ranking. In nine of the products analyzed, imports from Mexico rank lower than those from Japan, Taiwan, Korea, or Hong Kong, among others. These other countries constitute a high percentage of the U.S. import bill in these items. As noted, a difference may be found in the U.S. content of imports from such nations versus imports from Mexico.

Our study also shows that 65% of the plants have U.S. ownership of more than 90% of capital, and ten more constitute U.S.-Mexican joint ventures with Mexican participation below 50% (table 7.5). Only eight plants in the sample have ownership interests from other countries, half of these with Japanese participation. The maquiladoras are thus in large part a U.S. operation, sourcing components with large U.S. inputs for North American-based plants.

For a total of thirty-six maquiladoras we obtained more detailed data. Our criterion for this sample included choosing all the operations of the Big Three, and all other producers with non-U.S. capital in their structure (excluding Mexico). General Motors is the assembler most involved in maquiladoras, employing close to 38,000 workers. Wire harnesses represent most of its plants; it also engages in other activities of maquiladoras as

Table 7.6
The highest U.S. imports from the Mexican maquiladoras (1982–1990)

Product	1982 Mexico Imports/tot. U.S. imports	1982 Mexico Ranking	1982 Other countries Country	1982 Other countries Ranking	1990 Mexico Imports/tot. U.S. imports	1990 Mexico Ranking	1990 Other countries Country	1990 Other countries Imports/tot. U.S. imports	1990 Other countries Ranking
Locks of base metal	3.4%	(6)	Japan	(1)	13.7%	(2)	Japan	59.6%	(1)
			West Germany	(2)			Taiwan	13.6%	(3)
Nickel-cadmium storage batteries	49.7%	(1)	Japan	(2)	25.2%	(2)	Japan	59.7%	(1)
			Hong Kong	(3)			Hong Kong	5.7%	(3)
Windshield wipers	0.0%	*	Canada	(1)	77.3%	(1)	West Germany	8.8%	(2)
							Japan	4.2%	(3)
Radio-tape player combinations	0.0%	*	Japan	(1)	40.6%	(1)	Japan	29.5%	(2)
			Hong Kong	(2)			Korea	14.0%	(3)
Radio-broadcast receivers	24.2%	(2)	Brazil	(1)	64.1%	(1)	Singapore	14.9%	(2)
			Japan	(3)			Japan	12.8%	(3)
Insulated ignition wiring	74.0%	(1)	Taiwan	(2)	73.7%	(1)	Philippines	6.7%	(2)
			Japan	(3)			Taiwan	5.3%	(3)
Safety seat belts for bodies	10.3%	(4)	Japan	(1)	64.5%	(1)	Japan	24.9%	(2)
			Canada	(2)			Canada	9.3%	(3)
Radiators, for motor vehicles	2.5%	(5)	Japan	(1)	22.4%	(2)	Canada	49.3%	(1)
			West Germany	(2)			Japan	9.2%	(3)
Mufflers and exhaust pipes, for vehicles	0.1%	*	Canada	(1)	31.3%	(2)	Japan	32.8%	(1)
			West Germany	(2)			Canada	8.0%	(3)
Steering wheels, steering columns	n.a.				22.6%	(2)	Japan	44.5%	(1)
							Canada	20.9%	(3)

Product	%		Source(s)		%		Source(s)	
Parts of trailers and semi-trailers	13.7%	(2)	Japan (1) / West Germany (3)		9.3%	(3)	Taiwan 22.4% (1) / Canada 15.2% (2)	
Accesories for automatic regulatos	n.a.				16.3%	(2)	Japan 33.7% (1) / West Germany 9.3% (3)	
Seats of a kind used for motor vehicles	n.a.				60.8%	(1)	Canada 32.8% (2) / Japan 13.0% (3)	
Parts of seats of a kind used for vehicles	n.a.				14.3%	(3)	Canada 64.1% (1) / Japan 18.2% (2)	
Other parts of seats	n.a.				20.6%	(2)	Canada 34.1% (1) / West Germany 11.0% (3)	
Lighters	0.0%	*	Canada (1)		51.4%	(1)	Taiwan 14.1% (2) / Korea 13.4% (3)	

Notes:
*Below 7th. place as a U.S. source of imports of this product.
n.a. The exact match for this product to the Harmonized Tariff System in 1990 was not found.
Source: Data base provided by SECOFI from the U.S. Tariff System.

described above. Ford's and Chrysler's participation is significantly smaller (table 7.7).

With the exception of Honda's plant, Mexican components represent at most 4.8% of production value with a mean of 0.3%. The total Mexican value added in this sample constituted on average 22% of total production value. The Big Three employ a total of 53,000 workers in all their analyzed maquiladora operations. For this sample of U.S. auto makers, close to 80% of total production value is represented by imported materials, while Mexican components represent less than 1%. The wage bill is about 10% of the total value of production. This is relatively good news for U.S. labor, given that these ratios would differ significantly in overseas operations.

Other U.S. component imports from the Mexican auto parts industry outside the maquiladora sector have shown significant growth but their future is not certain, at least in their present condition. Between 1982 and 1989, auto parts exports multiplied five times in value. North America represented nearly 80% of total Mexican auto part exports in 1990, but the Mexican share of total U.S. imports trails the share of several other countries. Parts exports are concentrated among a small number of companies and include very labor-intensive products and those in which Mexico has some other competitive advantage. There is an absence of firms exporting high-technology parts, and a lack of international competitiveness in medium-technology parts. It seems that most of these exports constitute low-technology products.

To further explore this issue, we undertook the same type of analysis as with the maquiladoras looking at highly exported Mexican auto parts in the U.S. Import Tariff (table 7.8). We can confirm the above observations. With the exception of safety glass, Mexican imports represent around 5% of U.S. total imports. Mexico ranks significantly lower than Japan or Canada for most of these. Absent further foreign investment in the auto parts industry, most of the auto parts sector that produces for the domestic Mexican market is likely to be replaced by imports from the United States.

Prospects for the Domestic Market

The oil bonanza period between 1977 and 1981 significantly benefited the Mexican automobile production. Passenger car production grew at an average of 25% per year. Total vehicle production peaked in 1981 at close to 600,000 units, with automotive GDP representing 7.1% of total manufacturing GDP. Nonetheless, as in the previous twenty years, increased production was tied to higher imports and a sectoral trade deficit, which in

Table 7.7
Survey of Mexican automotive maquiladora plants (data for May 1991)

Owner and production	Plants surveyed	Number of employees	Mex'n comp./ prodn. value (%)	Value added/ prodn. value (%)[1]	Import. com./ prodn. value (%)
Big three	27	53,509	0.2%	20.9%	79.1%
Wire harnesses	14	29,458	0.5%	27.7%	72.3%
Seat covers, vinyl boards and interior trim	5	9,336	0.0%	28.5%	71.5%
Gasoline injectors and engine controls	1	2,931	0.0%	23.5%	76.5%
Radios	1	4,137	0.0%	4.8%	95.2%
Bumpers	1	1,224	2.3%	58.2%	41.8%
Ceramic magnets	1	771	0.0%	90.6%	9.4%
Windows, glass	1	380	1.0%	60.8%	39.2%
Climate controls and radiators	1	1,301	0.0%	22.5%	77.5%
Steering columns	1	2,764	0.1%	14.5%	85.5%
Catalytic converters	1	1,207	0.0%	61.0%	39.0%
U.S. joint ventures					
Korea-U.S.: Metallic structures	1	6	0.0%	40.0%	60.0%
Germany-U.S.: Plastic springs	1	53	0.4%	4.4%	95.6%

Table 7.7 (continued)

Owner and production	Plants surveyed	Number of employees	Mex'n comp./ prodn. value (%)	Value added/ prodn. value (%)[1]	Import. com./ prodn. value (%)
Other countries					
Japan:					
Wire harnesses	2	4,381	0.2%	59.5%	40.5%
Honda, seat covers and body parts	1	236	27.9%	48.1%	51.9%
Jap-Mex: Electrical components	1	52	1.7%	80.7%	19.3%
Panama:					
Cassete players	1	13	0.0%	1.2%	98.8%
Speed counters	1	44	0.0%	54.3%	45.7%
Canada:					
Leather wheel covers	1	663	0.4%	21.0%	79.0%
Total of sample		58,957	0.3%	22.0%	78.0%

Notes:
Total production value is defined as the sum of value added plus imported components.
1. It includes Mexican components.
Source: Own calculations based on data provided from SECOFI.

Table 7.8
Some of the highest U.S. imports from the Mexican auto parts industry (1982–1990)

Product	1982 Mexico Imports/tot. U.S. imports	Ranking	1982 Other countries Country	Ranking	1990 Mexico Imports/tot. U.S. imports	Ranking	1990 Other countries Country	Imports/tot. U.S. imports	Ranking
Toughened (tempered) safety glass	0.2%	*	Canada	(1)	28.8%	(2)	Canada	36.2%	(1)
			Japan	(2)			Japan	14.5%	(3)
Windshields of laminated safety glass	53.2%	(1)	Canada	(2)	37.9%	(1)	Canada	31.1%	(2)
			West Germany	(3)			West Germany	5.9%	(3)
Bodies (including cabs)	0.2%	*	Canada	(1)	2.1%	(6)	Canada	56.6%	(1)
			Japan	(2)			Japan	12.1%	(2)
Bumpers and parts thereof	36.3%	(1)	Japan	(2)	5.2%	(4)	Canada	62.3%	(1)
			West Germany	(3)			Japan	18.2%	(2)
Brakes, servo-brakes and parts	1.9%	(6)	Canada	(1)	3.6%	(5)	Canada	43.5%	(1)
			Japan	(2)			Japan	25.7%	(2)
Gear boxes for vehicles	12.9%	(4)	Canada	(1)	0.3%	(6)	Japan	52.6%	(1)
			Japan	(2)			Canada	23.7%	(2)
Road wheels and parts and accessories	10.2%	(6)	Taiwan	(1)	5.3%	(5)	Canada	34.4%	(1)
							Japan	20.1%	(2)
Clutches and parts thereof	n.a.				3.9%	(7)	Japan	51.2%	(1)
							Canada	12.3%	(2)
Parts and accessories of bodies	0.0%	*	Canada	(1)	5.0%	(4)	Japan	61.1%	(1)
							Canada	16.8%	(2)

Notes:
*Below 7th. place as a U.S. source of imports of this product.
n.a. The exact match for this product to the Harmonized Tariff System in 1990 was not found.
Source: Data base provided by SECOFI from U.S. Tariff System.

1981 explained close to 40% of the national deficit. The period of high inflation and fall in per capita real income until 1988 seriously affected the domestic market. From 1981 to 1983, total passenger car sales dropped 43%. A slight recovery in the following two years was followed by two worse years, leaving domestic passenger car sales at a ten-year low of 154,152 units in 1987.

The stabilization of the economy since 1988 and special policy measures, such as the "Auto Popular" Decree and certain price controls, have created a significant recovery in domestic sales, more than doubling the 1987 sales figure with 352,608 passenger cars and 550,000 vehicles in 1990. This year was the third in a row with a growth rate above 30%.

Automotive imports closely followed the production swings of the 1980s, reflecting domestic sales and exports (figures 7.13 and 7.17). Nonetheless, the introduction of the less restrictive automotive decrees in 1989 marked the end of six years of trade surplus in this sector. The partial deregulation and increased openness of the auto industry made imports of components alone jump from $1.7 billion in 1988 to $4.6 billion two years later. The data seems to suggest a fragile trade surplus and an inevitable dependence on imports of components for both exports and the growing domestic market.

Although Mexican nominal imports have somewhat changed over time, we see an almost constant proportion of imports from the United States. Comparing the import structures of 1982 and 1990, we find a nonsignificant variation of proportion of materials used in the production of auto parts, engine components, and auto parts themselves. All of these numbers are above 70% (table 7.9).

As for passenger car imports themselves, manufacturers have been mostly importing luxury cars during this period of adjustment (table 7.3). Partial explanations are the actual limits on the amount of imports, and the higher profit margin obtainable from these cars, which would otherwise not be produced in the country in such short runs. In 1990, the Big Three accounted for 68% of the imported units sold, equivalent to 88% in value. However, in thinking about these numbers, we should consider possible uncertainties about the final terms of the Free Trade Agreement and the fact that the period of observation is still very short in relation to production decisions.

The likely bright future of the export-oriented sector is not shared by the rest of the parts and vehicle plants in Mexico. These plants are the result of decades of import-substitution policies, oligopolistic protection, and restricted entry conditions, all of which impeded technological pro-

Table 7.9
Mexican automobile import structure

Imports	1982 U.S./Total (%)	1990 U.S./Total (%)
Components used in parts production	71.6	73.0
Liquids, glass, metal parts, wheels, etc.	72.3	72.5
Engines, bombs, filters, mechanical systems	70.9	72.4
Metallic structures, "pullers"	92.4	97.8
Engine components and parts	82.3	83.7
Auto parts	76.0	73.6
Parts in Chapter 87 (automobiles)	75.8	74.7
Boards, seats, and interior trim	77.6	67.7
Chassis and bodies	98.5	88.9
Vehicles	96.4	86.1
Tractors	100.0	91.3
Buses	36.5	85.7
Passenger vehicles	99.4	87.9
Trucks	90.5	98.5
Special vehicles	96.7	64.8

Source: Data base provided by SECOFI from the U.S. Tariff System.

gress. These vehicle assembly plants operate in very short runs, far below world scale (around 250,000 units), aiming at a small closed market with scarce opportunities for competition. Levels of technology are low, there is little use of robotics, and antiquated equipment dominates the environment. The organization of production and labor-management relations are far from current lean production techniques or their closest equivalents in non-Japanese firms.[11]

Nevertheless, for a variety of reasons which include Volkswagen's shutdown and the strategic decisions of U.S. producers responding to some changes in demand, these plants have exported some models in recent years. Contrary to expectations, some plants have achieved higher productivity and quality performance levels than similar plants in other developing countries. It is nonetheless clear that the arrival of a free trade area will create extraordinary pressure on these plants, which will need to undergo substantial restructuring in order to remain open. Among several possibilities is the specialization of some of them on particular models that are produced in small runs, due to their own characteristics or to market demand conditions. This may be happening already, with some luxury models produced and exported in 1990 (table 7.3). Substantial growth and enlargement of the plants is another option. This is unlikely, as it would entail the modernization of the whole infrastructure of the plant when their location near Mexico City in the geographical center of the country makes exports more difficult.

III The Potential Demand for Automobiles in Mexico

The Mexican export boom discussed above is made possible by the relatively open U.S. economy. Since the trade barriers to Mexican autos entering the United States are small, while the barriers to U.S. finished vehicle exports to Mexico are large, the opening of the Mexican auto market to U.S. producers will be one of the largest effects of a free trade agreement. The inefficient operations of the traditional plants in the center of Mexico suggest that the "new" Mexican market will be largely served by existing plants in the rest of North America.

In this section we consider the potential size of the Mexican market by examining the current demand for automobiles in Mexico. We estimate a simple demand system, depending on prices and national income, for various types of autos in Mexico. The estimated model parameters allow us to predict the demand for autos in Mexico as prices fall and as income rises under a free trade agreement. Although the current size of the Mexican market is small, our parameters are consistent with a prediction that a fall in prices to world levels, together with a rise in national income, will produce a substantial increase in Mexican auto demand. If the free trade agreement is restricted to North American producers, then this substantially increased market will be an important source of revenues for these firms.

The partial equilibrium approach of this section contrasts with the related general equilibrium work of Hunter, Markusen, and Rutherford (1991). That paper attempts to solve out for all of the equilibrium responses to a free trade agreement, including new demand levels, output prices, input choices, and industry wages. Such an ambitious undertaking necessitates heroic assumptions on the nature of production and demand. Also, the parameters of that model are selected by a combination of arbitrary guesses and calibration to a very small amount of data. For example, the authors treat all automobiles as a homogeneous good and assume a constant demand elasticity equal to one.

Our approach is strictly partial equilibrium, but we allow for product differentiation and provide econometric estimates of demand elasticities. The econometric approach provides a clear path from the data to the results and allows us to calculate standard errors for model parameters and for projected demand. Rather than attempt to solve out for new equilibrium outcomes, we provide a series of projections for Mexican automobile demand under alternative hypotheses about post-free-trade prices and growth in income. The approach of Berry, Levinsohn, and Pakes (1991) could be used to extend the partial equilibrium approach of this chapter to include a much richer model of product differentiation and an explicit calculation of new (partial) equilibrium outcomes under free trade.

The data for our analysis are constructed from a monthly series of product-level prices and sales for the eleven-year period 1980–1990. These data were kindly made available to us by the Mexican automobile dealers association. The Mexican auto dealers group their autos into four categories, "popular" (which at the end of 1990 includes the Volkswagen beetle and a local version of the Nissan Sentra), "compact" (which includes the VW Jetta and Ford Topaz), "sports" (such as the Ford Thunderbird), and "large" (or "luxury," which includes the Ford Taurus, GM Century, and Chrysler New Yorker, but no U.S.-style luxury cars such as Cadillac or Mercedes). As mentioned above, until 1990 Mexican law required that all of these automobiles be produced in Mexico, and only very limited imports are now allowed.

For the purposes of this study, we have aggregated the product-level monthly data into quarterly data on three product groups: popular, compact, and a combined "luxury" category, including both large and sporty cars. We combined the two more expensive types of cars because of the relatively small sales and sporadic production of the sporty models. For 1990, average prices (in U.S. dollars at 1990 exchange rates) and unit sales of these three types of cars are as follows (note that these sales figures differ slightly from the production numbers above):

	Popular	Compact	Luxury	Total
Sales	174,704	127,674	27,618	329,996
Prices ($)	15,824	30,574	45,383	23,191

Relative to the United States, these figures are notable for the high level of prices and for the extremely low level of demand (about 0.34% in annual per capita auto sales.) Both of these factors suggest the potential for a much larger market under free trade.

To consider this potential market, we suppose that the demand for autos of a particular type depends on the average prices in the three classes, on national income, and on the prices of alternative uses of income. We posit two broad alternative uses of income: savings and the consumption of other goods. Other goods are treated as the numeraire, as prices are adjusted for the Mexican consumer price index (CPI). We include as the "price" of savings the real rate of interest on three-month Mexican treasury bills (RATE). National income is proxied by gross domestic product (GDP.)

Estimates of Demand

As a particular functional form for demand, we adopt a constant elasticity framework in which the demand for product type j at time t, q_{jt}, depends on the prices of all the product types, p_{jt}, and on aggregate demand factors, x_t:

$$\ln(q_{jt}) = x_t \beta_j + \sum_k \eta_{jk} \ln(p_{kt}) + \varepsilon_{jt}, \tag{1}$$

where η_{jk} is the elasticity of demand for product j with respect to the price of product k, and ε_{jt} represents unobserved demand factors that are assumed to be uncorrelated with x_t. Consistent with the discussion of the last paragraph, the terms included in x_t are a constant, the logarithm of real quarterly GDP (indexed with 1980 GDP equal to 100) and the real three-month T-bill rate. Over the course of the sample, the GDP index varies from 96.3 to 128.5 with a mean of 109.8.

Table 7.10 presents OLS estimates of the parameters in (1) for each of the product classes, with the cross-price elasticities all constrained to be zero. These results are consistent with priors, in that an increase in GDP is associated with increases in demand, while increases in interest rates and prices appear to decrease demand. For each product class, price elasticities

Table 7.10
OLS demand results, by type; dependent variable is: ln Qty (standard errors in parentheses)

	Popular	Compact	Luxury
Const	2.14	−6.60	2.07
	(2.32)	(4.13)	(4.02)
LnGDP	2.60	4.14	2.95
	(0.64)	(1.12)	(1.13)
Rate	−0.75	−1.01	−0.89
	(0.14)	(0.21)	(0.23)
LnPrice	−0.67	−0.45	−1.08
	(0.21)	(0.27)	(0.29)
R-SQ	0.63	0.52	0.59

of demand are estimated to be either inelastic or approximately unit elastic. However, these OLS estimates ignore the time-series nature of the data, the effect of cross-price elasticities, and the correlation of prices with the unobserved demand characteristics, ε_j. This latter feature of the data will tend to bias our results in the direction of inelastic demands.

Instrumental variables methods are the well-known solution to the correlation of prices with demand errors. The choice of instruments describes the "experiments" that reveal movements along a given demand curve; a question naturally arises as to the availability of such instruments. Luckily for our econometric analysis, in the 1980s the Mexican government itself conducted a sequence of "experiments" (or policy changes) that altered input prices and competition in the auto industry. We take variables proxying for these experiments as our instruments.

We consider two types of relevant policy changes. For much of the 1980s, the government set a special"controlled" exchange rate, which was available for many commercial transactions. (Toward the end of our data, the controlled exchange rate coincides with the market exchange rate.) Changes in this exchange rate affect the input costs of auto producers by altering the cost of imported inputs. (The exact nature of the change in perceived input costs is complex, as for much of this period auto firms may import only by exporting in equivalent amounts.) The controlled exchange rate is therefore one instrument for prices. Also, as outlined in section III, during the time period of our analysis the government announced two new decrees affecting automotive production and competition. These decrees took effect in 1984 and 1990. Furthermore, at the end of 1987, the government launched a new "stabilization" effort under which it tried to reduce the real prices of automobiles.

Thus, as proxies for different government policy regimes, we use as instruments four time-specific dummy variables. These dummy variables cover the periods 1980–1983, 1984–1987, 1988–1989, and 1990 respectively. The first of these is omitted to avoid collinearity with the constant in x. In addition to the x vector, we therefore use four instruments for prices: three time dummies plus the controlled exchange rate.

We will not present a dynamic model of automobile demand in Mexico, but we will acknowledge the time series nature of the data with an assumption on the serial correlation of the unobservables. In particular, we assume that ε_{jt} follows a linear first-order autoregression:

$$\varepsilon_{jt} = \rho\varepsilon_{jt-1} + v_{jt}, \tag{2}$$

where v_{jt} is assumed to be independently distributed across time and to

Table 7.11
Demand system results; instrumental variables (standard errors in parentheses)

	Popular	Compact	Luxury
Const	3.30	−5.69	−2.64
	(4.81)	(5.05)	(4.29)
lnGDP	3.40	3.98	4.55
	(1.33)	(1.51)	(1.26)
Rate	−0.17	−0.87	−0.51
	(0.39)	(0.19)	(0.36)
lnPrice Pouplar	−2.80	1.08	—
	(0.91)	(0.62)	
lnPrice Compact	1.08	−1.49	—
	(0.62)	(0.51)	
lnPrice Luxury	—	—	−1.55
			(0.44)
serial correlation	0.47		
	(0.22)		

be mean independent of exogenous data, z (consisting of x and the four instruments described above). Our estimation method requires no further assumptions on the properties of the unobservables, such as homoskedasticity or assumptions on the correlation of the errors across product types at a given time.

Estimating the demand system with an unrestricted matrix of price elasticities yields very imprecise estimates of the elasticities. Table 7.11 provides a set of estimates that impose symmetry on the matrix of elasticities and constrain the cross-price elasticities between luxury autos and other autos to be zero. This restriction is not rejected by the data and, given that some restrictions are necessary for precise estimates, appears relatively reasonable. These estimates indicate once again that demand increases in GDP and decreases as interest rates raise. A 1% increase in GDP is associated with a greater than 3% demand increase for each product type. The estimated own-price elasticities are negative as required, and are significantly different from zero. In contrast to the OLS results, the estimates imply elastic demands for each product type. The large value of the own-price elasticity for "popular" cars is consistent with the large sales response to recent price cuts for the Volkswagen Beetle, as discussed above. The estimated cross-price elasticity between popular and compact autos is positive, although not precisely estimated. As expected with quarterly data, the estimated serial correlation parameter (of 0.47) is positive and significantly different from zero.

Table 7.12
Actual and projected Mexican auto sales (standard errors in parentheses)

	Popular	Compact	Luxury	Total
Actual fourth quarter 1990 sales	53,027	24,263	7,964	85,254
U.S. Prices + 20% Tariff	98,458 (36,678)	50,302 (21,183)	27,422 (13,949)	176,182 (56,642)
U.S. Prices No Tariff	139,093 (66,743)	54,644 (28,742)	37,432 (23,833)	231,169 (95,976)
5 years 3% Growth (U.S. Prices)	239,141 (161,916)	103,091 (78,008)	77,266 (64,230)	419,497 (245,933)
5 years 5% Growth (U.S. Prices)	356,080 (297,019)	164,338 (154,184)	131,587 (130,084)	652,004 (468,290)

Implications of the Estimates

These estimates imply a large effect of price decreases and of increases in national income. Post-free-trade demand will depend on aspects of the industry that we have not addressed (such as production parameters and the nature of competition) and on the details of the free trade agreements. We will therefore present estimates of demand under several hypotheses about prices and income.

Hunter, Markusen, and Rutherford (1991) note that producers may price discriminate across different countries if consumers are not allowed to trade across borders (and thereby arbitrage away any price differentials). They suggest that, depending on the terms of the free trade agreement, this may limit any decline in Mexican prices. However, the own-price demand elasticities estimated here are considerably higher than the unit elasticities assumed by these authors; this will limit the size of producer markups and thus limit the size of price differentials across countries.

Table 7.12 presents results for predicted unit quarterly sales under different scenarios. The first row of the table gives actual fourth-quarter of 1990 sales. The second and third rows of the table consider the effect of a decrease in prices to U.S. levels. For the purposes of these policy experiments, we use prices that approximate the prices of similar automobiles sold in the United States, $8,000 for "populars," $12,000 for compacts, and $18,000 for large and sporty cars. The second row assumes that the Mexican government retains tariffs and taxes sufficient to raise Mexican prices 20% above U.S. levels, while the third row assumes that prices fall to match their U.S. counterparts. We see that a price decrease to U.S. levels more than doubles total Mexican demand.

Increases in Mexican GDP will further increase demand. Rows four and five of the table present two scenarios. The first is that GDP continues to grow at recent rates of about 3% per year for five years. The second is that the free trade agreement accelerates growth to 5% per year for five years. Of course, the effects of such a large increase in GDP are difficult to measure precisely, as indicated by the large standard error of estimated demand in the last row. However, the point estimates suggest that under the optimistic assumptions of 5% growth and U.S. prices, Mexican demand could reach more than seven times its present level. Even the relatively conservative estimates in the third row imply total annual sales in excess of 1.6 million, which is roughly 15% of U.S. annual demand. This may be a reasonable number for a country with a population one-third that of the United States. However, the standard errors of these estimates indicate a wide range of possible outcomes.

Some Caveats and Possible Extensions

The analysis of the preceding section could be improved in several directions. The constant elasticity demand framework is relatively simple and could be extended to consider product-level information in the manner of Berry, Levinsohn, and Pakes (1991). In an application to the U.S. auto industry, that paper shows how to combine explicit models of consumer utility with product-level variables to estimate a much richer set of cross-price elasticities. The lack of attention to product-level detail has possible empirical implications; for example, we may underestimate demand increases by leaving out the effect of increases in product variety.

The framework of this chapter does not distinguish consumer perceptions of short- versus long-run changes in GDP and prices; adding this distinction would be quite difficult, but could alter interpretations of the income elasticity parameter. A related point is that we have not modeled the durable nature of automobiles, which implies that past sales influence current demand. Also, the policy experiments of the last section do not attempt to solve out for a new pricing equilibrium, but rather assume that current North American price levels will prevail. This assumption becomes less realistic as the Mexican market increases in size and is problematic if producers are allowed to price discriminate across countries. Once again, the methods of Berry, Levinsohn, and Pakes (1991) could be used to solve out for new pricing equilibria with and without price discrimination.

The demand analysis of this section makes no attempt to estimate the location of the plants that will service the growing Mexican market. While some new plants may locate in Mexico to produce models that have particular appeal in Mexico, we should note that apart from the VW Beetle, the models currently produced and sold in Mexico are very similar to other North American models. Therefore, much if not most of the increased Mexican demand could be served from plants that serve the overall North American market. As we argue above, if these plants were likely to move en masse to Mexico, they would have done so already.

Finally, we should comment briefly on the possible role of used automobiles. If free trade in used cars is permitted, the relatively poor Mexican consumers would become a major source of demand for used cars from the United States and Canada. This would substantially drive up the price of used cars and lead wealthier consumers (in all countries) to trade in their old cars more frequently. In this case a more complicated trading pattern might emerge, with the increase in North American demand for new cars coming largely from U.S. and Canadian consumers, while a large portion of Mexican demand is satisfied by used cars. A large supply of recent vintage used cars could easily supplant any new vehicle production geared expressly for the low-priced Mexican market, particularly the VW Beetle. However, as noted, free trade in used cars need not fundamentally alter our conclusion of a large increase in North American sales, but only the distribution of new cars sales across different groups.

IV Conclusion

We have argued that well-established exporting activities, with high levels of technology, product quality, and productivity, are likely to remain on both sides of the border. On the Mexican side, this sector will probably be formed by the engine plants, the high-tech assembly plants, the U.S.-Mexican joint ventures in auto parts, and a few other auto parts producers with high efficiency levels. The maquiladora industry in Mexico will continue to provide a useful cost-reducing mechanism for all North American-based plants, although their current justification, avoiding tariffs, is likely to disappear under a free trade agreement. Highly labor-intensive components will continue to be produced in plants similar to current operations.

There are several factors that make Mexican production difficult, which explains why most production activities will not simply move to "the other side." Mexico's industrial infrastructure is weak in several areas. There is a shortage of suppliers of maintenance parts, which increases the risk of a partial halt in operations for long periods. Transportation systems, such as rail and highways are still unreliable, disrupting supply lines and final prod-

uct delivery. Skilled labor is not abundant, at least in the medium run, and
additional training will be required for some tasks.

Mexico's role for the U.S. automobile industry could involve the opening of production activities of small models that compete directly with the
large number of similar cars imported from Japan or East Asia, sometimes
even by Ford or General Motors themselves (Kia, Geo). The benefit from
this strategy consists in the additional sourcing of components with high
percentages (close to 80%) from the United States, itself. Ford's restructuring of its Hermosillo plant points in this direction. Most importantly,
Mexico, as Canada with the implementation of the Auto Pact, offers the
opportunity for production diversification and rationalization.

Finally, the dynamics of the domestic Mexican market itself, expected to
reach 1.5 million units of annual sales in six to ten years, represents an
important possibility for export growth from U.S.-based plants. As Canada
did in the 1960s, Mexico could offer the opportunity for the creation of a
large new market just next door.

Appendix

The model defined by equations (1) and (2) can be rewritten in terms of the
model parameters, θ, and the data as

$$v_{jt}(q, x, p, \theta) = \varepsilon_{jt}(q, x, p, \theta) - \rho\varepsilon_{jt-1}(q, x, p, \theta),$$

where

$$\varepsilon_{jt}(q, x, p, \theta) = \ln(q_{jt}) - x_{jt}\beta - \sum_{k=1}^{3}\eta_{jk}\ln(p_{kt}).$$

Note that the model parameters are $\theta = (\beta, \eta, \rho)$, where η is a vector with
up to nine elements. Estimation is based on the moment condition

$$E(v_{jt}(q, x, p, \theta)/z) = 0,$$

where z is the seven vector of instruments discussed in the text. We sim-
plify our use of instruments by first regressing observed prices on the
seven instruments and creating predicted prices from the estimated coefficients. These predicted prices, $\hat{p}$, would be the optimal instruments for the
elasticities if expected value of price, conditional on z, were linear and if the
v's were i.i.d. (see White, 1984). In any case, they will provide consistent
and asymptotically normal estimates. Let the constructed instrument vector
be

$$\hat{z}_t = (x_t, \hat{p}_t).$$

We then choose the value of the parameters that minimizes the sample correlation between the errors and the instruments. The objective function is therefore

$$\min_\theta \frac{1}{T}\sum_t v_t(q, x, p, \hat{\theta}) \otimes \hat{z}_t.$$

The asymptotic variance, $V(\theta)$, of the resulting estimator is standard from White (1984).

The outcome of each of the "experiments" in table 7.12 can be written as the linear combination of the estimated parameters

$$\ln(\hat{q}_j) = \ln(q_j) + \delta'\theta,$$

for some δ. The variance of the estimator of log quantity is therefore

$$\text{Var}(\ln(\hat{q})) = \delta'V(\theta)\delta.$$

By the usual first-order expansion, the variance of the predicted quantity is

$$\text{Var}(\hat{q}) \approx \hat{q}\text{Var}(\ln(\hat{q})).$$

Notes

We are grateful to Armando Soto of the Mexican Automobile Dealers Association (A.M.D.A.), as well as to Luz Maria De la Mora, Humberto Jasso, Edilberto Jimenez, Octavio Rangel, Pino and Raul Valrejo of the Mexican Office for the Negotiation of the Free Trade Agreement, who kindly made data available to us. The opinions presented here are those of the authors alone. Of course, any errors that remain are our own responsibility.

1. See also Womack 1991 for a useful discussion of many of the issues discussed below. While Womack relies heavily on interviews with industry participants, we rely more on government and trade association data and, in our final section, on econometric analysis.

2. Of course, the increasing share of U.S. production is in large part a result of the robust recovery of the U.S. economy over exactly these years. A peak-to-peak comparison of, for example, 1978–1988, would produce somewhat different results.

3. Once again, this is influenced by cyclical factors.

4. Honda started its U.S. operations in 1982, and was soon followed by Nissan (1983), Toyota (1986), Mazda (1987), and Subaru-Isuzu (1989).

5. Only in Australia (included under "others") did American automobile output decrease in this period.

6. For a good description of the negotiation process between manufacturers and the Mexican government, consult Bennet and Sharpe (1985).

7. See Lopez-de-Silanes (1991) for a more detailed analysis of the past automotive decrees and their effects on the Mexican industry.

8. This constitutes a significant change since the previous 60% content rule was measured at production costs. Further discussion of this issue is also found in Lopez-de-Silanes (1991).

9. Data is from United Nations trade statistics.

10. Most of these products were chosen from the automotive products chapter in the U.S. Tariff Schedule (Chapter 87). Nonetheless, we also looked at all those products that are identifiable as pertaining for the most part to the automobile sector, but find themselves classified in other chapters of the Tariff Schedule. We included some of these items since several of them constitute a large part of U.S. imports from Mexico.

11. An analysis of current production processes and techniques is provided in Altschuler et al. (1985).

References

Altschuler, A. et al. 1985. "The Future of the Automobile: The Report of International Automobile Program." Cambridge, MA:MIT Press.

AMDA, "Cifras del Sector Automotor en Mexico, " several issues.

AMIA, "La Industria Automotriz de Mexico en Cifras," several issues.

Banco de Mexico, "Indicadores Economicos," several issues.

Bennet, D., and Sharpe, K. 1985. "Transnational Corporation vs. The State; The Political Economy of the Mexican Auto Industry." Princeton: Princeton University Press.

Berry, S., J. Levinsohn, and A. Pakes. 1991. "Automobile Prices in Equilibrium." Mimeo, July.

Bozz-Allen & Hamilton and Inforec. 1987. "Industria de Autopartes," Mexico, Bancomext and SECOFI study.

Hunter, L., J. Markusen, and T. Rutherford. 1991. "Trade Liberalization in a Multinational Dominated Industry: A Theoretical and Applied General Equilibrium Analysis." Mimeo June.

Lipsey, R., and R. York. 1988. *Evaluating the Free Trade Deal*. Toronto: C.D. Howe Institute.

Lopez-de-Silanes, F. 1991. "Automobiles; Mexican Perspective" in "U.S.-Mexican Industrial Integration; The Road to Free Trade," edited by Sidney Weintraub. Boulder, Co: Westview Press, Inc. Survey of Current business, various issues.

White, H. 1984. *Asymptotic Theory for Econometricians*. New York: Academic Press.

Womack, J. 1991. "A Positive sum Solution: Free Trade in the North American Motor Vehicle Sector," in Strategic Sector in Mexican-U.S. Free Trade. The Center for Strategic and International Studies, Vol. VIII, No. 6, Washington, D.C. World Motor Vehicles Data, various volumes.

Wards' Automotive Annual, various volumes.

8 Opening the Financial Services Market in Mexico

Peter M. Garber and
Steven R. Weisbrod

Ideally, the North American Free Trade Agreement will remove restrictions on banks' ability to operate across borders within the free trade area. This means that foreign financial institutions from within the area will be subject, without discrimination, to the same rules and regulations that are applied to domestic banks so that U.S. banks would be free to establish branches and own subsidiaries in Mexico.[1] In trade disputes with other countries, the position of the U.S. government has been that the United States has a comparative advantage in service-oriented industries such as banking and finance. Thus it argues that if U.S. banks are free to enter markets within a free trade area, they will play an important role in the economies of the countries within the free trade area.[2]

In this chapter, we investigate whether this proposition is likely to hold in Mexico—that is, given free entry, whether U.S. banks will play a major role in the Mexican financial system. We restrict our analysis to the impact of free entry on local financial markets. Since Mexico does not impose capital restrictions on its citizens, Mexicans can already freely use the services of United States, Mexican, or third-country financial institutions outside Mexico. Thus Mexicans currently can hold dollar-denominated bank deposits in banks in the United States or in the offshore branches of U.S. banks.

Moreover, the ability of large U.S. corporations to obtain financing for their Mexican operations will be little affected by the right of U.S. banks to enter the Mexican market. These corporations have for some time raised capital on a worldwide level rather than on a country-specific level. Thus they are likely to issue securities in liquid dollar markets and use swaps to hedge currency risk. They backstop their access to securities markets by holding liquidity lines with large U.S. banks. Since a local presence of a U.S. bank beyond a representative office, which is already permitted, is not

Table 8.1
Reprivatization process, Mexican commercial banks (figures in U.S. $millions)

Bank name	Total assets	Total liabilities	Total equity	Sale price	Sale price to book	New owners
1. M.M.M.	$2,626.5	$2,529.9	$98.6	$261.8	2.66	PROBURSA Group
2. BANPAIS	$1,124.9	$1,065.2	$59.7	$180.6	3.03	MEXIVAL Group
3. BANCA CREMI	$1,851.5	$1,742.2	$109.3	$372.1	3.40	GPO. GUADALAJARA
4. BANCA CONFIA	$2,386.5	$2,288.8	$101.0	$376.3	3.37	ABACO Group
5. BANORIE	$349.6	$322.5	$27.1	$111.2	4.10	GRUPO MARGEN
6. BANCRESER	$3,152.9	$3,097.3	$55.6	$140.7	2.53	ROBERTO ALCANTARA, CARLOS MENDOZA
7. BANAMEX	$23,961.9	$22,232.8	$1,729.1	$4,553.4	2.63	ACCIVAL
8. BANCOMER	$19,821.0	$18,151.0	$1,670.0	$4,990.0	2.99	VAMSA

necessary for any of these activities, it is likely that the free trade agreement will have little impact on such corporations.

By some measures, Mexican conditions appear right for foreign entry into banking. For example, real return on bank equity in Mexico has been quite high over the last few years—much higher than it has been for banks in the United States. Also, the prices that Mexican buyers paid in 1991 for the eight of the eighteen nationalized banks that were privatized were quite high, as indicated in table 8.1.

This evidence has led to two major arguments concerning why U.S. banks will find entry into Mexico attractive. One is that profits and prices are high because the system is monopolistic: the top three banks hold 65% of the loans. The second is that the Mexican banking system is inefficient. Potential returns then are even greater than actual returns. According to this argument, U.S. banks have better internal management systems for controlling risk and better technology to provide the services associated with banking—primarily processing payments.

In this chapter, we take a different view of why the banking system is profitable. We argue that banks in Mexico play an even more crucial role in supplying liquidity to the economy than banks in the United States. Compared to the United States, Mexico is an illiquid market. A much higher percentage of its wealth is held in assets for which ready, liquid markets do not exist. The operation of the government securities market, the most liquid of all Mexican securities markets, indicates that it is a much less liquid market than in the United States. Thus liquidity is a scarce commodity in Mexico, and the marginal value of additional liquidity is greater in Mexico than in the United States. This leads to greater real bank returns in the Mexican market.

There is, however, still a question about whether the marginal value of liquidity is high because of artificial restrictions on the ability of the market to create liquidity. If this were true, foreign bank entry would reduce the cost of liquidity, benefiting the foreign banks that enter and the Mexican financial markets.

The price of liquidity is high because the tools necessary to create liquidity are in scarce supply, and they cannot be readily imported by foreign institutions. Also, domestic banks are in a better position to create liquidity than foreign banks; consequently, they will earn rents because of the shortage of a valuable skill that is not especially tradeable. U.S. banks will play the marginal role they have played in all developing financial systems, including Mexico—they will provide short-term dollar-denominated liquidity to the system, a service they already supply.[3]

To make the argument, we divide the chapter into three sections. The first briefly compares how wealth is held in Mexico and the United States. We also present historical real returns in banking compared to the United States. In the second section we compare the role played by banks in the market for Mexican government securities with the role U.S. banks play in the U.S. government securities market. Through this comparison, we show how the Mexican market depends more heavily on settlement of transactions in bank deposits than does the U.S. market. That is, Mexican banks end up intermediating the government securities market to a much greater extent than in the United States.

The frequency with which market transactions are settled in bank deposits is the measure of the liquidity of a market. Markets that must frequently settle in bank deposits are illiquid. When a security seller demands payment in a bank deposit rather than effectively undertaking a swap through a same-day security purchase, he demands to hold an asset that maintains its value in terms of the unit of account to avoid the risk that securities prices will change. We explain why Mexican investors want access to bank deposits—that is, why they have a greater demand for liquidity than their U.S. counterparts.

In the third section, we consider the competitive position and future prospects for Mexican banks. Because the government securities market is shrinking relative to the economy, liquidity will become even more scarce. This, in turn, will increase the economic value of the banks, which explains the high prices paid for the banks that have been privatized. Banks create liquidity from illiquid assets by skillfully choosing their customers and managing their behavior. Thus banks with the best understanding of their customer base will command the highest prices. Foreign banks will not pay the same high price for Mexican banks as Mexicans because managing customer liquidity is, as always, primarily a local business.

1 An Overview of the Mexican Financial Market

Table 8.2 summarizes how Mexicans and U.S. residents hold their wealth. Financial claims (bank deposits, bonds, notes, and bills) held in private hands (excluding currency) relative to GDP is over four times greater in the United States than in Mexico. Stock market capitalization relative to GDP is more than twice as high in the United States as in Mexico.[4] These data indicate that much of the wealth of Mexico is held in a form that is not publicly traded. Thus much of Mexico's wealth is illiquid, meaning that

Table 8.2
The liquidity of the Mexican and U.S. economies

| | (Year-end 1990) | |
	Mexico	United States
Financial claims to GNP	41.3%	169.7%
Dom. banking deposits to GNP	22.0%	58.5%
Dom. Banking dep. to fin. claims	51.0%	34.5%
Stock market capitalization to GNP	26.3%	59.8%

Notes: Mexican financial claims are M4 less currency as reported in IMMEC, *Commercial Banking System Sectorial Studies*, July 1991, p. 26. Mexican bank deposits are Captacion Directa less repurchase agreements for banks' own accounts reported from Comision Nacional Bancaria, *Boletin Estadistico de Banca Multiple*, March, 1991. U.S. financial claims are from the U.S. Flow of Funds. They exclude currency and government debt held by government agencies. Domestic banking deposits are also from Flow of Funds. They include thrift and credit union deposits. Stock market capitalizations are reported in Comision Nacional de Valores, *Banking and Financial Institutions in Mexico*, August, 1990, p. 17.

wealth holders cannot convert their assets into goods and services or other assets without going through a good deal of expense and trouble.[5]

In an environment in which financial forms of wealth are scarce, we would expect households to hold the relatively small amount of financial wealth they own in very liquid form. Thus we find that the ratio of bank deposits to financial wealth is about one and a half times what it is in the United States. This figure excludes from the data repurchase agreements made with securities owned by the banks, amounts that are substantial for Mexico and relatively inconsequential for the United States. We will discuss the reasons for this later.[6]

The illiquid market for wealth in Mexico relative to the United States is associated with higher real returns on bank equity in the Mexican market. Comparative real returns on bank equity are displayed in table 8.3. We also include the ex post real return on federal funds in the United States and three-month *cetes* (short-term government bills) in Mexico in the table. This indicates that in Mexico the real return on bank equity was substantial relative to an investment in cetes. We now turn to an explanation for why the returns in Mexico have been high, and judging from the prices paid for banks, are expected to remain high.

2 The Role of Banks in an Illiquid System

According to table 8.4, on March 31, 1991, securities made up about the same percentage of assets on Mexican bank balance sheets as they did on

Table 8.3
Real return on bank equity, Mexico and the United States

	Real bank ROE Mexico	Ex post real cetes rates	Real bank ROE United States	Ex post real Fed funds rate
1988	41.10%	17.45%	9.12%	3.17%
1989	17.30	25.39	3.34	3.11
1990	26.10	8.44	1.67	2.00
Average	28.17	17.09	4.71	2.76
Avg. real ROE less Avg. real interest rate		11.08		1.95

Notes: Real return on Mexican bank equity is calculated by subtracting from net income the amount of nominal capital necessary to maintain a constant real value for the previous year's equity. Reevaluation reserves are counted as contributions to real equity, but any deductions from capital reserves during the year are not counted due to lack of data for 1988. Thus, real returns are somewhat overstated. Also, we had no way to evaluate the loan portfolios of Mexican banks so we could not make any adjustments for appreciation or depreciation of the value of the loan portfolio. American bank real ROE equals nominal ROE for all banks less the inflation rate as measured by the consumer price index.
Sources: Comision Nacional Bancaria, *Boletin Estadistico de Banca Multiple,* March 31, 1991, Comision Nacional de Valores, *Banking and Financial Institutions in Mexico,* August 1990, p. 81, and *Federal Reserve Bulletin,* July 1991, p. 510.

Table 8.4
Asset and liability composition of Mexican and U.S. banks (March 31, 1991, as a percent of total assets)

	Mexico*	United States
Loans	60.1%	60.7%
Securities	20.1	21.0
Deposits	57.2**	77.8
Repurchase agreements for own account	8.2	2.8
Memo: Repo agree. to securities	40.8	13.2
Memo: third-party security resale agreements to assets	16.1	N.A.

*Excludes third-party security resale agreements from assets.
**Does not include repurchase agreements for own account (Reportos por Mesa de Dinero).
Sources: Comision Nacional Bancaria, *Boletin Estadistico de Banca Multiple,* March 31, 1991. *Federal Reserve Bulletin,* August, 1991, pp. A72 & A73 (U.S. Assets, Domestic Only).

domestic balance sheets of U.S. banks. This figure is net of third-party security resale agreements, which are purchases of securities with an agreement to resell at a fixed price.[7] However, Mexican banks enter into repurchase agreements with about 40% of the securities they own outright, whereas U.S. banks only enter into repurchase agreements with about 13% of the securities they hold.[8] We use this difference in the role of investment securities to contrast the role of Mexican banks and U.S. banks in providing liquidity to securities markets.

Securities Dealers in the United States

We begin by considering how securities dealers finance their inventories on a normal day in a very liquid market in the United States. Assume a securities dealer, dealer A, purchases a $1 million U.S. Treasury bill from a customer, customer A, and dealer B receives an order from a customer, customer B, to purchase a $1 million Treasury bill. Customer B does not want to accept market risk by purchasing a Treasury bill outright; he only wants to hold an interest-earning asset that maintains its value in cash overnight. Hence, customer B wants to enter into an overnight repurchase agreement with dealer B.

The inventory financing problem for dealer A is solved by the order customer B places with dealer B. Dealer A enters into a repurchase agreement with dealer B. That is, dealer A sells a security to dealer B under an agreement to repurchase it the following morning. Dealer A holds a Treasury bill bought from his customer as an asset. As a liability he holds a repurchase agreement. Dealer B has an asset item, a security purchased under agreement to resell. Because he bought a security, he pays cash to dealer A in return for the security. Dealer A then sends the cash to the customer who sold him the security in the first place. Dealer B obtains the cash to send to dealer A from the sale of the same security to customer B, which appears as a liability item, a security sold under agreement to repurchase.

To close this chain, we can assume that customer A, who originally sold the T-bill, needed to raise cash to make a payment to customer B. Since customer B turned right around and purchased the Treasury bill sold by customer A, no one holds a bank deposit at the end of the day. All these transactions can take place because the electronic payment system and the book entry system for government securities in the United States, fedwire, guarantees delivery of good funds (reserves into a bank's deposit at the Fed) at the end of the day. Thus when customer A tells his bank to pay the

Dealer A

Assets	Liabilities
T-Bill $1 Million	Security Sold Under Agreement to Repurchase $1 Million

Customer

Assets	Liabilities

Dealer B

Assets	Liabilities
Security Purchased Under Agreement to Resell $1 Million	Repurchase Agreement with Customer B $1 Million

Customer

Assets	Liabilities
Security Purchased Under Agreement to Resell $1 Million	Net Worth $1 Million

Figure 8.1
End-of-day balance sheets

bank used by customer B (all this happens indirectly through dealers and their banks), customer B's bank is willing to let customer B use the funds that will be delivered that evening to purchase a Treasury bill. Everyone's end-of-day balance sheets are displayed in figure 8.1.[9]

Of course, customer A's bank must have enough confidence in customer A to let him make a payment if he does not yet have cash in his account. (He will ultimately receive the funds to pay customer B from customer B's purchase of his Treasury bill.) Customer A can provide his bank with the necessary confidence by covering the contingency of nondelivery of the payment by holding a bank line, which represents the right to borrow from his bank in just such an emergency. The market is liquid because customer A is very certain that he can find a market for his Treasury bill (in this case, customer B), so he will not have to draw his bank line down. Dealer A is willing to fund overnight with a repurchase agreement because he is confident that he can sell a bill the next day at a price relatively close to its purchase price plus accumulated interest—that is, major price discontinuities in the market are very rare events. He is exposed to the risk that interest rates may rise, but he views the market as liquid enough to take this risk. Dealer B is subject to the risk that his customer will fail to return his security if interest rates fall. Data from U.S. government securities primary dealers[10] indicate that, on net, primary dealers are in the position of financing inventory with repurchase agreements—that is, they take the same risk as dealer A. For example, in April 1991, repurchase agreements exceeded resale agreements by $67 billion, $482 billion in repurchase agreements versus $415 billion in resale agreements, indicating that dealers buy securities outright from their customers and finance their positions with repurchase agreements. Bank balance sheets play a very small role as purchasers of the securities sold under repurchase agreement by dealers: bank securities purchased under agreement to resell totalled only $23 billion as of March 31, 1991.[11]

We note that government securities dealers obtain very few of the securities that they purchase under agreement to resell (an asset item for the dealer) by engaging in agreements with banks. Less than 30% of the $92 billion in bank repurchase agreements (as of end of March 1991) were agreements with securities dealers.

Mexican Banks' Role in the Government Securities Market

Mexican banks enter into repurchase agreements for a much larger share of securities that they own outright than their U.S. counterparts. Market participants in Mexico—that is, securities dealers—would rather engage in resale agreements (the bank's liability is the dealer's asset) with banks than with other securities dealers. How does this affect the example of the securities trade introduced in the previous section?

Recall that dealer A buys a security outright from customer A and funds it with a repurchase agreement with dealer B who, in turn, sells the security under a repurchase agreement to customer B. In Mexico, it is likely that a bank will play a much larger role in the transaction than in the United States. First, it is more likely that customer B will enter into a resale agreement with a bank (a repurchase agreement from the bank's point of view). This would obviate the role of dealer B.

For this to happen, the bank must obtain the security in the first place. It could buy it outright, or it could engage in a resale agreement (an asset item for the bank) with dealer A. From dealer A's point of view, this would be like taking out a bank loan collateralized by the security. There is some evidence, which we discuss below (see footnote 17), that securities dealers commonly borrow money from banks through this device.

The Role of the Bank in Providing Liquidity

By entering into a resale agreement with a bank, customer B is in the same position as if he had held a deposit with the bank. He holds a promise from the bank that cash will be delivered the next day, or whenever the agreement matures. Since the transaction between customers A and B could have taken place with dealers as intermediaries, it is apparent that the promise of a bank to deliver cash is more believable than the promise that a securities company will deliver cash. This means that customer B thinks that, if market interest rates should rise sharply, the bank is more likely to deliver cash for the security than a securities dealer. We now consider the question of why this might be so.[12]

Assume, as before, that dealer A promises to repurchase a security from dealer B. Overnight, the market experiences a liquidity crisis—that is, there is an upsurge in the demand for those claims, such as short-term deposits, that maintain a fixed peso value. However, to keep the agreement, dealer A must deliver cash or bank deposits to dealer B. To raise the cash, dealer A needs to find a market for the security at a price that is reasonably close to the amount of cash he must deliver to dealer B. In a liquidity crisis, he might not be able to do this. If dealer A cannot raise cash to pay dealer B, dealer B will not have sufficient cash to keep his agreement with customer B. Hence, customer B, who thought he held a liquid claim, will suffer a loss in capital value on his investment and a loss of access to cash in a liquidity crisis.

However, if customer B had entered into a resale agreement with a bank, his liquidity risk would have been much lower. In a liquidity crisis, the demand for deposits that can be immediately converted into cash—that is, can be used for payments purposes at their face value—increases. Bank funding costs decline, or at least do not rise by as much as the funding costs of a dealer, because, with the increased demand, the interest rates on deposits fall relative to other rates.[13]

While the bank takes a loss on the repurchase agreement—it must still repurchase at a price above market—its position in the deposit market implies that it will have the financial strength to keep its end of the bargain. Even if it cannot create a deposit to fund the repurchase of the security (perhaps because of reserve constraints), it can better afford to sell the security in the open market and take the loss because it experiences a relative decline in the cost of its deposits. This enhances the value of the bank, leaving it in a stronger position to absorb the loss in the value of the security it might have to sell in the open market.

Why do deposits increase in value (pay a relatively low rate of return) during a liquidity crisis? First, they represent a claim on something that maintains its capital value in terms of the monetary unit—the clearing deposits (noninterest—bearing reserves) held by banks at the central bank. Mexican banks are not subject to a reserve requirement to hold a certain amount of deposits with the Bank of Mexico, but they in fact hold about 1.8% of their assets on deposit for settlement purposes. This is more than twice the amount of deposit reserves held by American banks as a percent of assets, even though U.S. banks are subject to a 12% reserve requirement on transaction accounts.

Claims on a reserve account at the central bank are valuable in a liquidity crisis because they maintain their value when all other securities prices are falling. The central bank could intervene in the securities market to maintain the value of securities, but in a liquidity crisis, by implication, it has chosen not to support securities at their old value. That Mexican banks keep relatively high balances with the Bank of Mexico when they do not have to, and that customers prefer to enter into repurchase agreements with banks, indicate that there is a stronger demand for deposits at the central bank in Mexico than in the United States. This implies that Mexicans expect liquidity crises to be more frequent and more severe than U.S. residents expect them to be. That is, Mexicans expect more discontinuities in securities' prices than do U.S. residents. We conclude from this evidence that Mexican securities markets are more illiquid than those in the United States.

The value of the bank is tied to its value as a creator of liquidity. It produces liabilities that maintain a fixed value in terms of the unit of account. When these liabilities increase in value during a liquidity crisis, the bank is in a better position to absorb losses for its customers. It also has the central bank as a backup. As long as the market believes that the banks are in the best or perhaps unique position to supply liabilities fixed in terms of the unit of account, the banks will act as intermediators in other securities markets.

The major difference between securities markets in Mexico and the United States is that market participants in the United States are much more trusting that dealers will meet their obligation than they are in Mexico. This makes U.S. securities markets more liquid than Mexican securities markets so that the role of banks is less important in the United States. Dealers in the United States need only convince their customers that they have *access* to bank credit because they hold credit lines with banks. In Mexico, customers, both dealers and the public, more frequently want the assurance of actual bank assets and liabilities.[14]

The Mexican Liquidity Requirement

Before proceeding to a discussion about the value of Mexican banks and the role of foreign banks in the Mexican market, we digress somewhat to discuss the bank liquidity requirement. Until August 1991, Mexican banks had to hold 30% of their deposits in the form of bondes and cetes.[15] In an illiquid market, such a requirement need not be a binding constraint on investor behavior because much of the government debt would wind up on bank balance sheets anyway.

As of March 31, 1991, Mexican banks actually held about the same proportion of their assets in securities as did U.S. banks. Mexican banks were, through March 1991, also actively engaged in selling securities through repurchase agreements. Though accounting convention requires that they continue to be posted as assets, the securities sold under repurchase agreements were unavailable to meet liquidity requirements, indicating that banks held more securities than they needed to meet the requirements. In fact, our argument in the previous section presumes that the real constraint on liquidity was the ability of banks to increase deposits at the Banco de Mexico, even though there are no reserve requirements constraining clearing balances.

Government peso-denominated debt, however, is shrinking rapidly relative to GDP. In 1986 it represented 36.5% of GDP; by year-end 1991 it fell to 20.8% of GDP. This has occurred because inflation has reduced the real value of outstanding debt, and the government deficit is falling as a proportion of GDP. It was 16.1% of GDP in 1986; in 1990 it was 3.8%. In the context of a shrinking public debt relative to GDP, the liquidity requirement is likely to become binding.

A binding liquidity requirement for banks would have the effect of making the cetes market as liquid as the deposit market. For example, if a liquidity crisis occurs, the banks can expand deposits only by purchasing more cetes. Thus the impact of the liquidity crisis on one particular market, the government securities market, is reduced. The crisis, consequently, falls more heavily on other markets since deposit expansion is subject to the additional constraint.

If securities dealers believe that the government securities market can weather a liquidity crisis, they will start making repurchase/resale agreements in government securities among themselves rather than depend on banks. Through March 1991, evidence indicates that the liquidity requirement was not sufficiently binding to cause this behavior. That is, investors bought securities from banks under resale agreements (bank repurchase agreements) because they feared the illiquidity of the government securities market. However, in August 1991 apparently the price of cetes rose above the price of deposits as banks scrambled to meet liquidity requirements at the end of the month.[16] Cetes had evidently become more liquid than bank deposits, at least on the last day of that month.

The Banco de Mexico responded to this situation by reducing the liquidity requirement on old deposits and eliminating it on new ones.[17] In effect, the Banco de Mexico moved to restore the primacy of short-term bank liabilities as the most liquid instrument in the economy.

Why is this a sensible policy? In determining at what price to purchase assets in a liquidity crisis, banks make judgments that affect the long-term prices at which various borrowers can access securities markets. If, due to regulation, the government securities market is more liquid than it ought to be, other creditors suffer. An investment in government securities will appear attractive for regulatory reasons, raising the price of government securities relative to the securities issued by other borrowers.

3 The Competitive Environment and the Role of Foreign Banks

In August 1991, the Mexican government sold Banamex, the largest commercial bank in Mexico, to a securities dealer for over 2.5 times the book value of earnings. This price was surprisingly high; if earnings maintain their current level, the real rate of return on the investment will be about equal to the average ex post real return on three month cetes over the last three years. (See table 8.3. A price 2.5 times book will decrease real ROE measured on accounting value of equity from 28.17% to 11.27%, which is about equal to the ex post real return on cetes.) The winning bidders either anticipate a decline in the real return on cetes or an increase in the profitability of banks.[18] In this section, we argue the position that bank profitability will improve. We also consider whether foreign banks can take advantage of these returns.

Forces Leading to Increased Profitability

Although banks participate in the government securities market to maintain market liquidity, they are not the sole holders of government debt. As of year-end 1989, the commercial banks held slightly over 50% of the *bondes* (floating rate government notes) and cetes not held by government entities or the Banco de Mexico. In comparison, U.S. commercial banks held about 15% of Treasury and agency securities not held by government entities or the Fed (as of March 31, 1991). This is further evidence that the Mexican government securities market is less liquid than the U.S. government securities market. U.S. banks not only engage in fewer repurchase agreements than Mexican banks relative to the securities they hold; they hold a much smaller percentage of the total outstanding. Thus U.S. investors are willing to take the capital risk in the government market, whereas Mexican investors are not.

The market for private business debt in Mexico is less liquid than the government securities market because a greater percentage of private debt ends up on bank balance sheets. For example, commercial paper,[19] an open market substitute for bank loans, is dwarfed by bank loans.[20] In April 1990, the ratio of commercial paper to bank lending was about 6% in Mexico,[21] much smaller than the 50% of government securities that is in nonbank hands. Of course, the business loan market in the United States is also less liquid than the government securities market, but again, it is more liquid than its Mexican counterpart. The ratio of commercial paper to bank loans is 27% in the United States.

Will the decline in government borrowing and the concomitant increase in private borrowing lead to a greater dependency on banks for liquidity? Two factors are at work. First, private borrowers are less liquid than public borrowers as long as the debt is issued in the currency that public borrowers can create. Second, stabilization of macroeconomic policy, of which debt reduction is a part, will lead to less fluctuation in securities prices. Thus, the markets for all securities will become more liquid.

Liquidity under a Fixed Exchange Rate Regime

To analyze the impact of a stable macroeconomic policy on the liquidity premium in Mexico, we consider what might happen to Mexican financial markets if Mexico were to adopt a credible fixed exchange rate between the peso and the dollar. In this case, the liquidity of U.S. financial markets would be available to Mexicans. For example, Mexican consumers could hold dollar money-market mutual funds as liquid assets without fear of exchange rate risk. Corporations might issue commercial paper in the large, liquid money markets of the United States. Would these opportunities reduce the role of banks in providing liquidity and therefore reduce future bank profits?

The liquidity premium on yields paid by issuers in the United States is lower than in Mexico because U.S. investors can more easily find markets for their securities when they decide to sell them. If Mexican investors can sell their securities in the same markets, the cost of holding securities rather than bank deposits should decline in Mexico. This should cause an increase in the demand for securities relative to bank deposits. However, if Mexican investors on average have less certain cash flow than their U.S. counterparts, they may find that they have to sell securities more frequently than U.S. residents. Even though the two sets of investors would face the same liquidity premium, the expected cost to Mexicans of holding a relatively illiquid asset would be higher. Consequently, Mexicans would hold more bank deposits than U.S. residents.

Likewise, while Mexican firms would be able to tap U.S. money markets for funds, they might find a less welcome reception. If Mexican firms experience less certain cash flow, they will have to use bank lines more frequently when they roll over their commercial paper. Moreover, investors might find it difficult to sell outstanding commercial paper of a firm that is experiencing cash flow difficulty. Thus, investors are likely to demand more frequently that Mexican firms meet their obligations by delivering bank deposits rather than issuing commercial paper.

Experience in other markets indicates that stabilization of macroeconomic policy is not sufficient to make illiquid borrowers liquid. For example, in the United States, commercial paper did not become a viable alternative to bank loans until the early 1970s. Firms must establish records of meeting payments commitments before investors are willing to hold their short-term liabilities (commercial paper) rather than bank deposits. Firms with liquid balance sheets must exist in great enough numbers such that the commercial paper market itself is liquid. This means it must be large enough to support a network of dealers that can finance inventory with repurchase agreements. No other market in the world has developed commercial paper as a substitute for bank loans to the same extent as the U.S. market.

In summary, the Mexican market will become more dependent on banks for liquidity because the government debt market is shrinking as a percent of GDP and private firms are less liquid borrowers than the government. Private debt will hardly circulate at all, so liquid securities other than bank deposits will become quite scarce. This conclusion rests on the assumption that banks are in the unique position among private financial intermediaries to make the liabilities of illiquid borrowers liquid. We now turn to investigating why this is so.

How Banks Manage Liquidity

Earlier we indicated that the public trusts the liquidity of bank deposits because banks hold reserves created by the central bank. Thus the public is willing to hold the liabilities of banks at a lower interest rate than it holds the liabilities of other financial intermediaries or borrowers. Nevertheless, if a bank creates liabilities that promise payment in reserves without properly managing the assets it purchases with those liabilities, it will suffer loan losses that could throw the bank into bankruptcy. The central bank will be forced into two choices: the it can lend to the troubled bank through the discount window or it can permit the bank to fail.

The first solution risks inflation and a misallocation of scarce investment resources. For example, if banks believe they will be bailed out by loans from the central bank, they will be prone to take excessive risk—this is the usual moral hazard problem with the financial safety net. The experience of the U.S. thrift industry provides ample evidence for this.[22] The second solution might cause the market to become skeptical of the liquidity of bank deposits, which would leave it without a domestic liquid asset.

Banks are the best investors to create liquidity in the private sector. Because banks produce liquid liabilities backed by reserves on deposit at the central bank, they can exercise a unique form of control over borrower behavior. Firms hold their transactions accounts with banks, so banks have the means to control a firm's ability to make payments. If the bank is in doubt about the ability of the firm to repay a loan, it recalls the loan on a technicality, with which loan agreements are amply supplied.[23] If the firm cannot generate cash, the bank can seize any deposits and incoming payments. It can also prevent the firm from making payments. Such acts can quickly force a borrower to renegotiate with its bank.[24]

Of perhaps greater importance than access to central bank liquidity is the establishment of banks that are skilled at converting the securities of illiquid borrowers into liquid deposits. We would not be surprised to see a banking system develop along the "main bank" concept in Japan. That is, a bank develops a strong relationship with selected corporate clients and maintains responsibility for that client's liquidity. In return, the bank is given wide discretion to influence management decisions.

Central bank policy must be geared to ensure that the skill of imparting liquidity to assets is profitable. This includes discouraging discount window borrowing and preventing a reliance on deposit insurance as a means of creating liquidity. In other words, the best policy in an illiquid market is to let the institutions that are skilled in creating liquidity earn high profits. If the market believes that this is government policy, the increasing illiquidity of Mexican securities markets should lead to higher expected bank profits.

Evaluating the Mexican Banks

The argument outlined above is consistent with a higher price for Mexican banks than current spreads justify. However, a high price could be consistent with many stories, including an expected decline in the real return on cetes. To distinguish our proposition from other possible stories, we consider what our view implies for relative prices across banks. Specifically, we discuss the relative values of the three wholesale banks and their future roles in the Mexican economy.

First, we assume that the market believes the government will pursue a policy that permits banks to profit from creating liquidity. This means that the banks best able to monitor management behavior will end up with the lowest loan losses and the lowest cost of funds. The latter result will obtain if the market trusts the liquidity of the deposits of less risky banks more than it does the liquidity of deposits of riskier banks. For example, even if the government promises that bank deposits in failed banks will eventually be paid, if they are not immediately payable, deposits in less risky banks will be more liquid than deposits in riskier banks.

A less risky bank's promise to deliver credit immediately to its customers (under credit lines and commitments) will be more believable than the promises of riskier banks. Therefore, less risky banks will be able to sell credit lines at higher prices than do riskier banks.[25]

These advantages of the less risky bank over the riskier bank will lead the less risky bank to obtain the highest-quality customers. A nonfinancial firm's reputation in securities markets is partly a function of the reputation of the bank on which it depends for liquidity so potential customers will compete to become a customer of the less risky bank. A less risky bank that has a reputation for skillful monitoring will try to preserve the reputation by being selective as to who its customers are. It will be selective by charging higher interest rates on credit products to its customers than its competitors would charge the same customers. However, because it will obtain the best customers, the return on its credit products, before adjusting for risk, will be lower than the return of other banks. The less risky bank will also pay less interest on liabilities than the riskier bank.

Based on these criteria, we can rank the value of the various Mexican banking franchises by analyzing the cost of bank liabilities and the revenues earned on bank asset portfolios. In table 8.5 we provide the ratios of interest income and interest expense to average 1990 assets for the three largest banks, Banamex, Bancomer, and Serfin (which we will refer to as

Table 8.5
Mexican bank income, expense, and balance sheet items (as a percent of assets)

	Interest[1] income	Interest expense	Net int. margin	Securities[2]	Repurchase agreements[3]
Banamex	21.87%	16.33%	5.54%	36.91%	27.95%
Bancomer	32.60	24.96	7.63	25.30	16.64
Serfin	29.57	25.59	3.98	32.22	14.86
Merc de Mexico	32.64	28.84	3.80	50.61	38.67
Confia	30.07	27.30	2.77	47.75	33.32
Bancreser[4]	37.71	33.52	4.19	19.57	47.89
Oriente	41.66	33.54	9.13	47.43	34.99
Regional avg.[5]	34.34	37.17	7.17	32.38	22.65

1. Income and expense items are for 1990 divided by July 31, 1990 assets.
2. Securities include securities purchased under resale agreements for third parties. These items are as of March 31, 1991, so they are taken relative to assets on the same date.
3. Includes securities sold under agreements to repurchase for third parties as of March 31, 1991.
4. Bancreser reports a high percentage of securities sold under repurchase agreements but very few securities held. We think that it reports the asset counterpart to securities sold under repurchase agreements as other assets (*otros activos*).
5. Excludes private banks.
Source: Comision Nacional Bancaria, *Boletin Estadistico de Banca Multiple*, March 31, 1991.

wholesale banks), for regional banks on average, and for a select group of individual regional banks. Using one year's worth of data is not generally appropriate for this kind of analysis, so our results can, at this point, only be suggestive.

Banamex has the lowest interest expense among the wholesale banks. Its interest expenses are also lower than those of any of the regional banks. It might be argued that Banamex's funding costs are low because it funds a greater percentage of its assets with repurchase agreements (including those for third parties) than the other two large banks.[26] We would expect repurchase agreements to be a low-cost source of funds for the bank because they represent secured overnight loans. However, in table 8.5, we have also included the interest expense of regional banks that have exceptionally high repurchase agreement funding ratios. The two regional banks with the highest repurchase funding, Bancreser and Mercantil de Mexico, also have interest expenses substantially above the regional bank average. This indicates that all customers, including repurchase customers, look beyond the repurchase agreement to the quality of the bank to determine the rate at which they are willing to lend. It appears that Banamex receives the greatest vote of confidence from its liability holders.

Banamex has a lower gross return on assets than the other two large banks and a lower rate of return on assets than any of the regional banks as well (see table 8.5). Again, it is difficult to conclude that this difference comes from the composition of its asset portfolio, which is less heavily invested in securities (including third-party resale agreements) than are those of many regional banks that earn very high rates of return on assets. Also, the return on assets of Serfin, the third largest bank, is too high relative to Banamex's to be explained by the difference in the percentage of assets invested in securities. We conclude that Banamex's loan customers are lower risk than the customers of the other banks.[27]

This conclusion is strengthened by the data in table 8.6. This table displays 1990 returns on average equity for the three largest banks and an average for regional banks before and after contributions to loan loss reserves. Among the three largest banks, Banamex has the smallest difference, indicating that its provision for loan loss in 1990 was relatively small. This could indicate that Banamex failed to add sufficient reserves to its loan loss account; however, because it also has a relatively low return on its asset portfolio, we conclude that it is making loans to low-risk borrowers. The regional banks have a relatively small difference between return on equity before and after loan loss provisions as well, but these banks also

Table 8.6
Real return on equity* before and after loan loss provision

	ROE before provision	ROE after provision	Difference
Banamex	39.10%	23.21%	15.89%
Bancomer	36.92	9.29	27.63
Serfin	54.44	27.17	27.27
Average regional**	39.01	21.21	17.80

*Calculated as in table 8.2, except includes changes in capital reserves. Based on average equity.
**Excludes private banks.
Source: Comision Nacional Bancaria, *Boletin Estadistico de Banca Multiple*, March 1991.

Table 8.7
Mexican bank loans and assets, real growth rates (Dec. 1989–March 1991)

	Assets	Loans
Banamex	13.1%	7.8%
Bancomer	5.8	24.3
Serfin	81.2	44.9
All banks	45.7	29.7

Source: Comision Nacional Bancaria, *Boletin Estadistico de Banca Multiple*, March 1990.

have relatively high interest incomes to assets (see table 8.5).[28] This indicates that, in contrast to Banamex, many regional banks have not made sufficient provision for loan losses.

Another comparison of quality involves the willingness of a bank to expand its customer base. The customer base and a bank's ability to manage the liquidity of its customer base is the valuable resource in the banking business. Developing a trusting relationship between the bank and its customers takes time. A bank's reputation is a valuable asset for its customer in an illiquid market. A less risky bank will not squander its reputation by expanding too rapidly.

Between year-end 1989 and March 31, 1991, commercial banking assets grew by 46% in real terms. Loan growth was less—30% in real terms—indicating that much of the expansion resulted from an increase in bank participation in the securities market through repurchase and resale agreements for the accounts of third parties. Loan and asset growth for the three largest banks and for all banks is displayed in table 8.7. Banamex experienced significantly smaller loan growth than the market and the other two large banks. This indicates that Banamex was less aggressive in soliciting new loan business than the other two, a fact consistent with the notion that it is more conservative in lending its reputation to new customers.

Notwithstanding the observation that Banamex is of higher quality, the market always needs lower-quality banks—that is, those willing to take some risk in providing liquidity to new firms. Nevertheless, their greater risk should generate lower share prices relative to expected returns.

The Sale Price of Banamex versus Bancomer

Banamex was sold to private investors in August 1991 for a price of 2.63 times book. Bancomer was sold in October 1991 for 2.99 times book— approximately 15% more relative to book (see table 8.1). Bancomer also sold at a higher multiple to 1990 earnings than did Banamex, both before and after additions to loan loss reserves. Between 1990 and 1991, net interest margin grew at about the same rate at the two institutions, but Bancomer placed tighter control on noninterest expenses than Banamex. Noninterest expenses grew by 88% at Banamex compared with 55% at Bancomer. Net earnings grew more slowly at Bancomer than at Banamex because the former made higher provisions for bad loans. Bancomer's noninterest expenses for the first three months of 1991 also exhibited slower growth over expenses for the same period in 1990 than Banamex's expenses.

Given the prices paid for the two institutions, the purchaser of Bancomer is probably projecting higher earnings growth for its bank than for Banamex.[29] The evidence to date is that the source of this projection is in noninterest expense growth. Banamex has the characteristics of the premier wholesale bank in Mexico, which is a valuable franchise in an illiquid market. However, to realize this value, the bank must control expenses.

The Securities Companies

As we indicated in the introduction, to date, securities companies have been the major purchasers of the banks that have been privatized. In this section, we look at why this has been so. First, we note that the nominal value of securities trading has been overwhelmingly dominated by trading in cetes (see table 8.8).[30] Also, we note that the balance sheets of securities firms have roughly expanded along with trading volume (see table 8.9 and compare asset growth with trading volume growth in table 8.8). However, the return on equity of securities firms has actually declined while the

Table 8.8
Trading volume in Mexican securities (trillions of pesos)

	1988	1989	1990
Cetes	836	997	1,970
Other fixed income	104	134	251
Equities	13	15	35
Total*	966	1,170	2,279
Cetes/total	86.5%	85.2%	86.4%

*Items do not sum to total due to missing items.
Source: Comision Nacional de Valores, *Banking and Financial Institutions in Mexico*, p. 78.

Table 8.9
Securities firms: Balance sheet and income items (trillions of pesos)

	1988	1989	1990
Assets	16.1	35.1	52.5
Capital	2.4	3.0	3.5
Return on equity	16.3%	15.8%	11.3%

Source: IMMEC, *Financial Summary*, June 1991, p. 44.

balance sheet has been expanding,[31] and firm equity has not risen to keep pace with growth in assets (see table 8.9).

Despite these rather negative balance sheet and earnings reports, the market value of securities companies' stocks increased by about 50% in real terms during 1990, which compares very favorably with the stock market performance of the industrial sector. Hence, the market saw expanding opportunities for securities firms despite the fact that the public securities market is bound to shrink relative to the rest of the economy. The market must have anticipated that the securities companies and the banks would be merged when the banks were privatized.

One reason that the securities companies are the major purchasers of banks is that there is no other source of private capital in the financial services industry. From newspaper reports, during the days of stringent controls on banks, the major securities companies, including ACCIVAL, the purchaser of Banamex, placed private debt with wealthy investors through trusts and mutual funds managed by them.[32] Banks' ability to lend was severely restricted by the government.[33] Thus the securities companies are familiar with the potential bank clients. It appears that ACCIVAL, while not the largest company in terms of assets, was one of the largest in terms of equity. It was also the leading placer of private debt. Thus it is not surprising that it bought the least risky bank.

The actual capital in securities firms at year-end 1990 totaled 3.9 trillion pesos in book value, considerably less than the 16.4 trillion pesos of book value capital in the banking system. To pay several times book in cash for the banks, the owners of the securities firms must have drawn on their own private capital as well as the capital in their firms. To have accumulated personal capital, the owners had to withdraw capital from their securities companies over the years, a supposition supported by the data on the increasing leverage of their balance sheets. Thus the owners of securities companies probably realized that the expansion potential of securities firms is limited.

The Role of Foreign Banks

The value of a bank, especially in an illiquid market, is determined by its customer relationships. The core of a well-run bank is its ability to create liquidity out of the loans it makes to its customers. Foreign banks must compete with the skills of domestic banks in evaluating and managing the behavior of managers of domestic firms. The record in several major markets indicates that domestic bankers are better at this than foreigners. U.S. banks with assets over $100 million that were foreign owned in 1990 earned an average of 28 basis points on assets over the last seven years. Domestically owned bank holding companies of a similar size earned an average of 62 basis points.[34]

In Japan, foreign banks were not prohibited from owning Japanese banks after World War II, but no bank tried to make such an acquisition.[35] Chase established a very profitable business clearing dollar payments and providing dollar liquidity during Japan's postwar recovery and development. However, the domestic market for loans to large corporations remained entirely in the hands of the large Japanese banks.

We have an example of how a foreign-owned bank, a subsidiary of Citicorp, operates in Mexico, and the composition of its balance sheet is consistent with the U.S. and Japanese evidence. This bank has recently experienced a large expansion in its balance sheet, increasing its assets from 122 billion pesos in July 1990 to 6 trillion pesos in March 1991. However, almost two thirds of the growth came from repurchase and resale agreements done for third parties rather than the commercial loan market. Its asset share (including third-party repurchase agreements) is about 2% of total banking assets as of March 1991. Its loan share is even less—0.3%. This indicates that it is difficult for foreign banks to enter the local peso

lending market. Citibank's customers are the top 200 Mexican corporations, for whom it does external operations and a loan booking business.[36]

Foreign banks likely will excel in those banking markets in which technical skills are of paramount importance, such as securities trading, foreign
exchange trading, and bringing dollar securities issues of the biggest
Mexican corporations to international public markets.[37] Since futures and
options markets in Mexico are precluded by regulation, there is a strong
feeling in Mexico that foreign financial and banking firms, with experience
in marketing risk management packages based on derivative instruments,
will have a major advantage once the market is opened. The Casas de Bolsa
and banks therefore want to develop derivative markets in as many instruments as exist in the United States; they also want some time to gain
experience before Mexico opens to trade.

Such a view hinges on the notion that derivative markets will thrive in
Mexico once they are introduced. Yet, such instruments flourish only in
markets that are served by the most liquid currencies and have large numbers of liquid borrowers and lenders. For example, options clearinghouses
in the United States can guarantee delivery of cash or securities to traders
at relatively low cost because they know that relatively continuous markets
exist for benchmark securities to close out a position on a defaulted contract. In illiquid markets for the underlying security, the cost of this assurance is much higher. In countries that maintain illiquid currencies or have
illiquid borrowers and lenders, such markets have not evolved and the
entire system leans on banks. It is not at all clear that the expertise gained
by foreign entities in the highly liquid dollar environment will give them
any competitive advantage in the illiquid Mexican environment.

Foreign banks will play their traditional role in developing markets—
providing short-term dollar liquidity, primarily through dollar loans to
domestic banks. The domestic banks will excel in managing the peso liquidity of most Mexican corporations. These corporations' access to dollar
liquidity will likely remain confined to short-term instruments such as trade
finance secured by the letters of credit of Mexican banks.

It is sometimes claimed that foreign banks have a comparative advantage
in developing retail and consumer lending markets, such as credit cards and
mortgage markets, which are underdeveloped in Mexico. The argument is
that they have the experience to provide the technology and organiza-
tional skills to develop consumer lending markets that rely on statistical
data rather than personal customer knowledge to make credit evaluations.
These techniques were developed in the United States where there is a
long history of data to relate income, age, and education variables, for

example, to loan default rates. Also, there are established files of credit history on consumers. Much less of this kind of information exists in Mexico, implying that personal, rather than statistical, credit evaluation will be the norm for some time in this market. Consumer markets are illiquid, not for lack of technique and skill, but for lack of the type of data and historical experience available in the United States that make credit scoring a reliable method.

We note that some of the most optimistic views about liquidity in the consumer loan market have been found wanting in the United States as well. For example, no-income-verification mortgages have had higher loan loss experiences than anticipated.

Equipment leasing is a retail market that foreign banks have actively entered. In this market, the finance company retains title to the equipment it finances. If the secondary market for the equipment is fairly well developed, and the lessee can be prevented from destroying the equipment, this business can be done with little local knowledge. Thus, foreign bank operational skills will be more important than the local knowledge of the domestic banks.

In summary, it has been argued that the technical skills (managing interest rate risk, establishing management information systems, automated processing, etc.) of the foreign banks will permit foreign banks to offer banking services at lower cost than the domestic banks. From our point of view, the major factor affecting a bank's success is its ability to manage customers. If the technical skills of U.S. banks are an important source of improved profitability, these skills can be purchased from the banks or consultants who can design and implement the systems. We note that the evidence on noninterest expenses does not suggest that the major Mexican banks are grossly inefficient. For example, noninterest expenses at Mexican banks equaled 69.7% of net interest revenue plus noninterest revenue in 1990, whereas in the United States the (approximate) same ratio was 68.1%.[38]

Integration of Commercial and Investment Banking

Another factor that has been mentioned as a reason for the attractiveness of Mexican banks to domestic investors (and to foreigners as well) is that commercial and investment banking are no longer legally separated as they are in the United States. The argument for legal separation in the United States is based on the alleged dangers of conflicts of interest. Banks learn confidential information about borrowers in their role as liquidity providers unavailable to public market participants. If banks could trade in public securities for their own accounts, they might be tempted to profit by sending false signals to other market participants about what they know. The experience of U.S. banks in trading the junk bonds of clients with whom they have banking relationships indicates that the market, as well as the regulatory authorities, is concerned about potential conflicts of interest.

In an illiquid market like Mexico, the problem of conflict of interest is much less of an issue. For most borrowers, banks are the only source of credit. Therefore, there is no public market in which a conflict of interest can arise. As we indicated earlier, as the government securities market shrinks, the role of securities dealers will decline.

Conclusion

In this chapter we have argued that bank returns are relatively high in Mexico because the market is illiquid. Prices for banks are high relative to current returns because investors expect that the market will become even less liquid in the future because the government securities market, which is more liquid than the market for private securities, is shrinking relative to GDP. Foreign banks cannot exploit the potential profit opportunities as well as domestic investors because creating liquidity from securities issued by illiquid borrowers tends to be a local problem.

Notes

We are grateful to Eduardo Creel, Juan Manuel Perez Porrua, Ignacio Trigueiros, Miguel Cano, Andres Lederman, Liliana Rojas Suarez, Rudiger Dornbusch, and Sweder van Wijnebergen for extremely helpful conversations and data on the evolution of the Mexican financial and banking markets.

1. Currently, total foreign ownership of the newly privatized Mexican banks is limited to 30% of a bank's shares with a 5% cap on ownership by a single foreign entity. Thus, Mexican institutions and individuals have been the principal buyers of the banks recently sold by the government. Foreign banks with the exception of Citibank currently can open neither branches nor subsidiaries in Mexico. Foreigners cannot own more than 30% of a Casa de Bolsa nor can they control the board.

What form an opening of trade in financial services will ultimately take is problematic. Presumably, subsidiaries of foreign banks may enter with some control on the size of their capital. The Canadian case serves as model for this. There will probably be some transitional period even for such a limited opening. U.S. banks, of course, are pressing for rights to establish branches to do an investment banking business, to offer derivative instruments (now banned even to Mexican banks and securities houses), and to access the payment system. Throughout this paper, however, we will take the extreme case and assume that the Mexican market will be completely open for foreign financial subsidiaries.

2. Since the limited 1989 agreement with Canada, however, U.S. banking assets in Canada have increased by only 20%, though the agreement was still restrictive.

3. In some countries, such as Chile, U.S. banks have played an important role as deposit takers because they have been more sound than domestic banks. Nevertheless, they do not play a major role in the loan markets; instead they lend wholesale on the interbank market or security lending.

4. Also, the bulk of shares are closely held except in the recently denationalized companies.

5. The stock market itself is relatively illiquid. The U.S. Securities and Exchange Commission is concerned about he liquidity of the Mexican market; it recognizes only eleven Mexican stocks as having a ready market status.

Various regulations increase the illiquidity of the market. For example, banks cannot lend on security collateral, so market makers cannot get ready financing of position. NAFIN (Nacional Financiera, the largest development bank) does finance broker-dealer positions, as one of its functions is to promote development of the capital market. The Comision Nacional de Valores (the securities market regulator) itself does not know how much credit is channeled to carry positions in securities markets. NAFIN can borrow from banks, so indirectly the banks finance securities market activities.

Casas de Bolsa are brokerages only: they cannot take positions on their own account. However, if NAFIN and the CNV determine that there is a liquidity problem, they can temporarily relax the rules against the brokerages acting as principals. (The mutual funds managed by the brokerages as separate entities probably do an informal dealer business, since they can always have a presence in the market.)

6. Prior to 1989, repurchases were considered an activity of a security firm, so banks were prohibited from engaging in them. The repo business was then left to the Casas de Bolsa, and banks could not use them for funding. Repos are allowed only in government debt and bank securities deposited at INDEVAL (a securities depository). Under the liberalization of 1989, both banks and securities firms were allowed to do repurchases. Nevertheless, prior to 1989 banks openly did repurchases, though not on their books. The Banco de Mexico overlooked this activity because it gave depth to the government securities market. The 1989 liberalization caused these surreptitious repos to appear suddenly on the books of banks. Thus, we lack a long time series on repo development. Banks use repos in the interbank market—there is only a very small market in unsecured interbank lending—and to acquire funds from brokerage houses.

7. Bank assets (or liabilities and net worth) include repurchase (liability items) and resale agreements (asset items) for securities that banks execute for their customers. They make up almost 15% of bank assets (or liabilities and net worth). Since it is unclear to us whether banks quarantee the fulfillment of these obligations, we do not include them in table 8.3 comparing asset and liability compositions of Mexican and U.S. banks.

8. A repurchage agreement is a sale of a security for cash under an agreement to repurchase the security at a fixed price at a specific time in the future. It is a liability item on the balance sheet of the bank selling the security. The asset item usually remains the security itself.

9. Since May 1991, the Banco de Mexico has provided an electronic payments system. Before this, the central bank provided only a paper check-clearing service. The system now allows unlimited daylight overdrafts on bank accounts. Security firms have accounts at the central bank but they are not permitted to have overdrafts. They use such accounts because some payments to various government trusts must come only from a central bank account. Casas de Bolsa do not access the payments system directly. They must pay with checks, and therefore must go through banks. Banks, however, permit Casas de Bolsa daylight overdrafts without charge.

10. As reported to the New York Fed. Data appear in the *Federal Reserve Bulletin*, Table 1.43. The data that appear in this paragraph are from the August 1991 *Bulletin*.

11. The securities affiliates of major bank holding companies play a significant role as dealers in the government securities markets. However, we are concerned with assets held directly on the bank balance sheet for reasons we explain later.

12. Customer B might want to hold a security under a resale agreement rather than a deposit if he wants to sell the security outright to bet on an increase in interest rates.

13. For example, in liquidity crises in 1980 and 1981 in the United States, interest rates on overnight loans to large corporations rose relative to the Fed funds rate. Fed funds are a bank liability with the same characteristics as a demand deposit that is available on the following morning.

14. Securities houses can operate independently of banks, only depending on them occasionally for liquidity, when markets in the securities they trade are fairly liquid. In illiquid markets, securities companies and banks effectively become one organization. Securities houses developed in Mexico because the government securities market is somewhat liquid, and banks were subject to onerous restrictions that made it profitable to create independent, much less regulated securities firms.

15. There is no Banco de Mexico discounting operation for banks. However, if a bank is overdrawn at the end of the day in its clearing account, it effectively gets an overnight loan from the central bank at a severe penalty rate of three times the market rate on twenty-eight-day cetes. In addition it is subject to nonpecuniary penalties and "moral suasion."
There is a Banco de Mexico discount window operation only for securities firms between 2:00 and 2:30 P.M. It is used to give securities firms some ability to raise funds from the central bank. The overnight lending, however, is at the same penalty rare faced by banks for overdrafts. Hence, it is used only for emergency purposes.

16. Requirements need only be satisfied on the average of monthly deposits at the end of the month .

17. In response to the crisis, in September 1991, the Banco de Mexico changed the liquidity requirement to 25% of deposits on hand as of August 1991. Marginal deposits have a zero liquidity requirement. During this crisis, it became apparent that many of the securities held to meet the liquidity requirement were purchased from securities firms under resale agreements. Thus banks actively engage in resale agreements as well as repurchase agreements for their own accounts.

To satisfy the liquid asset requirement against deposits, banks can count deposits at the Banco de Mexico, vault cash, cetes, and *bondes*. Banks can use the nominal (face) value of their cetes holdings to meet the requirement, so in fact the liquidity requirement is actually less than the 25% requirement, given the current 15% annual discount rate on cetes. No private paper can yet be counted because such paper is not deemed liquid. In the past, the Banco de Mexico paid up to 50% of the cetes rate as interest on bank clearing accounts in the central bank. Now that there is no minimum reserve requirement on clearing balances, the Banco de Mexico pays an interest rate of zero.

18. We assume that expected growth in assets and net income, holding spreads constant, does not affect the return required by investors on book value of equity. This must be the case as long as investors require compensation for the increased risk if banks use growth to increase their leverage ratios. Under this assumption, bank stock prices can rise above book value only if the market expects an increase in spreads or if the discount rate declines.

19. Regulation channels the issue of CP to the Casas de Bolsa. When a party issues CP without intermediation by a registered financial intermediary (i.e., a Casa de Bolsa), he pays a 15% value-added tax on the interest payment. Therefore, a company will not engage in direct issue of CP. To issue without a tax, the issuer must register the issue; this requires depositing the paper in depository, INDEVAL (Instituto Nacional de Deposito de Valores). But only securities firms and financial intemediaries have accounts in INDEVAL, so a nonfinancial firm cannot register an issue unless a securities firm agrees. Thus commercial paper must be underwritten through a financial firm.

20. Various limitiations preclude a liquid secondary market in commercial paper. Securities firms can be brokers but cannot take a position in commercial paper. Banks are also prohibited from making a market. The rationale for this prohibition is that the government wanted to make a strict demarcation between the activities of banks and investment banks—it wanted to avoid having banklike investment banks through a dealer portfolio of short paper. In addition, it prohibited bank dealing because it wanted to avoid the appearance that banks were guaranteeing the paper of industrial groups.

The secondary market for CP is further proscribed because financial intermediaries other than banks and Casas de Bolsa, called nonbank financial intermediaries, are permitted to enter a dealer business only in bank paper (Hacienda and Banco de Mexico ruling interpreting Ley de Instituciones de Credito).

21. The commercial paper market really developed in 1988. Banks marketed the paper, but it is unclear if there was any bank guarantee of it. With the freeing of interest rates in 1989, much of the commercial paper activity returned to bank

balance sheets. Banks themselves worked liked Casas de Bolsa money market mutual funds, placing their own funds and the funds from the trusts they operated into the commercial paper they marketed.

Commercial paper developed through the repo market. Casas de Bolsa guaranteed repayment of commercial paper. The public viewed this guarantee as riskier than bank liabilities like Bankers Acceptances because of government guarantees of the banks.

22. The major Mexican banks may be more conservative than the U.S. saving and loans, even if government policy implies bankruptcy protection. The banking franchise in an illiquid economy is more valuable than a savings and loan franchise in the United States. Thus the shareholders stand to lose more in a bank failure in Mexico than thrift shareholders stand to lose in the United States.

23. For example, on October 3, 1991, RJR Nabisco announced its intention to raise equity to pay off its bank loans. Its balance sheet had been heavily saddled with junk bond debt and bank loans. It stated that bank loan covenants so restricted the firm's freedom of action that it could not expand in what it sees as profitable markets—particularly Europe. The chief financial officer indicated that he thought operating with so much bank debt had put the firm in a straightjacket. See *New York Times*, Oct 4, 1991, p. D1.

24. If a bank has the means to seize a payment, it will make it its business to determine when payments are expected to arrive before granting additional loans. An example is the bank seizure of a payment from Polly Peck International reported in *Financial Times*, October 4, 1990.

25. For example, Morgan Guaranty now has such an advantage over many of its New York wholesale bank competitors. Morgan has the capital to meet regulatory guidelines so potential borrowers know it can create loans when other banks may not be able to.

26. We had to include third-party repurchase agreements in the numbers because the interest income and expenses include them.

27. It is interesting to note that, among U.S. banks, regionals have a lower cost of funds and a lower return on assets than the wholesale banks in New York. For example, in 1990, regional banks (with assets greater than $5 billion) earned 9.33% on assets and paid 6.02% on liabilities compared with 10.17% and 7.69% respectively for large New York City banks. It appears that wholesale banks in the United States are riskier than regional banks. This is caused by the fact that the wholesale banking business in the United States is shrinking.

28. The profitability of the regional banks is not a result of a local monopoly. Hacienda controls branching by the national banks, but is very liberal.

29. The higher price for Bancomer relative to book could be partially due to inflation accounting in Mexico. Asset revaluation seems to be concentrated in December. Thus the further a purchase is made from December, the greater the deviation of book value of assets from market value of assets. This effect is not

eliminated by measuring book and purchase price in dollar terms because the dollar value of the peso has not fallen to reflect the high Mexican inflation rate. That is, the peso has experienced an appreciation in real terms.

30. In the United States, government securities trading represents 95% of the volume of trading on the New York Stock Exchange and the government securities market.

31. The return on equity is reported by the Casas de Bolsas. Although it is not clear from the table whether the returns are real or nominal, since the peso returns and the dollar returns match, we assume they are adjusted or inflation. (If they were not adjusted, the dollar capital would increase faster than the peso capital, and this is not the case.)

32. See Dianna Solis, "Buyer of Banamex Stake Brings New Blood to the Mexican Bank," *Wall Street Journal*, August 27, 1991.

33. See S. Ramachandran, *The Reform of the Mexican Banking System*, World Bank mimeo, for a description of how the Mexican government used the banks to control access to credit.

34. The banks classified as foreign owned may not have been foreign owned over the entire period covered. In this case, the data would indicate that foreigners are not successful bidders for the best banks in the market.

35. As is the usual case with Japan, no one really knows what the attitude of the ministry of finance would have been had a foreign bank tried to buy a major Japanese bank.

36. Opinion in Mexico is generally that the market segment for foreign banks will be with large firms, especially in dollar-based operations. In this area, foreign banks have a technical advantage plus a greater ability to circumvent regulations. There are currently forty five foreign bank offices in Mexico, serving primarily as loan-booking offices. They can make loans in foreign currencies to Mexican entities that will be booked offshore. They can neither take nor solicit deposits for offshore entitites. Of course, nothing prevents a Mexican firm from telephoning a bank in New York and establishing deposit services.

37. The ban on options on securities and on indexes has pushed the potential market for these instruments out of Mexico, with some options now trading over the counter in Europe. For example, an option on Telefonos de Mexico began trading in New York in September 1991. U.S. subsidiaries of Mexican banks and brokerages can always deal in options in New York, but they would like to have a domestic business as well. Similarly, the ban on margin buying of securities has pushed trading of major issues to New York. For example, traders can buy Telefonos de Mexico on margin in New York.

38. For Mexico this ratio was calculated as Costo de Operacion divided by the sum of Margen Financiero plus Ingreso neto por servicios plus otros ingresos netos. The data are from CNB, *Boletin Estadistico de Banca Multiple*, March 1990. For the United States, this ratio was calculated as the sum of salaries, occupancy expense,

and other operating expenses divided by net interest margin plus noninterest income. The data are from *The Federal Reserve Bulletin*, July 1991, p. 517.

References

Banco de México. *Informe Annual, 1989, 1990.*

Comision Nacional Bancaria. 1991. *Boletin Estadistico de Banca Multiple,* March.

Comision Nacional de Valores. 1990. *Banking and Financial Institutions in Mexico,* August.

Federal Reserve Bulletion. July 1991.

Macro Asesoria Economica. 1991. *Realidad Economica de Mexico—1991,* Mexico City: Macro.

Natella, Stefano, and Justin Manson. 1991. *The Mexican Banking System.* CS First Boston, May.

Ramachandran, S. 1991. "The Reform of the Mexican Financial System." World Bank, mimeo.

Solorio, Efrain. 1991. "Reporte Sobre la Eficiencia de la Banca Multiple Mexicana." Direccion General de Planeacion Hacendaria.

Trigueros, Ignacio. 1991. "Los Servicios Financieros y el Acuerdo de Libre Comercio." Working Paper, ITAM, August.

Index